The Politics of Academic Culture

Foibles, Fables, and Facts

Heinz Eulau

Chatham House Publishers, Inc.
Chatham, New Jersey

THE POLITICS OF ACADEMIC CULTURE
Foibles, Fables, and Facts

Chatham House Publishers, Inc.
Box One, Chatham, New Jersey 07928

Copyright © 1998 by Chatham House Publishers, Inc.

Publisher: Edward Artinian
Production supervisor: Katharine Miller
Cover design: Lawrence Ratzkin
Composition: Bang, Motley, Olufsen
Printing and binding: R.R. Donnelley & Sons Company

Library of Congress Cataloging-in-Publication Data

Eulau, Heinz, 1915–
    The politics of academic culture : foibles, fables, and facts
        p.   cm. —
    Includes index.
    ISBN 1-56643-061-5 (pbk.)
    1. College teachers—United States   2. College teaching—United
States.   3. Education, Higher—United States.   I. Title.
LB1778.2.E95   1998
378.1′2′0973—dc21   97-33756
                                                                CIP

Manufactured in the United States of America
        10   9   8   7   6   5   4   3   2   1

Dedicated, in abject deference,
to six libertines of academic wit —

Bernie Grofman
Chuck Jones
Bill Keefe
Nelson Polsby
Bob Salisbury
Lee Sigelman

Also by Heinz Eulau

Micro-Macro Dilemmas in Political Science: Personal Pathways through Complexity. Norman, Okla.: University of Oklahoma Press, 1996.

Politics, Self, and Society: A Theme and Variations. Cambridge, Mass.: Harvard University Press, 1986.

Contents

A Nonmandatory Preface
with Some Thanks

Ever since I reached academic maturity, people have asked me what I do when not "working," or, as they so imaginatively put it, "what are you doing for fun?" I'm not sure why they ask this silly question. They apparently want me to tell them that I read mystery stories, listen to classical music, cultivate fuchsias, and have my Tanqueray on the rocks with a twist but without vermouth, genuine Italian, or cloned Napa. I do these things, but I can't say that I do them "for fun." When I reply that it is fun to observe and record the funny things *they* are doing, like asking me what I am doing for fun, they tell me that this is a rather funny answer. They really don't mean "funny" as I use it; they mean "weird" or something like it.

I have never been able to distinguish between work and leisure because I have always found in the observation and explanation of mammalian behavior, especially the social and political conduct of the human species, all the fun I need to tolerate the academic life. And that's why the directory on my faithful IBM XT designates this book as "funbook" (well within the eight-letter limit for a file name).

When I was somewhat younger, about half as old as I am now, I read a book with the semiacademic title *Fads and Foibles in Modern Sociology and Related Sciences* by Pitirim A. Sorokin (1956). The Harvard professor didn't like what was going on around him in sociology, especially at Harvard. It wasn't a very good book, and, until I looked at it again forty years later, I had forgotten what was in the book. But the title had stayed with me all these years. And when I set out on the current expedition, I found in my old-time, hard-copy vertical files a folder marked "Fads and Foibles." The first deposit in the folder is the outline for a projected piece entitled "The Little Footnote and the Big Footnote." It was written at a time, I think in the early 1960s, when I was deep into doing bibliographical essays of one sort or another. These essays, it seemed to me, were nothing but collections of inflated footnotes based on extended footnotes, which, in turn, reflected shorter footnotes until they reached the form of a nonfootnote reference in the text like (Eulau 1915). This reference was to the author's birth certificate, which, of course, is in German; and though it is not signed or even cosigned by the author, it unmistakenly attests to his authorship and early promise in the business of having fun. As I recall now, my intention was to do some research that would undergird this view of a rather peculiar academic compulsion—to footnote everything *ad infinitum*. I never got around to it, and I do not propose to revive the topic in this book, which, believe it or not, is garnished by only one footnote, cover to cover.

To get back to Professor Sorokin's book. Its title notwithstanding, it is not what you might expect, a funbook to read. On the contrary, it is a rather mean-spirited book. Professor Sorokin put his fingers on some of the silly things we social scientists do, like using unnecessary jargon, spinning extravagant ideas, or making claims to truth of doubtful veridicality. But instead of good humor, he displays a bad temper. As far as I can make out, apart from his dislike of "numbers" (especially in survey research) and "experiments" (especially in group dynamics), his major complaint seems to have been that his younger colleagues did not pay much attention to or cite their predecessors' work, including, of course, his own magnificent contributions to sociological knowledge. Reading Professor Sorokin on the topic of fads and foibles isn't much fun, therefore; but I want to emphasize (most emphatically) that the contents of this (my) book are in no way related or indebted to, inspired by, or stolen from the sociologist's vendetta of forty years ago.

In my perpetual and persistent efforts to document the fun, foibles, and fumbles of academia, there is a major difficulty. Much of the relevant documentation is only in my head, hence mere opinion and rather randomly distributed over various parts of the brain. There is no particular reason, therefore, why you should read this at best nonmandatory preface first and the book's Prologue or its sixteen chapters in some orderly fashion. In fact, like the disks and tracks on my CD player, one can "shuffle" the chapters and read them in random order. Nevertheless, I do not recommend total abandon. The Prologue *does* introduce the reader to the author's preprofessorial career by way of some true and untrue documentation, and it tries to set the "tone" of the enterprise. If, randomness notwithstanding, the chapters are numbered, it is not to test your commitment to transitivity—one preceding two, two preceding three, and so on into infinity. The numbers are there only to increase your reading pleasure by telling you where you are in case you like to do some shuffling without getting lost. Say you first read chapter 5 and you reach a point where you are invited to "see" chapter 3 or chapter 8; you can now safely read all of chapter 3 or of chapter 8 before returning to chapter 5, in the firm knowledge of not having missed anything. Or you may not want to return at all to the point of departure and give up reading the book altogether.

With a fine nose for what is politically correct and what incorrect, Susan Zlomke played havoc with parts of the original manuscript and saved me from much embarrassment potentially caused by my frequently irreverent candor. Thanks!

What is still so oddly called a ms. had, at the low end of its title page, where normally one finds the name of the publishing house, this provocative sentence: "A Splendid Manuscript in Search of a Distinguished Manufacturer." I knew all along that I wanted Ed Artinian, majordomo at Chatham House, to publish this book. He is a man of keen intellect as an editor and publisher, of unfailing memory in matters of our profession's fads and foibles, a devoted friend of political science and of many political scientists, a discriminating connoisseur of the better things of life, and an indefatigable producer and seller of distinguished texts.

Though the word "inspiration" would be much too strong, I have enjoyed the occasional contributions made to our otherwise dismal professional discourse by six practitioners of wit whose mastery of humor, irony, satire, and repartee, in prose or verse, has made, at least so far, my own survival in the never-never land of academia more bearable than it would otherwise have been: Bernie Grofman, a.k.a. A [*sic*] Wuffle; Chuck Jones; Bill Keefe; Nelson Polsby, a.k.a. Arthur Clun of Pontefract College; Bob Salisbury, and Lee Sigelman. I dedicate this book to them to express my appreciation but also to make sure that they cannot review it, unless they be accused of that most heinous of literary crimes—conflict of interest.

Abbreviations

AAAS   American Association for the Advancement of Science
AAUP   American Association of University Professors
ACLU   American Civil Liberties Union
ACE   American Council on Education
AJPS   *American Journal of Political Science*
APSA   American Political Science Association
APSR   *American Political Science Review*
CCRP   City Council Research Project
CNPS   Caucus for a New Political Science
EB   *Encyclopaedia Britannica* (15th ed., 1974)
ICPSR   Inter-University Consortium for Political and Social Research
IPSA   International Political Science Association
MJPS   *Midwest Journal of Political Science*
NAS   National Academy of Science
NCAA   National Collegiate Athletic Association
NIMH   National Institute of Mental Health
NSF   National Science Foundation
NWU   New World University
PB   *Political Behavior*
PS   *Political Science* (APSA house organ)
SCRL   Stanford Campus Residential Leaseholders
SDS   Students for a Democratic Society
SPSS   Statistical Package in the Social Sciences
SRC   Survey Research Center
SSRC   Social Science Research Council
UC   University of California (Berkeley)
UCLA   University of California (Los Angeles)
WCPS   Women's Caucus for Political Science

Prologue

The Origins of a Career:
Selected Documents
for an Academic Résumé

I. An FBI Memorandum

From: Special Agent Smith, FBI, Frisco
To: Director, Immigration and Naturalization Service
Subject: Eulau, Heinz Hermann Friedrich
Date: 1 April 1940

Subject of inquiry request is well known in these parts. Subject arrived Frisco through Golden Gate 30 April 1935 on Dollar Line "President _____" (unidentified, possibly "Lincoln"). Unknown whether ship controlled by Wall Street financial interests. According to Berkeley (California) police report, subject known to have spent first night sleeping on Live Oak Park bench in referenced police jurisdiction. Awakened by Sgt. on duty, subject claimed unable to return to Frisco where staying at YMCA because ferry service unavailable after 2 A.M. Said he liked honeysuckle smell in air and sky full of stars. No alcohol. Plans to study at Cal.

Subject later seen by neighbor entering home of one Professor (of Agriculture) Butterfield about 10 A.M. Interviewed by Agent Brown on tip from local police, Butterfield reported subject to be friend of his niece Clara, en route to Lincoln, Nebraska, to enter university. (Later inquiry shows no obvious connection between "President Lincoln" of Dollar Line and city of Lincoln, Nebraska). Father is missionary in Philippines. Evidently met subject on ship and had good time. Spent evening bar-hopping in Frisco with other shipmates, including subject, to celebrate arrival in U.S. Present whereabouts unknown.

According to informant "A," who knew subject at Berkeley International House, subject attended high school graduation with Butterfield family on football field. Subject shocked by experience. Found orange and blue and gold uniforms and hats making music "odd." Had to be told about school's marching band, evidently unknown in subject's home country except, he told informant, in Strauss and Lehar operettas. Strauss well known, harmless prewar Austrian composer; no info available on Lehar, possibly Hungarian communist. Subject amazed by senior class queen on rumble seat of Chevy circling field running track. Reported to say custom is un-American. Thinks independence from England great mistake made by founding fathers. Subject seems well familiar with American history, but opinionated. Other I-House resident (informant "B") overheard subject: "Had the thirteen colonies remained in the British Empire, Americans could have had real queens along with real kings and real palace guards and real scandals and a much better legislature than Congress."

Subject now studying political science at UC. Known to be something of a radical moderate. Seen buying *New Masses,* communist magazine, but no evidence of reading it. Associates with socialists but does not seem to belong to any org. With 10,000 others, took Oxford pledge in fall '35 mass meeting at UC gym. Associates with foreign elements at I-House. Subject seen at Sather Gate listening to leftist speakers, but did not intervene when, during 1936 presidential campaign, Norman Thomas pelted with eggs by members of football team (claim not substantiated by any witness). Attended cocktail parties in defense of Spanish democracy. Used to wash dishes at Alpha Phi (sorority) house and spoke at Kappa Kappa Gamma (also sorority house) about Hitler invading Rhineland. Subject seems to be partial to sororities.

In pol sci seminar subject said to be something of a pain-in-the-neck, according to Professor David Prescott Barrows, a.k.a. "the general," department chairman for life and former commander of California National Guard, known for taking care of '35 longshoreman insurrection in Frisco. As undergraduate, more often seen in Berkeley hills reading Hemingway to coeds than in classroom. Has several girl friends, usually from So. California and with car, preferably convertible. Seems to have settled down since working for higher degree. After about three years at I-House, lived in apartment with one Robert E. Ward and one other (red-haired) person of Scotch-Irish descent. Ward known for Serbo-Croation sympathies, but no evidence of political activity in apartment. Neighbor reports many parties there, but no complaints filed with Berkeley PD. According to Ward, subject has "modest talent and an unshakeable commitment to boozing" and is especially fond of combination of Fog Cutters and Tonga Taboos at local tavern called Trader Vic's. Ward also reports that subject has "truly impressive gift for the more acrobatic flourishes of dancing the schottische or polka at the William Tell and for singing rousing German ditties on the ski slopes of the High Sierras."

Bureau recommends continuing observation of subject as war approaches.

Director's Note: Any similarity between this highly unreliable report and our usually highly reliable "raw" reports from the field is altogether noncoincidental.

II. From Subject's Diary

It's about ten o'clock, and I'm exhausted. Think it's April 7, must be 1940, but am not sure. Anyway, became a naturalized citizen today. Had dinner in S.F. with Fred D. and Madeleine L., who were my witnesses at naturalization hearing. I flunked the citizenship test the first time I took it as, I think, any good political scientist should have done. That was about two weeks ago. It was just too silly. Here's the dialogue between the judge and me:

> *Judge:* How many branches of the government are there?
> *Eulau:* Five
> *Judge:* What?
> *Eulau:* Yes, five.
> *Judge:* Is that what they teach you over there in Berkeley?
> *Eulau:* No, but I read it in a book.
> *Judge:* What book?
> *Eulau:* By somebody with the name of W.F. Willoughby. He says that there are not only the traditional executive, legislative, and

judicial branches. There are two new branches, the bureaucracy and the electorate.

Judge: Well, young man, you go back over there to Berkeley and study some more, and come back here in a couple of weeks.

Two weeks did go by, and we went back to San Francisco to the courthouse. It was rather embarrassing that I had to ask F. and M. to do this twice. We were there on the dot of ten, and evidently as a reward for having flunked the first time my name was called first. I turned out to be the very model of a modern applicant for citizenship before an audience of people who, as far as I could hear, spoke only Polish or Italian or Greek, and who were sitting on the long and hard benches still studying some little red, white, and blue book, which, I suppose, contained the Constitution. This time the conversation went like this:

Judge: Nice to see you again, Mr. _____. How do you say your name?

Eulau: Ulau, like in Ugene, Urope, Uclid, Uphrates, Ucalyptus, Unuch.... (*Eu can never be sure how long it takes for people—even a professional like a federal judge—to get it, unlike "Heinz." People get that name right away: "like in 57 varieties," they will say when polite or, when lost for words, "like in catsup."*)

Judge: That's enough (*He is clearly a quick learner*). Now tell me, how many branches of the government are there?

Eulau: Three.

Judge: Good! What do you do over there in that Bureau of Public Administration? I know Sammy May. Do you?

Eulau: Oh, yes. He's my boss. And I write reports for the legislature up in Sacramento, like "The Importation of Chinese Egg Products into California" or "Horse Racing Laws in the 48 States," or . . .

Judge: Hold it right there. What'd ye find out?

That's where he stopped and we talked about horse racing and its regulation, and what not. That probably gave my fellow applicants some extra time to bone up on the Constitution before their turn came to inform the judge about the number of branches.

III. A Ph.D. Examination

UNIVERSITY OF CALIFORNIA
GRADUATE DIVISION
PROGRAMME OF THE
FINAL EXAMINATION FOR THE DEGREE
OF DOCTOR OF PHILOSOPHY
OF
HEINZ HERMANN FRIEDRICH EULAU
A.B. (University of California) 1936
M.A. (University of California) 1938
Monday, May 5, 1941, at 1:30 P.M. in Room 114
University Library

COMMITTEE IN CHARGE:
Assistant Professor Eric Cyril Bellquist, *Chairman,*
Professor Raymond Garfield Gettell,
Professor Robert Joseph Kerner,
Associate Professor Charles Aikin,
Professor Eugene Irving McCormac.

No contemporary doctoral examination *programme,* if that institution still exists anywhere, can match the elegant British spelling of what Americans think of as a "program." It attests to French culture reaching well beyond the British Isles, not only to Quebec or Louisiana but also to California where, heretofore, only Spanish and barely traceable Russian influences have been identified. It takes a great state university—that is, the university being great, the state large—to uphold tradition. The *programme* was printed at university expense, though even back in 1941 the impoverished candidate had to pay a fee for any expenses incurred in exiting from academic bondage, like having the degree posted by mail if not willing to shake hands with the president and some dean.

Of the five committeemen in charge, only the first two were really known to the warrior of this defensive action. There is no doubt in his mind that the three others had absolutely nothing to do with the dissertation whose "defense" presumably was the object of the *programme* arranged for the early afternoon of 5 May 1941. Fortunately, the English word "defense" differs from the French *défense* only by the *accent d'aigu* to be placed on the first "e," hence not requiring further etymological elucidation. As a matter of fact, the ensuing attack on the candidate's work, pursued in orderly manner around the table, was highly informed in any conceivable dimension. The high point in the *programme* came with Professor Kerner's turn. He had presumably been the third or "outside reader" of the dissertation, appointed by the dean of the graduate division. The candidate was certain, on what evidence he had, that the professor had not read the masterwork he was to attack. He had it on his desk for several weeks, and when the candidate came to pick up the signed copy, the prof had to pull it out from under a stack of a dozen other manuscripts. It wasn't signed yet, but he signed it without a word exchanged with the candidate who, like many other Ph.D. candidates before democracy came to have the professoriat in its grip, was dismissed with equal grace. Professor K. launched his attack by mercilessly asking bibliographical questions about other bibliographical questions in his own specialty of historical bibliography. The candidate finally blew up and said, "Professor Kerner, I know *my* bibliography at least as well as you know yours."

After the candidate had left the room, his somewhat nonacademic, out-of-line reply caused some rumpus among the committee in charge because Professor K. wanted to flunk him, and some of the other members were not happy with his performance in this part of the *programme*.

All I knew about Professor K. at the time was that he taught Russian history. The real source of his ire, I was told later by my dissertation adviser, was that I had taken all kinds of courses in Spanish and Latin American history but none in Russian history, and there was something like a minor war going on in the Department of History among various territorial factions. However, I once attended a public lecture given by Kerner in the cavernous auditorium of UC's Wheeler Hall. Kerner was holding forth on the current (1939) German invasion of his beloved Czechoslovakia (he fancied himself to have been one of the country's creators, having had some role in drawing its boundaries at Versailles). He was pounding the lectern in front of him and shouting, "documents, ladies and gentlemen, documents." At this point a voice was heard from the auditorium's back row: "Yesterday's *New York Times*, Professor Kerner?" It came, the candidate noted, from a political science teaching assistant not otherwise identified at the time or identifiable now.

The day after the examination I reported Professor K.'s misdemeanor during the *programme* to a more kindly and my really favorite historian with whom I had done Latin American politics and who had read the thesis as a favor to me, the white-haired Herbert I. Priestley, director of the Bancroft Library and author of *The Coming of the White Man.* HIP's comment on the episode was short and enthusiastically nonacademic: "what can you expect from that goddamn bibliography compiler." That's how I learned about academic comity at the professorial grassroots.

IV. An Academic at War

DEPARTMENT OF JUSTICE
WASHINGTON, D.C.

July 25, 1941

Mr. Heinz Eulau
Special Defense Unit
Department of Justice

Dear Mr. Eulau:

You are hereby appointed an Assistant Analyst in the Special Defense Unit, Office of the Attorney General, Department of Justice, for temporary service for a period not to exceed three months, effective with your entry on duty. Your salary will be at the rate of $2,600 per annum in Grade Caf-7, payable from the appropriation for "Salaries, Special National Defense Unit, Department of Justice."

You should execute the required oath of office, personal history statement and Form 3464a.

Respectfully,

[signed, Francis Biddle]
Acting Attorney General.

Note to File

Until I recently retrieved this letter from some hiding place, I did not know that I had been what the letter said I was. I had come to Washington in June 1941 to work in Harold Lasswell's Division for the Study of Wartime Communications, Library of Congress, where the outfit was housed, according to my entry in *Who's Who in America* and any other *résumé,* of which there are many different versions, depending on the occasion for which they were written. But all of them have me as "research associate, Library of Congress, 1941–42" or something like it. So much for either my youthful naiveté (I thought I was doing "basic" research in symbol analysis, paid out of Rockefeller Foundation funds), or the reliability of "Marquis," whoever he or she was.

Some of us at the Library of Congress had in fact been physically transferred—soon after Pearl Harbor—to an old, dilapidated brick building on Pennsylvania Avenue and D Street, opposite the Justice Department, with neither heat in winter nor air conditioning in summer, calling for sacrifice to what everybody now called the "war effort." And we actually did "applied" research on "organizations and propaganda" for the Justice Department. By then my three-month probationary appointment had been transformed into "for indefinite service during the present emergency," but I still slaved away at the $2,600 salary, equivalent to an assistant prof's salary in those preinflation years. I don't know what made the authorities upgrade me a year and a half later to the magnificent title of "senior" O&P analyst, but I had become the "chief" of the Spanish section after the transfer. Or, perhaps, it was because by now once "acting" AG Biddle had become just plain AG Biddle.

The AG was a great believer in civil liberties. So, at one point, they put some of us to work on taking care of the dangerous ideas found in the periodical *Social Justice,* mouthpiece of the fascist Detroit radio priest Father Charles Coughlin. He had published, in literal translation, excerpts from Nazi propaganda minister Goebbels's speeches without any attribution to their source. This violated all kinds of laws, like the Foreign Agent Registration Act and what not. Anyway, Biddle, being a great liberal, stopped Coughlin by advising the Postmaster General to take away the fourth-class-mail privileges, which the holy father enjoyed for sending *Social*

Justice to the faithful around the country. The expectation was that it would be too costly to send the paper by first-class mail, and that it would wither away. This circumvention of the First Amendment was successful, the whole thing was in the spirit of the laws, the paper ceased publication, and at night all of us could sleep better.

DEPARTMENT OF JUSTICE
WASHINGTON, D.C.

July 28, 1943

Mr. Heinz H.F. Eulau
War Division
Department of Justice

Dear Mr. Eulau:

You are hereby placed on indefinite leave without pay as a Senior Organizations and Propaganda Analyst in the War Policies Section of the War Division, Department of Justice, commencing August 25, 1943, due to your having been inducted into the United States Army.

Respectfully,

[signed, Francis Biddle]
Attorney General.

V. Peredishka (Time-out): Becoming a Journalist

THE NEW REPUBLIC
40 East 49th Street
New York, N.Y.

August 26, 1943

Dear Mr. Eulau:

Are you going to be in New York in the near future by any chance?

If so, I wish very much that you would come in and see me. We have in mind a little project on which you might be of some help to us, if you were free and wanted to.

Cordially and sincerely,

[signed, Bruce Bliven]

Note to File

Careful reading of this letter shows that I had just about twenty-four hours to get out of public service into private employment in the public interest. As the army had sent me back to the department, and as I had had enough of the paradise that was Washington at war, I jumped at the opportunity that Bliven so vaguely hinted at. What it initially involved was, in fact, the preparation and editing of a special issue of the *New Republic* on the following year's presidential election. I stayed on for almost three years in which I became an assistant editor of this "journal of opinion," until returning to academia in the autumn of 1947. That's when the fun, foibles, and fumbles really began.

1

My Forefathers and Other Falsifiable Stories,
or
A Little Lie Can Get You Further Than You Think

There are some things absolutely and undeniably true. For instance, like most other humans, I was born on this earth. I say like "most" of them, because there are some academics who think they were born elsewhere and hence godsends to the rest of us. In addition to all kinds of other marks of distinction, you can easily spot them because they write holier-than-though memos to their less virtuous colleagues (see chapter 7). Whatever, whether one's roots are divine or profane, they are undeniable; or, to put it more elegantly, *sum ergo cogito* and not, as that seventeenth-century French savant and rationalist wanted us to believe, *cogito ergo sum*. That makes me into something of a philosophical realist.

The Need for a Birth Certificate

It is also true that I was born in Offenbach am Main, in imperial Deutschland, then at war, on 14 October 1915. This truth is more difficult to document than the fact of birth as such—not for me, of course, but for anyone else. I still have the *Geburtsurkunde* (birth certificate) that I needed to get out of Germany and into the United States. For some reason, you have to prove that you were in fact born somewhere before being admitted as a legal immigrant.

Once upon a time, in the early years of World War II, some insensitive people, aware of my accent, would ask me, "Where do you come from," meaning where was I born? Even though there was little anti-German hysteria in the country, as there had been during World War I, I sometimes had the sense that, under the circumstances, the truth could be something of a dangerous thing. So I did some marginal lying. By an act of mental exertion I simply crossed the German-Swiss frontier and would say "Basel" where, I knew, there were some resident Eulaus, in case anyone wanted to check up on me in that city's telephone book.

There was a second time when I told a little lie to the "where are you born" question. One late evening, dead tired and driving back from Tijuana, I was asked the invasive question by a particularly patriotic border policeman. "In Brooklyn," I said. By this time, maybe a dozen years after the Second World War's end, my accent had become less Kissingerian, so that it was difficult to make a clear distinction between German-German and Brooklyn-German. Satisfied, he waved us on. Now, this lie was born from bitter experience.

In 1945, after peace had broken out, I used to meet my future wife (with the nice name of Cleo, bestowed by her father for a reason never extracted from him) on weekends in Buffalo, halfway between New York, where I was working, and Cincinnati, where she was interning as a clinical social worker. This equidistance meant that the *Ohio State Limited*, leaving both terminal cities at 4:00 P.M., would arrive in Buffalo around midnight, making it possible for us to register at the local hotel as Mr. and Mrs. Smith.

One day during one of our rather venturesome and possibly even illicit get-togethers, and not wedlocked—registering in hotels as man and wife was both necessary and illegal—we went up to visit Niagara Falls. Thinking of nothing much but clearly in love, we crossed the bridge into Canada to see how things looked from abroad. Returning across the bridge and reaching the American frontier post, we were asked *the* question. "In New York," Cleo could truthfully say. Not to be outmatched as a teller of truth, I responded, equally truthfully, "in Germany."

Did I have a naturalization certificate or a passport on me, the nosy custodian of America's spatial integrity asked. "No," I said, "but I have a social security card." "No good," he said, producing a deep depression in me. I had believed, at least until then, that the social security card as a passport to old age was as good as a passport across borders or even better because it did not have to be renewed every five or ten years.

In despair and just about ready to jump off the bridge, I heard him say, "Just go back across the bridge to the Canadian post and ask them to deport you to the United States *as an American,* and we will let you come back in." Dubious, I asked, "What if it doesn't work?" "It will work," the man assured us. So we trotted back to Canada, I had myself deported with a piece of paper in hand saying that the Canadians didn't want me. It was evidently more accept-able to my new friend on the American side of the border as satis-factory evidence of my U.S. citizenship than the social security card.

If all this sounds absurd, well, it was an absurd experience. Perhaps even more absurd was what I read on the Canadian depor-tation order—that, under this or that Act of Parliament I must never set foot in the country again. I have lost the document and, therefore, cannot say for what crime I was being deported. I have been to Canada at least a dozen times since, on one occasion as an agent of the U.S. government.

Demographics and the Risks of Lying

In the country's demographics, the learned professions do not ag-glutinate to statistically overwhelming numbers; the cohort of col-lege and university professors do so considerably less, with the pro-fessors of political science being physically invisible in the mass and statistically insignificant. Being invisible and insignificant, I gener-ally lie about my profession when the risk involved is minimal.

There was a great opportunity for relatively low-risk lying in the years before jet travel came in, when I took the *Zephyr* from Oakland to Chicago. This is a three-day trip, but after you have moved through Feather River Canyon in California and some pic-turesque parts of Utah and Colorado, it is dreadfully dull. I once took daughter Lauren along, when she was ten or so, and she sent her mother a crayon drawing of her father with the punch line, "All Dad does is . . . Read, Drink, and Smoke."

When you travel alone, you cannot stay cooped up in your roomette for an entire day, and so you visit the Pullman Parlor. There, under the influence of some beneficial elixir, fraternity among like-minded travelers inevitably leads to the "what'ye do for a living?" Well, in this critical situation, I'm inclined to begin with a little lie, like "I'm a college dean," because deans are always good subjects for a little prevarication. You can then complain that professors and students aren't what they used to be.

More often, though, it was the academic in me that made me tell the truth by admitting to professorial status. But then comes the ticklish follow-up question, "And what do you teach?" If I tell the truth—that I teach political science—I am likely to be in for a long speech by my new friend. He tells me all he knows about politics or politicians and what he likes or dislikes about what he calls "Washington." Or, alternatively, having taken a political science course in college, he tells me that political science is not a true science.

To get out from under all this I like to resort to a really big lie, the biggest I can think of: "Oh, I'm an astrophysicist." That will cut off any further talk along this line. And the risk of being found out as a big liar is very, very small. The probability of my encountering an astrophysicist in a Pullman Parlor on a particular day in a particular month of a particular year is zero to the nth degree. If someone babbles on about the stars and astrology, I will say, with authority, "You don't know what you are talking about." I can't say this when someone tells me about politics. For, in this populist democracy of ours, everybody is entitled to his political opinions, no matter how wrong.

A Jew in the Haystack

In the demographics of the census I should be one among the 5 million people or so who are identified as Jews. Being somewhat intimidated by demography as a scientific enterprise, I don't know whether the census makers think of Jews as a religious category, as an ethnic or racial group, as a cultural entity, or what. The Jews I know, most of whom are of the secular sort, think of Jewdom as a "community of fate," but I don't think demographers are very happy with this psychologically inspired and hence "not real" conception of a difficult-to-specify aggregate. I seem to remember that, some decades ago, there was a debate over whether the "religion question" should be included in the decennial census. I am for it because the census gives one a wonderful opportunity to lie. Asked about my "religion," I can unhesitatingly say "Jewish," even though

I have been a secularist ever since I had to learn ancient and rather useless Hebrew in order to be bar mitzvahed at age thirteen and become an elder in the tribe of Levi to which, I had been told, the Eulaus belong. So much for a lie that, as far as I can tell, is not likely to lead to criminal prosecution.

Now, the great thing about being "Jewish" is that you can't lie about it. That was the real lesson I learned from having been a Jew who lived in Germany but did not think of himself as a "German Jew" but as a German, until the Nazis came to power in 1933 when I was seventeen. My father never learned this. He was an awfully upstanding and compulsive German, decorated in World War I with a medal known as *Das Eiserne Kreuz* (Iron Cross), though his was of the "third class." He began to sport it when the Nazis conquered the country in 1933, but being a Jew the *Kreuz* didn't do him much good.

I had some trouble in identification. Overground, I joined a Zionist youth group; underground, I belonged to a Spartacist cell. The group was named for the insurgent Roman slave leader Spartacus, and the name was clearly designed to evoke the memory of the *Spartakusbund*, the underground revolutionary group during World War I that became the basis of the interwar German Communist Party. Our cell of six met once a week in the backroom of a *Bierstube*. The only thing we actually "did" was to distribute handbills or fliers telling the really nonexistent "democratic masses" that the anti-Nazi revolution was just around the corner. We distributed these things in the darkness of night at some risk, and I had to invent all kinds of little lies to get out of the house. In summer 1933, six months into the Nazi regime, two of us were sent on a mission to establish contact with like-minded groups elsewhere—whatever it was that was being "minded." The trip's cover was a walking tour through the Black Forest. I dropped out after this quixotic excursion; the hopelessness of the cause was not worth the risk I was taking.

Shortly afterward, I was shipped out and, in my own mind, soon stopped being a "German," though in my student days, living in Berkeley's International House, I was considered a German. There was no overt anti-Semitism in California, at least not among my middle-class acquaintances. Hence there was no reason to deny or proclaim being "Jewish." I discovered my being an "American Jew" when I went East in 1941, not in the big cities of Washington and New York but in the countryside where I encountered signs—"No Hebrews Admitted," and such. The issue came up in a direct, personal encounter only once when Cleo and I were booted out of a motel on Lake Winnipesaukee in New Hampshire. That was on our honeymoon in 1946. Although there was no sign at the entrance when we checked in, somewhat later the proprietor came down to the lake where we were sitting and asked, "Are you Hebrews?" Perhaps I should have lied. But I couldn't and didn't. That's when I really learned that you simply can't lie about being Jewish because "they" (the gentiles, or *goys*) won't let you. It's the story of the "Jewish people" everywhere. It makes us into a community of fate.

My only trouble, from time to time, is with some other Jews who won't let me be the sort of Jew I am. Should I say that I don't like to go to religious services, even on the high holy days, and not even for "cultural reasons" or "tradition's sake," some will disapprovingly shake their heads, individually or collectively. I do like a good Seder, if the talk is well informed as it is when the celebrant is a friend of ours, who is a professor of Jewish Studies at Stanford (he is a kind of historical sociologist or sociological historian). The evening's ritual centers in the reading and talking about a book called *Haggada*. Although "haggada" really refers to an entire literary genre, the book read at Pesach is about the exodus from Egypt and full of little lies disguised as anecdotes. The story appears in hundreds of versions in Hebrew and many other languages and is accompanied by commentaries of rabbis cribbed from Talmudic and Midrash sources. Children play an important role in the reading of the *Haggada*.

The Curse of Cheating and Repentance

As a secularist, I do not feel that a single "Day of Atonement" (Yom Kippur) is enough to take care of confessing and seeking redemption from all the sins committed in the other 364 days, even if I should fast—a rather silly ritual because I can think better when the stomach is full than when empty. Moreover, I do not find my openly confessed little lies either embarrassing or shameful. After all, a general prohibition against impersonal lying is not even to be found in the Decalogue (it only prohibits "bearing false witness against thy neighbor"). But what of more serious trespassing of the moral order? Cheating, for instance, especially in pursuit of academic laurels?

I must confess to having cheated once, as an undergraduate on an examination in Anthropology 100 or 101, I cannot remember the exact number. This particular course, taught by Professor Robert Lowie, was devoted to facts like the body hair of the Ainu and the size of Bantu teeth, exciting topics all. Obviously, I am doing Lowie an injustice in this brash description. Like most undergraduates, I never knew anything about most professors' reputation or lack of it. Lowie was one of the "greats" in early American anthropology. I just happened to take the wrong course from him. His "objective tests," calling for true-or-false answers, were truly exciting opportunities for cheating. To make sure that there would be no cheating, two sets of the test were handed out, alternating from one seat to the next so that you could not benefit from turning your head to the left or the right. Then there were persons called "proctors," hired graduate hands—a despicable species long extinct —who marched up and down the aisles to make sure that no cheating was going on.

As the test was held in a large lecture hall with seats that ascended from the pit in front to the top row, it was rather easy to lean and look over the right shoulder of the person one seat below to your left or the left shoulder of the person one seat below to your right—something the good Professor Lowie overlooked in installing his security measures. So great must be my well-cultivated sense of guilt that I have retained a vivid image of looking over the shoulder of the fellow on the left and following his pen as he put "*x*s" in what I hoped were the boxes with the correct answers. I can't recall what grade I got on this particular test, but the course grade was a barely passing *D*. Without cheating, I am sure, there would have been a test grade conducive to an *F* in the course as a whole, no graduation, no graduate work, no Ph.D., no professor, and, now, no professor emeritus. I have never regretted this episode and, when the time came to make up for my misdemeanor, I did so in kind.

The occasion was an essay examination I gave when teaching at Antioch College. One of the students in the class was sick and bedded in the college infirmary. He wanted to take the test there. This was not unheard of at the Antioch of the 1950s where take-home examinations, guided by some honor code, were the order of the day. As a teacher, I really never cared much about grading until the grade inflation of the late 1960s called a halt to my lassitude and laxity in the matter. One day, after having assumed the department chair, I discovered that one of our assistant professors, only recently arrived from Berkeley but "unfinished" as a Ph.D., had an enrollment of 300 in his undergraduate seminar on political theory, and that all 300 had been given a grade of *A*. We summarily fired him ("let go" is the polite version) as soon as the academic year was up. He didn't appeal.

But back to that other fellow in the Antioch infirmary. He handed in a paper that deserved an *A* if ever a paper deserved that grade—except for the fact that it was plagiarized verbatim from some book that I happened to have read not long before. As I don't like public scandals and the travail going with them, to be expected in cases like this one if I had reported the incident to some authority, I just wrote a big *D⁻* on the paper's front page, made no further written comment, and had it returned to this fellow. There never was any follow-up conversation about it between us, but I think he got the message. And I felt good about it: after all, my own indiscretion back in 1935 or 1936 had been redeemed.

Because I never felt that grading was all that important as an incentive for serious study, I would tell my students that I assumed they were all "*A* material" and that they could only work their way down the alphabetic ladder but not up. This recollection is somewhat at odds with that of Dan Goldrich, now a professor at the University of Oregon, who on an appropriate occasion reminded me of something I had altogether forgotten. He confirmed that I was in fact full of disdain for the conventional *A* to *F* (for "flunk") grading system because it did not permit enough critical elbow room. My *causa operandi* and remedy were evidently different from what I recall as my *modus operandi*. Writing about a year in which I first offered "Politics and Society" as a ten-credit course in 1952–53, Dan reminisced:

> For me [the course] has set the standard. One was challenged to put in incredible hours, learn to theorize, prepare oneself to put forth newly generated, vulnerable ideas in class discussion after having barely managed to put them together in all-night efforts. The sense of challenge, of creation, and of cooperation in the effort among us was its own reward. I've always felt that people who haven't had a crack at such experience have been denied something of incomparable value.
>
> Lest I wax sentimental, I call to mind the grade received on my first paper in the course. On the horrendous scale adopted, from *A* to *Z*, I got an *R*. Mercifully, I plodded through the alphabet across ten weeks, during which time the rewards did seem also to shift toward the intrinsic.

Then there was the case of the cheerleader in my early years at Stanford who needed a good grade in summer school to avoid flunking out of school. He was taking my course, and one day he arrived with a case of Gallo wines, not California's best, to put it mildly. Evidently his father had something to do with the Gallo company. I told him to take it back to his dorm, but encouraged him to bring it back *after* I had deserved it by his having received a good grade, and *that* depended totally on his performance and not on my enjoyment of wine. As I remember it, his grade, given by a course assistant, was satisfactory to him and the university, but his wine was not quite up to snuff. The case stood in our cellar for a number of years, its three bottles of white gradually used up in cooking, a somewhat dangerous step for us to take. When, some years later, we moved, I left the rest of the case behind. Resisting evil in the academy is rather easy because, unlike in politics or business, the lures offered make for the smallest of payoffs (see chapter 3).

Stealing a Scarlet Promotion Letter

The challenging thought of academic hypocrisy brings me to my last confession and involves a most serious infringement of what is called "professional ethics." I must say, first, though, that all the stuff I have read about professional ethics has never touched me very much. I don't know why this is so. Perhaps I was born naive and cannot help myself to be otherwise. More likely, I have a hunch it has something to do with some cultivated tendency to assume that most academics are honest but occasionally stray off the reservation, and usually on reasonable grounds that no code of ethics can anticipate.

There is the case concerning the promotion of a young colleague. As always, letters about him and his works had been solicited from any number of highly respected and respectable experts in his field of specialization around the country. All of them were most laudatory: he was clearly more than a "promising" fellow and, in fact, quite accomplished, and so on and so on. Then, at the very end of the evaluation process, just after our committee had decided to recommend his promotion to department and dean, there came a letter from a rather distinguished colleague. In no uncertain terms, it made mincemeat of our candidate's books and articles. The letter was all too passionate, and, it seemed to me, altogether unfair. What to do?

There's nothing like experience in such matters, code of ethics or no code of ethics notwithstanding. My mind wandered back to one of my very first experiences at Stanford. The effort was made to attract a very-well-thought-of and productive senior political theorist. That was in 1959. I had known him for several years, and we had dire need of him to uplift an obsolete operation, though he was no great admirer of my own kind of behavioral research on politics. He had come to visit and given a splendid seminar, everybody was happy with him, and I had shown him the sights. We had driven into the hills behind Stanford, and he was very excited by the opportunity to join us. Excellent letters had come in, the chairman had called a meeting, and the department had unanimously voted to recommend the appointment. I called our candidate in the evening to tell him the good news—that the recommendation was going forward to the dean and that it was only a matter of a few weeks before he would receive official word.

Then, the very next day, in the afternoon, another meeting was called. A new letter had come in, from the man's chairman (at a midwestern state university); it thoroughly castigated the candidate as a "troublemaker" and all that sort of thing. Our spineless chairman asked the tenured faculty to rescind the recommendation and not go forward with the appointment. Lambs that we were, we voted the chairman's way. I had to make a second telephone call within twenty-four hours.

I remembered this episode some fifteen years later, and it answered my "what to do?" in the promotion situation. I put the letter in my hip pocket, took it home, tore it up, and never told anybody about it until many years later. I had no doubt that my action was a breach of "normal" conduct; but I also knew that the letter was pretty wrongheaded and unjust and that routine had to give way to some higher appreciation of deviance.

2

The *Curriculum Vitae* and the Iron Law of the Academy, *or* Blowing Your Own Horn Doesn't Hurt Anybody Else

One of the more redeeming prospects of academic life is the competition for fame and fortune. There is a serious qualification to be made, though. The opportunities for fame are considerably greater than the opportunities for fortune. What fortune comes our way is largely due to one of two factors: either you marry into it or you write an extraordinarily successful textbook. Few academics are successful in doing both.

Fame can come in many ways. One is of particular interest because it is not dependent on any objective assessment of accomplishment but on your own ability to create the celebrity so rightfully yours. This involves blowing your own horn and requires you to be a master in constructing your *curriculum vitae* to your own greater glory—not the real one (which would not need italics) but the one that requires a mountain of paper.

The Iron Law of the Academy

In general, academics are modest people, generally shying away from the celebrity status so much sought after by Hollywood stars, professional athletes, or what used to be called "café society." Modesty, of course, is not an absolute value but constitutes a span that is more or less elastic from one profession to another. In the academy the span is exceptionally unpliant, occasioning some concentration at the less modest pole.

I became embarrassingly aware of this phenomenon when I had to prepare for the site visits I often made at the height of my physical strength but decline in mental health. The to-be-visited departments, not leaving anything to chance, would send the visiting committee reams of what some of them called "dossiers" for their twenty-five or more faculty members, some of them weighing a couple of pounds or so, making literally and metaphorically "the package" previously promised by some dean who had solicited your service. "We will send you a package, for sure," the dean would say.

Exploring just a handful of these documents led me inevitably to the "iron law of the academy." There is, I discovered, an inverse relationship between the length of an academic's self-presentation in his or her print-encoded professional *apologia pro vita sua* and his or her reasonable scholarly accomplishment. The relationships covered by the iron law hold even after being controlled for age or formal professorial status, and so on.

To get a truly scientific handle on the iron law, I perused hundreds of entries in the biographical directory of the American Political Science Association (APSA). The vast preponderance of cases tends to support the iron law. It predicts (and seems to prescribe) that the more undistinguished one's career, the more newsprint is needed to present it. There is no formal model for the law, but the empirical evidence is overwhelming, at least at the aggregate level, some inconvenient outliers notwithstanding. For reasons only psychoanalytically fathomable, a few very smart, creative, and productive scholars inflate their selves to near-busting point. And some others, equally qualified, cultivate and convey an air of mystery.

Reading what students modestly call their résumés, but what in academese is more grandiloquently called c.v. for short, even if it is long, requires some skill because one must read not only what is on the lines but also what is between them, and there one may find more than meets the eye. "Reading between the lines," then, means that what's on the lines is at best a guide to what's between them. The iron law thus gives license to inflation of the academic self, including the option to do double-spaced typing. C.v.s in the latter mode are clearly intended to be more impressive because they are bulkier, but few experienced c.v. consumers are fooled by this ruse.

Degrees Earned

The standard c.v. begins, reasonably enough, with the subject's (as that term is misused by psychologists) education, usually in the form of a highly stylized and hence economical section called "Degrees Earned," including B.A. (or, perversely, or reversely, A.B.), M.A., and Ph.D., or any of the other degrees constructed from the letters in the alphabet. It is a sign of universal academic modesty that no c.v. producer in any of my files or directories has made use of the actual words the degree letters stand for. Newspaper reporters, when they want to be condescending, are inclined to address some academic big shot they dislike as "doctor," spelling it all out. The best-known example is, of course, Herr Doktor Henry (nee Heinz) Kissinger, the diplomatic oracle ("Herr Doktor, isn't it true that . . . ?"); but, then, he is no longer an academic identifier.

There are two more or less ambiguous indicators of how these curricular "earnings" can be evaluated, especially in the case of the Ph.D. One is the year of earning, the other the institution that either took the candidate's money or paid for his or her schooling. Depending on the c.v. interpreter's own sense of snobbishness, he or she will value a Ph.D. from, say, Harvard twice as much as a degree from Yale, or vice versa, not to mention a distinguished institution of higher learning, like New World University.

Anyway, one does this sort of reading between the lines and draws one's conclusions about the degree's "value" or, more accurately, future earning capacity. The trouble is that such conclusions may be very mistaken. As anyone should know, NWU at the time of our candidate's attendance was not only in possession of the NCAA's national basketball title but also in the forefront of the "new math" or the "new evolution theory" or the "new institutionalism" or whatever else was new or post-something or other. Hidebound Harvard and stodgy Yale were notoriously behind in all these innovations. This sort of unlicensed intrusion into the traditional rank-ordering of degree-giving institutions is worrisome. It obviously calls for a differential discount rate for each degree earned, and as one cannot find the rate *on* the lines one must find it *between* them. With some luck, one can find some basis for setting the discount rate elsewhere in the c.v., but the cost is high and makes for c.v. inflation.

The *Cursus Honorum*

The academic training route may be uphill, downhill, or flat. B.A., Swarthmore, M.A., Princeton, and Ph.D., Harvard, is a monotonously flat route. All kinds of inferences are possible. Born with a silver spoon in his or her mouth to start with, or, alternately, with a high IQ that made him or her a sure winner of lucrative scholarships, fellowships, or sundry other emoluments, this academic regular learned all that is to be learned at Swarthmore. The further and presumably higher schooling at Princeton and Harvard did not add much. One way to prove that it did is to inflate one's c.v.

Even more revealing is the unobtrusive-appearing date at which a degree was earned. Fortunately, the typical c.v. does not reveal the date of the high school degree, though it usually informs the reader that the c.v.'er was in fact born on a certain date at a certain place—in an expanded c.v. city, state, and country. Year of birth is something very important to know because it permits one to make a reasonable estimate of a person's "progress"—a metaphor, surely—up the academic career ladder. But suspicion can take over quickly: how is one to assess a B.A. obtained at the precocious age of eighteen as against a B.A. completed at the advanced age of twenty-eight, all other things being equal? As both ages make for a great deal of doubt about the c.v. writer's true qualities, the only way to reduce ambiguity is to seek for an explanation between the lines. Of course, the clever c.v. writer provides some on-line information in this regard, which has the further advantage of contributing to c.v. inflation. For instance, the eighteen-year-old *Wunderkind* will report having gone to the Bronx High School of Science, where one can skip classes if one's father or mother taught one calculus and Latin at home; and the twenty-eight-year-old B.A. hang-back boy or girl will report having fought for God and Country in some faraway war. The median age of a trustworthy B.A. being twenty-two, of most trouble even to the most skilled c.v. diagnostician is the twenty-four-year-old B.A., who is likely to conceal having tasted and tested the secret pleasures of some watering place. Alas, whatever the case may be, unless an inflated c.v. is of help in pondering these otherwise imponderables, one can only speculate by relying on what one reads between the lines or on some gossip one can pick up.

Returning to the more generic aspect of all this, the cunning c.v. diarist will tell any spellbound reader why it took ten or fifteen years to complete the Ph.D. Not doing so is surely a missed opportunity for genuine inflation of the self and all kinds of obstacles in finding a teaching job at age forty-five. It is necessary, therefore, to seize one or two or more of the many other opportunities to impress the consumer of one's c.v.

Honors and Awards

The standard c.v. invariably includes a section on "Honors and Awards." It modestly follows the "Degrees Earned" listing but really strains to come first lest it be overlooked.

Mercifully, the standard c.v. does not list all the *A*s received on the way across the flatland, though a really good H&A section will list the one course that was flunked as a noninflated measure of achievement to offset the rest. Needless to say, this does not end the inflationary spiral; it's only the beginning. One's masterpiece of a Ph.D. dissertation has been universally crowned the "best" (most likely in a minuscule and refined field of specialization) by some department, a regional association, and/or, to cap it all, the national professional society. With an item like that on your c.v., who can doubt that you are a smart fellow, in spite of the dreary advance from Swarthmore through Princeton to Harvard?

As for the early honors and awards of those whose academic training route has been uphill or downhill, their c.v.s are likely to carry even more inflationary baggage. Take, for instance, uphillers moving from Eureka College—that training ground of American presidents—to the University of Chicago. They will account for a possibly prolonged journey by recounting their summer job as counselor at some YMCA or YWCA camp, pumping gasoline early in the morning before getting to school, or carrying grocery bags for elderly ladies in the afternoon after school (the school is Ulysses Simpson Grant High, of course, the "Simpson" being a clarification offered as a bonus for any c.v. reader unfamiliar with Civil War history). If modesty forbids listing these charitable doings under H&A, they can be shifted to a c.v. section on "Employment Experience." They still serve the critical function of boosting the length, if not the significance, of what is to be demonstrated as a whole.

Needless to say, one dutifully reports having made Phi Beta Kappa in college, if at all possible in the junior year, which is *ad valorem* to the discount rate. Then comes the news of having received, en route to the M.A. degree, a prize for an essay published in the *Journal of Irreproducible Results*. The Ph.D., finished in the world-record time of three years, was "earned with distinction," leaving no doubt that the candidate is not only bright but also (between the lines) a hard worker. This, however, might also be interpreted (between the lines) that the c.v.'er is a dullard and a bore.

Obstinately, even the most inflated c.v. does not tell much about what really matters, only about what does not. For instance, I graduated from the University of California with what, in the good old days, was considered an honorable undergraduate record —a clean and clear *C* average. To appreciate this accomplishment (which would never have gotten me into graduate school in our postmodern and enlightened era), it is important to know that there was no course in which I in fact received a *C*. There were only courses in which I scored *A* or *B*, and other courses with *D* and possibly even an *F*, though having no transcript of my undergraduate grades I cannot vouch for any of this. Now, what the *C* average conceals is not only that I lived "off" these outlying grades, so to speak, but also that I spent much time in the Berkeley hills holding hands with one or another of California's golden maidens and reading aloud Hemingway and F. Scott Fitzgerald. That sort of thing is difficult to squeeze into a c.v., on the lines or between them.

Fellowships and Grants

Then comes the important section on "Fellowships and Grants." The really talented c.v. artist breaks this section down into clearly separate subsections, thus adding some more altogether costless lines to the document. As for being a "fellow," a rather prestigious word and much to be preferred to "member" or "associate," one can say that one is or was a "fellow" of all kinds of institutions—a think tank, a professional society, a college (usually in England), or an "academy." Some of these fellowships are honorable enough;

one has been elected or selected by one's peers on the basis of merit. Other designations as a "fellow" can be purchased by subscriptions to a journal published by some "academy" or "association" that tries to act like one.

A fancy experience I had with this racket is of quite recent vintage. I received a two-page, single-spaced letter from the AAAS, dated 5 January 1996. Here are some excerpts:

Dear Member-Elect:

On behalf of the President and the Board of Directors of the American Association for the Ad-vancement of Science (AAAS), I am pleased to extend to you a special invitation of membership in the Association.

Your temporary Certificate of Membership and Membership Acceptance Form are enclosed. . . . When we receive it [the acceptance form], we'll immediately send you your first issue of *Science* and important information concerning your privileges and benefits as a AAAS member.

There followed all kinds of drivel—that "during the last several months, many noted scientists in various disciplines" have signed up; that my "name will be added to our membership roll, which reads like a Who's Who in the field of science"; that as a member I am "entitled" to receive fifty-one weekly issues of *Science*, an "international [*sic*] recognized journal"; and that compared to the institutional subscription price of $250, I will "save more than the annual cost" of my membership dues "just on [my] subscription to *Science* alone."

At this point I'm still on the first page of this terrific, ego-boosting letter, looking in vain for just how much the membership in AAAS would cost me these days. I don't find it in the letter, but I find it in small, light print on the Membership Acceptance Form. As a "regular member" it is $102, but given my current status, I might want to apply as a full-time student for $55, though this would require my fabricating a student ID number. And, before I forget it, the form informs me that "a membership in AAAS is being reserved in [my] name until February 23, 1996." After that date, what?

Now the hucksterism of this solicitation is so rampant that you may wonder why I even mention it and don't throw this stuff out with all the other junk mail inviting me to join this, that or the other organization. Let me make the story short. On the wall over my desk, along with other such memorabilia, all properly framed, there hangs a certificate (or whatever else this sort of thing is called) informing me that "Heinz Eulau was elected a FELLOW of the American Academy for the Advancement of Science in testimony whereof. . . ." Now, I achieved this distinction back in 1964 without having to apply for membership, though once enshrined, I subscribed to *Science*. I tried to read this journal once a week for a number of years, but rarely got beyond the news items because the great bulk of the science articles was devoted to science beyond my high school ken in physics and chemistry. The issues piled up beyond hope of catch-up. They even ran me one year for chair or something of section K (Social Sciences); I lost. So I stopped paying for *Science* to become the forgotten fellow of the AAAS.

Another way one can augment one's c.v. without too much effort, yet handy to puff up one's ego and sound more important than just being a simple professor, is to report on one's contribution to public enlightenment. Being called on by the press to provide some oral or aural bites of impartial and objective knowledge about parties, candidates, or issues in state and nation, it is fashionable nowadays to deny being a "professor" by referring to oneself or being referred to as a "political analyst." This ruse serves to inform the higher university authorities about how much one is in public demand as a political wizard. The alternative, I suppose, would be to refer to oneself as a "political professor"; but that sort of honest self-identification is clearly an academic taboo.

Grants, in turn, are much more prestigious than contracts. They usually involve applications for support of research designed by oneself for the benefit of the arts, humanities, or sciences. They have been presumably approved by some committee of impartial knowledgeables. Contracts involve research needed by some private firm or public agency; they are suspect, though not among professors of engineering and business administration.

As time goes on, this section of the c.v., in contrast to "Degrees Earned," is infinitely expandable. Its only limitation is that humility proscribes reporting the dollar amount received in a grant or contract, and that is the really significant item, given the long list of possibilities opened up by skill in "soft money" entrepreneurship. It translates into having a secretary, keeping a permanent tab at the Faculty Club, inviting friends from elsewhere to come in for a seminar, and, of course, jet-setting to cities with good museums and other amenities.

Publications and Papers

No section of the c.v. is more important, at least to the experienced critical eye, than "Publications." There are at least four separate divisions into which the evidence for one's devotion to the prescription of "publish or perish" can be cut—"Books," "Articles," "Reviews," and "Sundry." Of these, the last is by all odds the most interesting because, again, it is not only the progressively most expandable but also, by definition, the most heterogeneous. There are, first of all, the important "letters to the editor" of some newspaper, from the student-edited *Daily New Worlder* to the *New York Times*. There are also what the French call *feuilletons* written for the op-ed pages of the world press. These essayish contributions to higher learning in America may even require some thought. Finally, there are the "rejoinders" to the articles of others published in the more or less respected professional journals that serve to vent one's frustrations and hostilities.

When it comes to books, the skillful c.v. writer has all kinds of options to expand the length of his or her listings. There are, of course, the honest books, truly authored by the author. Here, appending to each entry two or three lines of praise from some book review will do the trick of making the list appear longer than it really is. Then there are the edited books, consisting of chapters mostly written by others. I have noted in recent years that, increasingly, publishers drop the "edited by," allowing the c.v. writer to give the impression that the book is wholly his or hers. And if the publisher is not forthcoming in this matter, the c.v. writer is not prevented from dropping the "edited by" anyway. At least I'm not aware of any sanctions, and I think I have it done myself here or there, depending on for whose eyes the c.v. was intended. Finally, the most rewarding way to increase the space of the book section is to give the impression that a collection or symposium in which the c.v. writer's essay appeared was edited by him and by him alone. This feat is easily accomplished by simply omitting the name of the editor or, alternatively, adding your own name to the editor's, as follows:

> "A Day in the Life of Congressman Vestibule," in *Congress at Bay* (Grizzly, NW: New World University Press, 1997)
> *or*
> "A Day in the Life of Congressman Vestibule," in R. Jones and C.V. Engineer, *Congress at Bay* (Grizzly, NW: New World University Press, 1997)

Although the c.v. thus swells by virtue of its own immanent laws of pathology, listing only the published stuff will not satiate the appetite for more pages that c.v. writers think their readers wish to absorb. Some jokers may list still unpublished, seemingly publishable, but really unpublishable monographs and/or papers under "Publications." The honest c.v.'er will set up a new section with the economical and revealing title "Papers." This title is okay as long as the reader is an academic who knows what's what; but if the c.v. is used in search of a nonacademic job, it will bamboozle the less enlightened outsider, say a bank president (to whom "papers" are known as "stocks and bonds").

The "Papers" section can make for a multitude of pages by listing, in religiously chronological order, "Unpublished Papers" or "Working Papers" or "Conference Papers." My very first post–Ph.D. c.v. included some real jewels of this sort. When I earned my keep as a research assistant in Berkeley's Bureau of Public Administration, I did a paper on "The Use of Chinese Egg Products in California Bakeries and Restaurants," prepared to amuse the California State Legislature intent on regulating this kind of un-American trade. Similar and even more outrageous early contributions to public policymaking have since been jettisoned from my now everbeing-shortened c.v., for the dual reasons of obsolescence and mature moderation. But, a long time ago, these items were of unquestionably functional importance in recommending me to all kinds of academic or nonacademic jobs. They were proof of some literacy and limited typing skill. "Working Papers" are impressive items because they tell the reader that the writer is a worker, and "Conference Papers" are obvious proof of being in demand as a conference-goer.

This section also allows inclusion of "remarks made" at the opening or conclusion of some learned panel discussion. Some c.v. writers even include "Miscellaneous Lectures" as a subcategory, and, most recently, it has become possible to list course syllabi as respectable contributions to scholarship. This can of course become a nuisance when hundreds of colleagues from across the country write in to obtain your valuable guide. I was greatly relieved, therefore, when in the dusting years of my career the enterprising Allan Kornberg of Duke University published *Political Science Reading Lists and Course Outlines*, with the alluring subtitle *Innovative Reading Lists from Leading Political Scientists*. Being asked to submit something to this audacious undertaking made my day, circa 1980, as it identified me and my co-teachers as both "innovators" and "leaders." One hardly dares to expect more from a modest syllabus.

Finally, the iron law requires topping all this with some futuristics under the heading "Work in Progress." There one lists six or more such "works," potentially ranging from a book one is actually working on or, if not, is thinking about writing, to some collaborative article presumably being prepared with one or more colleagues (who can be blamed if the particular work-in-progress is never finished), to a research proposal even more remote from reality and, at the moment, existing only in one's head, if something can "exist" there. My own current work-in-progress, I am happy to say, is largely of the nonexistent variety.

Community and University Service, etc.

Lest the c.v.'s reader suspect one of being a tedious bookworm, the standard résumé will include a number of sections that confirm one is not only a superior intellectual, honored and rewarded by scholarships, fellowships, grants, invitations to conferences in delightful locations, and so on, but also a "good citizen." What perhaps could suffice as a single c.v. section can yet be broken up or down into several self-standing units conducive to c.v. inflation —"Community Service," "University Service," "Professional Service," and "Consultation." Community service includes poll watching as a kind of minimal form of political engagement. Even though this strenuous activity recurs only periodically, it is not to be sneezed at as useless; it communicates a sense of civic responsibility and even republican virtue, as does more demanding service on the local water board. Then there are the three-second sound bites on the regional newscast, which prove your expertise on whatever it is you are said to be an expert on, or giving a talk at the Senior Center, or belonging to a church choral group, and other important community functions. And all these activities show your concern for good town-and-gown relations.

University service has endless possibilities for inflating the c.v., like being or having been on numerous committees or subcommittees at all levels of the university; or being an adviser to majors, nonmajors, or the football team (which guarantees one's occasionally being invited to sit on the bench next to the third-string quarterback). "Professional service" usually means being "involved" with the professional associations. As there are many of the mass organizations one can join (they are all "democratic," i.e., there are no criteria for excluding anyone willing to pay dues), one is able not only to list them as proof of professionalism but also to report holding office or several offices at once, being on some editorial board or several, running conference programs or panels, and so on.

The grab bag of professional missions to fill out an otherwise unfulfilled academic life is really inexhaustible: invitations to this, that, or the other event; "consultation," like talking with textbook sales persons who invade the office disguised as "editors"; briefing politicians who do not listen, or testifying before legislative committees whose members have made up their minds before you can enlighten them; serving on site committees studying "troubled" departments, or being called on as a referee of NSF or NIMH research proposals. All these activities give warrant to the proposition that the c.v. is a robust and persuasive test confirming, or at least not falsifying, the iron law of the academy.

3

Perks, Boons, and Boondoggles,
or
When Freebies Get You Less
Than Meets the Eye

The confusing thing, initially and as usual, is glottological. Perversely, "perk" is a shortened colloquialism for the stately word "perquisite," while "boon," a perfectly reputable word, has been lengthened into the reprehensible "boondoggle." It took me some time to figure out the semantic difference between the two words, but I still have trouble distinguishing in practice between the benefit I can get from a perk and the benefit that comes with a boondoggle, or boon, as I prefer to call it. Being more of a pragmatist than linguist, I am more concerned with the benefits of perks and/or boons than with their etymological origins and ethical aspects—whether on the up-and-up or more or less suspect. Nevertheless, I cannot refrain from sharing my definitional and etymological inquiries.

As an adjective, "boon," after various peregrinations through the Middle Ages, goes back to the Latin word *bonus* (*bona* and *bonum*, to make everybody happy), or "good." As an adjective, *Webster's* tells us, it is largely archaic, standing for "kind, generous, pleasant, etc.," though a further possibility is "merry" or "convivial." As being merry or convivial seems to be more *au courant* than being kind, generous, or pleasant, it is now used only in "boon companion" as a synonym for "close friend."

As a noun, "boon" also has its archaic side and refers to "a request or the favor requested." More modern, it seems, is to interpret a boon as a "welcome benefit" or "blessing."

The word "boondoggle" in its modern sense, according to *Webster's*, my boon companion as always, arrived circa 1935, the very year I arrived in California. This does not mean that the word did not have a premodern usage. It was evidently used to refer to an ornamental leather strap. The modern application refers to "a trifling or pointless project," and "now esp., one financed by public funds." I must confess that, without knowing it, I had once been a boondoggler paid out of NYA funds (at $.45 per hour) clipping newspapers for some Berkeley professor of International Relations who thought he was an empiricist.

There can be even more confusion for the illiterate. At first glance, boondoggle would seem to be a first and older cousin of "boondocks," a word that evidently entered our common language by way of military slang during World War II. I suppose that everybody knows that it refers to a wooded area, wilderness, or any remote rural or provincial region, where nincompoops either come from or are exiled to. What I didn't know, and most people probably don't know, is that this word has nothing to do with "boon" but comes from the Tagaloc *buńdok* "mountain." I didn't know all this when living in the boondock Philippines and before becoming a New Deal–supported boondoggler.

All this is very instructive, but does not help too much in disentangling the semantic difference between a "perquisite" and a "boondoggle." Definitially, a perk is clearly something that is "additional to" or "comes with" something else. Among the things it comes with are "status" and "position," or "the like." The latter may be a "prerogative" and even "right." All this suggests that perks are deeply rooted in Western feudalism.

Perks Are Not to Be Traded Off

Another way of saying all this is to say that perks, in contrast to boons, do not come cheap. They have to be earned. Contrariwise, boons are presumably what, in cultures other than the academic, are called "freebies" or "freebees" (I am at a loss to account for the difference in spelling). Some years ago, actually decades now, my distinguished colleague Richard Brody, in private life an internationally known chef, was credited with having invented a measure of political attitudes that became known as "tradeoff scale." It was Brody's sense of balancing coriander vs. paprika that led to his far-reaching discovery, though the classical example comes from economics and concerns the tradeoff between inflation and unemployment.

For some time now, ever since becoming obsessed by the follies and foibles of academe, I have thought about the price we academics must or should pay for the enormous portfolio of wonderful perquisites that come with our lifestyle. We can't have it all for nothing. What are we trading off for our short working hours, pleasant offices, high salaries, ever congenial colleagues, always stimulating discourse in faculty meetings, generous expense accounts when going to professional meetings, subsidies for sending our children to college, medical insurance above and beyond Medicare or Medicaid, rewarding retirement provisions, and so on (in case I have left something out)?

There are even some among us professors for whom everything in the university—even watching, week after week, a losing football team—is wonderful; napping through faculty meetings is the best kind of recreation offered by the university; the fare served at university receptions is the last word in gourmet cooking (after all, it is a free and particularly perky perk); and so on. They are particularly prone to pangs of conscience in the matter of tradeoffs.

The Truth about Perks

One day, before accepting the Stanford offer, I called on Professor James T. Watkins IV, the incumbent department chair, to suggest that $11,000 would be a more adequate salary than the $10,500 previously offered. It would represent a more propitious beginning for an "old blue" like myself in his relationship with an "old red" like the honorable chairman. For those not in the know: an "old blue" is a University of California (Berkeley) graduate; an "old red" is a facsimile in a different color at Stanford. Both come together once a year at a mass meeting called the "Big Game." I later discovered that at this time my salary was to be $500 more than the chairman's.

My haggling with Watkins was a major error, but I was eager to come back to California after fifteen years of exile in the East and Midwest, even though at that time Stanford was not Berkeley. Now, forty years later, Stanford, though still smaller, is at least equal and in some respects superior to Berkeley in matters academic. Palo Alto has a much better climate and now, I think, more coffeehouses and better restaurants than Berkeley (the city). "My dear Professor Eulau," Watkins, forever the gentleman, said, "you don't seem to realize that the sunshine we provide is worth more than $500." The dear Professor Watkins, *requiescat in pace,* really meant it.

My most hard-earned perk came in 1974 at a garden party given by my dean of the day, the psychologist Al Hastorf. It made me like him a lot, but I had liked him even before he put his arm around my shoulder, took me aside, and told me that I would be recommended to the Stanford Board of Trustees as the first William Bennett Munro Professor of Political Science. That was Dean Hastorf at his best: he didn't wait to have his secretary call me to make a mutually satisfactory appointment in his office. This kind of bureaucratic formality would have left me wondering what (in hell) the dean wanted to see me about, never a happy prospect, generically speaking. I had always thought of him as the "swinging dean." When you dropped in to see him to discuss some weighty matter (and top deans are only to be seen on the weightiest of matters), he would invariably get out of his swivel chair, walk from wall to wall, swing his arms, and say yes or no. It takes a gutsy dean to say yes or no, and I preferred dealing with this real dean rather than with whatever lieutenant served as what was and perhaps still is called a department's "cognizant dean." A cognizant dean does not and is not expected to give you a firm yes or no. He or she will take what you have on your mind "under advisement," which is bureaucratese for saying, "I must first talk to the dean before having any serious talk with you." So you might as well see the dean before seeing your subdean, though you are well advised, redundant though it is, to see this minor figure also, to give him or her something to do and maintain friendly relations.

But back to the arm around my shoulder. "Of course," the dean continued after the initial announcement and becoming more deanish, "this will not affect your salary. That's being set by your department chair and the dean as usual." Well, as I was the chair at the time, this meant that Dean Al would be setting my salary. I hadn't known before that in matters of salary all those wonderful-sounding name-chair professors were treated just like ordinary professors, at least at democratic Stanford. It seemed a rather depressing experience to have your job given a pretentious name without anything else. I was about to bolt to the table with the wine bottles when the dean grabbed me and said, "and no perks." I shrugged that one off by introjecting my pipe to where I usually held it because I felt speechless and, anyway, no answer was expected. I didn't find out until later that what he meant by "no perks" was "no secretary of your own." But as I hadn't ever thought much about perks, my usual equanimity returned just when I heard him say, "There's some money there to bring in some outside lecturers or have a conference." This cheerful news raised my adrenaline level, and we parted friends.

Nevertheless, the fact is that the lecturer or conference money that came with the named-chair title was not a real perk. It wasn't because its benefits were not mine alone; they had to be shared with students and colleagues. I don't think that a "collective good" like that can be considered a perk. But then I was informed of a really posh perk I could call all my own. This one came from the provost: beautifully designed stationery with my name and honorable title engrossed on sturdy sheets and envelopes, along with an engraving of one of Stanford's ever-changing emblems—in this case a sequoia tree. This sort of perk tells the recipient of the letter more about Stanford University than it does about the writer who uses this pretentious stationery. Not surprisingly, I thought of it more as a consolation prize than as some genuinely perky thing.

The Origin of a Chair

There is a follow-up story that can give additional insight into the culture of the academy. After the board of trustees had perked me up formally, I received a note from Chancellor (formerly President) Wallace Sterling inviting me to come and see him. I went and heard an interesting tale.

Before telling it, a few words about William Bennett Munro. He was a big-wheel professor at Harvard, where he had received his Ph.D. in 1900. They kept him on, and he became a prolific author of textbooks in American, comparative, and municipal government. His biggest money-maker, though, was a small primer for immigrants who would be taking the test for American citizenship. That was before World War I, and there were millions of immigrants floating about. In 1927 he became president of the APSA and, in his presidential address, "Physics and Politics—An Old Analogy Revisited," revealed himself as one of the period's leading "scientistic" political scientists.

I'm not sure what we can learn today from "three-button Benny," as Harold Lasswell once told me Munro was affectionately called by his contemporaries. Now, even if Munro is no longer memorable for the contents of his many texts, he ought to be memorable as an evidently successful investor of the royalties received from their sale. His biography records that in his later years, after having been brought to the newly founded California Institute of Technology to set up the social science program, he also served as chairman of the executive board of the Security–First National Bank of Los Angeles. I need not say more about this academic success story.

Now to Wally Sterling's tale. When he was a young assistant professor of history at Stanford, Sterling was visited one day by Professor Munro, who had a son at Stanford. The son, evidently a classical fraternity brother, got into all kinds of trouble, and Sterling had been recommended to Munro as someone who could keep an eye on the young fellow. Sterling evidently did and became something of a Munro family friend, often visiting in Pasadena.

After Benny had died, Sterling, now president of Stanford, continued his visits to Munro's widow, Caroline. On one of these visits the widow Munro asked him what she could do for Stanford. "Well," Sterling, according to Sterling, said to her, "I always have my little tin collection plate with me." And what he picked up was more than a dime. Apparently, Munro's will had provided for his fortune, or part of it, to go to some eastern university after Caroline's death, but it could be changed by her. Caroline, with Wally Sterling's encouragement, changed it with *éclat*. Her money soon came to Stanford and was administered for her as a life trust, to become the base for an endowed chair on her death.

I knew about the Munro money lying about for several years because, as department chair, I received every month the budget sheets for the empty chair. And I saw the money increasing as dividends on the investments were flowing in. By the time I was made the W.B.M. professor, there was not only enough money for my salary but a lot of money for lectures or conferences, this fund to be split between political science and history. (The original Munro will required a single annual lecture in political science and/or history to be named after the benefactor.) I made a deal with the chair of the history department, Gordon Craig, that one year we would get all the available dough, and the history department would get it the next year. That allowed me for several years to hold all kinds of conferences on all kinds of topics. In due time there was enough money in the Munro kitty to establish a second chair, named after Caroline Munro.

Practicing Retirement: A New Perk

To appreciate the benefits of perks, it is necessary to distinguish between two academic types (among several other dimensions)—the militants and the quietists. The militants never understand the notion of tradeoff, which implies paying some price for the perks offered by the university, whether you like them or not. Take retirement, that supreme perk of all academic perks. Along with everything else in academic life, retirement has become controversial: Which is the superior form of retirement—early retirement, normal retirement, or late retirement? Within each category, what is early or late and, especially, what is normal? The militants, as one might expect, don't want any retirement at all; that is because they do not understand the virtues of tradeoff. They think of retirement—early, normal, or late—as a punishment that cannot be compensated for by whatever joys retirement may bring. It cannot bring joy because it takes militancy away from them, condemning them to write letters to the editors of newspapers, from the *New York Times* down to the student-edited *Stanford Daily*. For the quietists, retirement is equally upsetting: they can no longer get what they had been used to—an occasional invitation by the university president to dinner in honor of a wealthy donor or passively absorbing the disappointment of not receiving the raise secretly yearned for.

I had not thought much about all this until retirement was

about to embroil me in these controversies. True, it had occurred to me that an all-too-sudden transition from a high level of activity to a low level might have disastrous consequences for my mental health. Being an experimentalist at heart, I decided that a little practice at retirement before it really happened might be helpful in absorbing the impending shock. It could also be helpful in doing some cost-benefit analysis of retirement-in-prospect. So, in anticipation of the joys and disasters to come, I canceled a course numbered PS128 for the spring quarter of 1986, my last term of service. And so it was that I could devote myself to the practice of retirement. It had to be full-time to meet all conditions required of a truly scientific experiment (except, of course, for receiving my usual full-time pay). I do not remember what the course was to be about, and it does not really matter.

I had totally failed to anticipate the possibly serendipitous effects of this otherwise very rational action. One day I received a memorandum, dated 6 February 1986, from the chair of my department, whom we had brought to Stanford only a few years earlier. I had thought of him as a great scholar, not a memo writer even of little notes signed "cordially"—something he cannot possibly have meant. Here's what the note said: "Dear Heinz, I see that you have decided to cancel PS128 for the Spring Quarter. This leaves you with teaching only two courses for the entire year. My own sense of this is that if you are on leave for one quarter you ought to be teaching three classes. With one exception this is what has happened in the past. Obviously, you will have to make up your own mind on this question."

I had no trouble making up my own mind. If this memo was designed to create a sense of guilt in me, it didn't; and if it was designed to get me into a fighting mood and make a militant out of me, it didn't do that either. I ignored it and practiced retirement.

The Perks of Retirement

Although the department chair tried to spoil my practice, the university did some wonderful things to ease the transition once I got off the payroll. There came a letter from the provost, who congratulated and thanked me for my "many years of outstanding service," and told me that I had "enriched the lives of [your] students and colleagues enormously" and that he hoped I would look back on the years "with a deep sense of satisfaction." He also wished me "a happy and rewarding future," leaving open my options as to what rewards I might claim.

All the old boys and girls get these or similar sentimental lines on retirement. Not so with the paragraph that constituted the heart of the letter and informed me of my new status. At the board of trustees meeting of 13 June 1986, the provost wrote, I would be named "the William Bennett Munro Professor of Political Science and, by courtesy, Senior Fellow at the Hoover Institution, Emeritus." Well, genuinely new about this was the designation "Emeritus." Moreover, I was told, there was a real perk connected with this indulgence: "The appointment will also be listed in the Commencement Program." The provost evidently tried to get me out of the house Sunday next, don a cap and gown, and schlepp with the other emeriti up and down the slippery-slope aisle steps of the open-air amphitheater. As I didn't go, I missed reading about myself in the commencement program.

Shortly afterward, I was informed of more perks waiting for me in the new status of "professor emeritus"—for years I thought that this kind of professor was one without merit as any non-Latinist might easily assume. The "e" in *e-meriri,* from which *emeritus* as the past participle derives, does not translate into "without" but only into the briefer "out." Hence "emeritus" has no odious connotation, and a professor emeritus is simply a professor who has been ousted after having "served out his time." (What would we do in the English language without the Latin past participle?)

Back to the avalanche of new perks awaiting me. I was informed by someone—might it have been the vice-president for finance rather than the provost?—that my new lofty status entitles me, free of charge, to an "A" parking sticker. This presumably meant that I can park at the most desirable locations on campus. What other university would ever give a retiree such an in-real-dollars highly valued perk? Reflection forced me to contemplate this unexpected generosity of the university. I figured out that the sticker really doesn't cost the university a thing. Emeriti are not likely to appear on campus before eleven o'clock (A.M., of course), if at all. On arrival they will find that all the reserved A-sticker spaces have been occupied by the ever-growing number of university administrators whose destiny is to swivel in their chairs all day long but without whom we professors could not do our own job. There is little that the university can lose by granting its emeriti this highly desirable perk.

In connection with this matter of emeriti getting safely around the campus in the face of students on bicycles without regard for pedestrians, I recently read somewhere that the good life at Stanford has been enriched by a new post in the Department of Transportation (one of the more splendid and useful nonacademic units). This department's function is to transport people into, across, and out of an ever larger, more labyrinthine campus. The new and, I understand, full-time position is for coordinator of bicycles. Obviously, without somebody watching over bicycles, bicyclists, bicycle lights, bicycle stands, bicycle lanes, and what not, our students could kill some absent-minded emeritus who mistakes a bicycle lane for a footpath.

Along with the A-sticker came another perk. If I let them know, they would mail to my home, also free of charge, the weekly faculty-staff company paper, then called *Campus Report* and recently rechristened *Stanford Report* (presumably so you won't forget just what campus you are on and get lost). The mission of this otherwise harmless paper is to see no evil in, speak no evil of, and hear no evil about the university. This perk lasted until 1994. In that year the publisher, evidently having lost the battle of the budget with the provost, asked for $25 per annum if I wanted to receive the paper by "slow mail," that is, with all the other junk we find in our mailboxes. So I had to give up this valuable perk and subscribe for a year. Then I received a renewal notice, telling me that my subscription was up with the last issue in September and that, should I wish to renew at some new rate (I cannot now remember how much), I should do so immediately, lest I would miss all the important news that make the campus such a thrilling place to know about and possibly even visit. Though tempted, I failed to subscribe for a couple of years. Then Cleo complained about it, and I recently resubscribed, this time for $50, in order to get the paper with its hot news by first-class mail.

The Director's Indian Gift

Some perks come your way in a relatively easy way. When I was appointed to be something or other (by courtesy) at the Hoover Institution (for War, Peace, Revolution, and the Good Life), I wasn't sure whether I should think of it as a perk or as an honor. The (by courtesy) thing hinted at an honor but, given the institution's reputation for radical conservatism, the honor was of some surprise to a radical moderate like myself. Was it a perk? Not at first, but it became one, at least for a while, until it turned out to have been an Indian gift. I'm still a senior fellow (by courtesy)—the courtesy always being extended by proper placement between curved parentheses [(...)] rather than before and after dashes [— ... —] or two simple commas [, ... ,], but for many years there had been nothing honorific or perky about being this type of a parenthetical fellow.

Then, one day, in the late 1970s, the director's wife, Rita Ricardo-Campbell, with the emphasis for obvious reasons on the Ricardo, herself an economist, and a pretty good one, asked me what kind of chair I wanted in my office. I didn't know that I had an office in the institution, but I assumed she meant one of the offices in a splendid new research building that was going up at the time. So I told her what chair I wanted, one with a high back, and shortly afterward I found myself and a Hoover-payrolled research assistant installed in the new building. I was reasonably sure by now that I should think of this transfiguration from a spiritually nominal to a physically real affiliation with Hoover as a boon. In fact, nothing was really expected of me, like, say, taking an oath to Milton Friedman or attending the four o'clock kaffee klatsches at which the economists discussed various versions of the flat tax.

It was a splendid office, and I spent as much time there as my teaching obligations permitted, with Vera McCluggage next door, editing *Political Behavior* and writing papers that failed to reflect what was said to be the "official" ideology of the Hoover Institution. Given this record of noncommittal quiescence and not being at best even a reluctant Hooverite, I was not surprised when, one nice day some years later, I received a letter from the director informing me that the little suite of offices was no longer mine. Period. I never inquired whether my being dumped was due to their needing the space for real, rather than genteel, fellows, or whether it was revenge for some *lèse majesté*. I continued to be a senior fellow, I don't know why, and my picture still appears in the institution's annual report.

Boons as Unearned Income

There is a third way to sort out perks and boons. Doing so shows that boons are not psychologically unalloyed blessings. They are like unearned income. They *do* make you feel guilty. A perk, even if not fully paid for by a tradeoff of some sort, is not likely to deprive you of sleep. A boondoggle does. What have I done to deserve being invited to this conference on St. Thomas to snorkel in the Caribbean? Why should I have been asked to spend a month at the Villa Serbelloni in Bellagio on Lake Como, presumably to do some serious writing, though everybody knows that very little of that can be done, with all the good food and wines being served and all the excursions to Bergamo, Varese, Lugano, and lots of other beauties beckoning?

All this turns me from the psychology-prone economist I pretend to be into the true-blue historian I have always been, only people didn't know it. There was in fact a time when a perk was really a perk. When I first came into the academic business and joined the American Political Science Association, this august professional society was holding its annual meetings in the week between Christmas and New Year's (when hotel prices were particularly cheap), rather than, as now, around Labor Day weekend (when they are still cheap). In those good old days, one would write one's remarks to be "delivered" on the back of an envelope while en route—by train, of course—to the convention city; in the new, bad days, one would have to "ditto"—purple ink being the preferred color—what came to be called a "paper" and send it to panel participants. Later, a sly executive director would even sell the papers to an ever-growing membership!

Change came in the early 1950s and much displeased the influential wives of the powerful professors from the great university cities of the American heartland, such as Ann Arbor, Columbus, Madison, and Urbana. Being able to go on a postholiday shopping spree at Saks Fifth Avenue in New York, Garfinkel's in Washington, or Marshall Field's in Chicago had been the not-to-be-sneezed-at boons that the ladies most appreciated. The fact is, of course, there were mighty few perks or boons to be had in academe in those modest years of yesterday before *Sputnik* changed the funding patterns of the university.

4

The Perplexing Perversities of Perjury,
or
Why Untruth Is Not Always
the Opposite of Truth

The really enjoyable things of academic life, now well behind, are really missed: no more rationally driven departmental faculty meetings hassling over this or that, mostly turf (see chapter 7); no more *bon vivant* search committees spending the dean's discretionary allowances to hire just the right kind of person whom we would want to "let go" after three or six years of servitude for not measuring up to snuff ("snuff" being us, the tenured faculty); no more thrilling report writing for some vice-president's or vice-provost's "eyes only" about the calamitous state of political philosophy; no more exhilarating office hours explaining the verities of political science to especially bright undergraduates in order to keep them from going to law school instead of becoming professors; no more stand-up comedy hours called lectures. And no more perjurious letters of recommendation for Ph.D. candidates who aspired to fellowships or professorships that they did not deserve.

Now, "perjury" is a pretty strong word, and I really don't mean it in the strict dictionary sense. In using it I was probably just carried away by the symphonic and alliterative opportunities created by this chapter's title. In fact, the alternatives Mr. Roget's *International Thesaurus* suggests—disinformation, deliberate falsehood, distortion, misrepresentation, prevarication, fabrication, and so on—would give a worse impression. For I have in mind something somewhat more subtle, like, perhaps, "bending the truth just a little bit" or "not telling all that could be told" or "drawing a fine line between fact and fancy." If I continue to employ "perjury" nevertheless, it is in these eupeptic senses, rather than in the dreary legalistic ones.

As is well known, the academic paper flow is irreversible and unabating, and the contents of file cabinets have an uncanny tendency to grow like weeds. To make room for the many manuscripts I still expected to write after retirement, the very first act on becoming a professor emeritus called for a merciless cleansing of the bulging letters-of-recommendation files that, with irresistible force, had accumulated over the years. Cleaning out files provides a propitious occasion for the kind of reflection impossible in the busy years when we academics are expected and generously remunerated to "think." So it was in one of those Archimedean "aha" moments that come with file-cleaning that I uttered the famous Greek's *eureka*: I had discovered the *quid* for the *quo* involved in all the great advantages I had enjoyed for so many years as an active professor.

The Costs of Perjury

Never had something become so clear to me: every benefit or pleasure I had ever had in my many years in academe was paid for by an act of perjury in a letter of recommendation written for students of all kinds, especially the hopeless ones whom we should have sent on their way before it was too late. No longer did I need to feel guilty about the pleasures of university life and the sundry perks that had come along from time to time. They had not been freebies after all but had all been earned. Perks and perjury, I now hypothesized in a truly scientific mode, are the necessary and sufficient components of a tradeoff scale yet to be created before the professoriat is again polled about their likes and dislikes in academic life (see chapter 3).

Unless a student is truly brilliant or beloved, writing letters of recommendation is a bore and, more often than not, an exercise in perjury. There are various strategies of avoidance. One strategy is just to decline writing a letter, but that always struck me as a failure of nerve and neglect of duty. A second strategy is difficult to execute—to explain to the less than brilliant student to apply only for things within the range of his or her limited capabilities, in which case I'd be glad to write an appropriate letter. The trouble with this alternative is that one may be altogether mistaken about the student's capacities; he or she may even become a college president or dean someday. And, more likely than not, this strategy gives rise to the kind of weaseling, canned letters that are the mode. The third strategy is to surround oneself only with brilliant students so that the letter-writing problem is no problem. But as at best only one in ten deserves this accolade, one may end up with no students at all. I eschewed this strategy of avoidance as cowardly. I always thought it to be a victory for humanity if I could extract a halfway passable dissertation from the less than brilliant student and help him or her get a job in a place where minimal talents would bring optimal good.

Now, reading over all the letters of three decades in the course of file cleaning, I had to decide which ones to keep and which ones to shred. The choice was relatively easy: I would destroy, first of all, those letters that, if revealed under some freedom of information act, might lead to a lawsuit accusing me of libel or slander for which I had no liability insurance. Liability insurance costing what it does (a lot), the most obvious candidates for liquidation were the most clearly perjurious epistles. Whatever letter was full of bias and/or ill will had to go. That left only a few in the drawer but had the salutary effect of not only creating file space but also erasing all memory of any possibly perjurious misdeeds on my part. Sued, I can honestly recall nothing. I can even avoid buying the liability insurance that might be needed if a former student should sue me retroactively for incompetence in the classroom.

The Wonderland of Perjury

The process of letter-of-recommendation writing has all kinds of starting points. Only some come to mind in this rather unsystematic investigation. It can be initiated by an institution in search of talent or in need of help on an internal promotion. It can be initiated by a student looking for a job or scholarship, or by a professor hoping finally to get rid of a student. It can be initiated by a colleague at your own or some other institution asking for your support in his or her application for a fellowship, a grant, or an award.

This journey into the wonderland of perjury begins with some requests seeking what are called "outside" letters of recommendation for hiring or promoting a colleague. The letters with this sort of request can be pretty dull and sometimes long-winded; this is quite unremarkable. One of the more honest letters I ever received came from a department chair seeking my perjurious help in the case of a lateral (within institution) appointment of a senior professor. This one was so unique that I want to quote its central paragraph in full, for it was candidly brief and did not go on forever specifying the virtues sought in a candidate:

> Several of my colleagues have suggested that you would be eminently qualified to provide an appraisal of Dr. _____'s *notable* contributions to the discipline. Your *favorable* comments will be used in endeavoring to induce our administration to respond affirmatively to the departmental recommendation (emphases added).

This letter is truly one of its kind. By telling me that the candidate's contributions were "notable" and asking me to make "favorable" comments, this solicitation surely gave me license to be a legitimate perjurer! What would they do if I were to write an unfavorable letter? My handwritten notation on the original: "I did not reply but sent letter [copy] on to _____" (name of one of writer's colleagues whom I knew well). End of this affair!

Four Categories of Perjury

As I read through all the letters of recommendation written for students, undergraduate and graduate, I can sort the perjurious ones into four categories of "pleasure" their writing gave me. In fact, the categories constitute a perfect ordinal and transitive scale. At the low end, the letter's opening paragraph includes the phrase "it gives me pleasure." This translates into a generally supportive and essentially warm endorsement—involving mild but not injurious perjury. It is the truest letter I used to write, and I called it, appropriately, my "grade D" letter. At the next level, the phrase becomes "it gives me great pleasure." This means a somewhat stronger but still not necessarily hot recommendation, but perjury is all too obvious and possibly punishable in a civil action. This was a "C" letter. In the third category (grade "B") , it would give me "very great pleasure" to write on the student's behalf. This admission clearly moves letter-writing pleasure across some hypothetical but inexorably moving equilibrium point of the perjury scale and means that perjury is blatantly self-evident and indictable in a criminal proceeding. Finally, there are a few letters that gave me "extraordinary pleasure" to send off. In these "grade A" letters perjury is so egregious and pervasive that I should have been hauled before the Ethics Committee of the American Political Science Association. As an example, take this one:

> It is probably only once or twice within a given four-year Ph.D. cohort that I write what I would consider a very strong letter of recommendation. It gives me extraordinary pleasure, therefore, to add (_____) to this very select group of persons among Stanford's Ph.D.'s in the field of American politics, broadly conceived, with whom I had something to do in the last twenty years. I rank her among the very best. . . . All of these were not only "promising" students but have delivered on their promises since taking their academic positions. I'm probably forgetting two or three others, but I hope the sample makes the point I wish to make.

How much more perjurious can one get? But this is not the end of it. The real secret is that I predicated the success of these letters on an inverse relationship between a letter's grade and the scholarly reputation of the school to which the letter went. Letters to Harvard, Yale, or Berkeley and the rest of the top ten were invariably of the "C" and "D" kind, while letters to the institutions of less repute were "A" or "B" letters. This "strategic preference" procedure was based on the further assumption that the lesser institutions were more in need of talent than the better ones and that our less brilliant students, destined to the lesser places in any case, were more in need of the letters that gave me very great or extraordinary pleasure to write.

It is no great secret that perjurious conduct in letters of recommendation is difficult to prove. These letters are presumably private and confidential, and what perjurious mischief they contain is a matter of guesswork. Guessing, in turn, requires multiple perjury on the part of the perjurer. The late Charlie Hyneman, a friend whose wry candor I appreciated, was an indefatigable perjurer in his letters of recommendation. His Ph.D. candidates at Indiana University were all geniuses, but you wouldn't know it until you had accumulated a sufficiently large and revealing portfolio of his often very long epistles. Charlie was a great teacher and scholar, and some of his students, as it turned out, did in fact become fine scholars. But his letters of recommendation were invariably and monotonously identical, with none of the refined calibration I invented for my own literary efforts in this line of academic work.

I cannot say just what pleasure I derived from employing the nuanced opening phrases about pleasure in my letters of recommendation, other than, perhaps their obscuring the perjurious nature of what followed in the letter's text. As I once wrote in one of them, letting my guard down, "You and I, having both written and received letters of recommendation of this sort, know how difficult it is to say anything meaningful about former students of ours, or others, that is not trivial. These letters all sound alike." This is from a letter that gave me "very great pleasure" to write. The "all-sound-alike" theme reverberates in this variation: "I would like to say something as a point of privilege. I just completed reading 125 files of applicants for an assistant professorship here. This comes to about 500 letters of recommendation. If I were to believe these letters, the country would be full of geniuses. I find it more and more painful to read and write letters of recommendation. They all sound alike."

In another letter I even searched my conscience—an action rarely required when writing perjurious letters: "Having written my fill of letters of recommendation, it becomes ever more difficult to write another one. What makes it somewhat easier in this case is that I have a warm personal affection for him that may bias my appraisal . . . , but which should not be written off precisely because it is by no means arbitrary or self-serving." Well, sometimes understatement pays off: the letter was a success. No! The candidate was and still is a success. He was hired by a first-rate institution, is still there, and has become a distinguished scholar. This was in 1971.

In the Wonderland of Ambiguity

There is an intersection where the high road and the low road of letter-of-recommendation writing cross. How to begin letters at this intersection always causes me some trouble, but I resolve it by informing the recipient that it gives me "considerable pleasure" to write. Decoded, that means that the letter will be ambiguous. "Considerable" can mean "large" or "much"; in this usage it is almost synonymous with "great." But it can also mean "worth considering" or "important" or "noteworthy." Interpreted that way, it alerts the letter's recipient to the possibility that the message may be on the up-and-up or honest, worthy of serious consideration. As I read over the relatively few letters in this genre, they indeed indicate some ambivalence; the letters are partly perjurious and partly honest. Let me cite from just one to illustrate what I have in mind: "She is bright and inquisitive, hardworking and pleasant, willing to learn and flexible. She is all that a teacher might ask for, above all perhaps a lively person who is responsive without being compulsive in responding. I can hardly say more." And I can hardly say, today, what being "responsive without being compulsive in responding" may have alluded to. But, then, this was addressed to a law school screening committee.

Another letter would report that I have "observed" the person in question for a number of years (suggesting that he or she has not committed any misdemeanor); that I'm "impressed" by his/her "progress as a scholar and teacher" (meaning I really haven't the slightest idea as to how he/she will work out over the long haul); that he/she was a member of a seminar "at a time when we were blessed with an especially bright and competitive group of graduate students," and that he/she was a "critical member of that group and did very well indeed" (in other words, kept up with the competition but was not one of the best).

A good cue for categorizing letters at the high-and-low road intersection is the use of the word "risk," as in the following: "He is certainly one of the younger scholars whose career can receive an enormous boost by being properly supported. Knowing the man, I think that supporting him would be a low-risk investment...." What does this say? The honest part of the passage says that the man's career *can* receive a boost by research support. The hidden and semiperjurious message is that so far he or she hasn't done much by way of research, though he or she might. The really perjurious part, evident to anyone skilled in reading such letters, is the suggestion of risk involved, even though it is judged to be low. "Why would Eulau bring up the risk factor at all?" some smart chair of an admission or grant-giving committee will ask. I gave the answer away in another letter where I demonstrated an unusual amount of candor: "Let me emphasize that in my own evaluation of candidates for promotion, I give as much emphasis to what they are likely to do in the future as to their track record (which some colleagues consider the less risky thing to do). I have always considered promotion a risky business, perhaps more often indicative of future failure than success. In the case of _____ I have the feeling that the risk of failure is very low." Of course, I did not qualify this prediction: that the chance of success in turn was not necessarily high.

The Truth Redeemed

Nonperjurious letters of recommendation are easier to code; o (zero) and 1 (one) suffice. The zeroed letters are those saying absolutely nothing; the "ones" are those that I would characterize as "positively critical" of the recommended person and his or her work. These are the truly honest letters. Because these letters are easily misread and misunderstood, you can write them only to persons whom you know really well, and on whom you can count for adequate interpretation to their colleagues who may not be attuned to irony or satire. Here is a specimen I once wrote to the chair of a department, an old friend. It involved my evaluation of a former Stanford student up for promotion. After promising a "disinterested appraisal," I had this to say:

> His attempt to exploit the data for theoretical purposes for which they were not necessarily collected was ingenious, though perhaps not as successful as one might wish for; but this reflects perhaps more on the data than on his ingenuity. I had some reservations about his theorizing in the dissertation because I felt that the data were not the right data for the purposes for which he used them,

but that only strengthens my regard for his ingenuity. In part, also, I had some doubts about his grip on the theoretical notions he tried to deal with, but his grip then was probably better than that of most graduate students, and his theoretical sophistication was certainly greater than that of most.

Without interpretation, a passage of this sort entering the field of vision of a dean who, say, is a chemist, would be disastrous. I could count on my friend, the chairman, that he would clarify it for a dean trained in reading the Periodic Table of Elements.

In another letter, written in behalf of a young woman with whom I had served on a research committee and of whom I thought very well, I noted that cultural anthropologists and perception psychologists had long tried to cope with the issues presented in one of her papers. In this regard, I continued,

> the discussion here strikes me as superficial. A few quotes from [two references] simply will not do. . . . Moreover, the attempt to get at the context of persons' cognitive structures by way of hypothetical situations . . . is likely to lead to several dead alleys. . . . I don't believe that asking a telephone respondent to place himself in the position of the President of the United States will yield valid and reliable knowledge about cognitive structures.

This letter was for the eyes and ears of a department that, I knew, would receive these comments in the supportive spirit in which they were intended. I'm sure George Orwell could not improve on such newspeak, where critical remarks have positive, and pleasing words have negative, value.

There are some letters that are difficult to put into any of the perjurious or honest categories because they involve some unclassifiable trickery. There is the request from a department for a letter evaluating someone whom they want to hire. I really do not think much of this person, but he or she is just the kind of person whom this department deserves. Here's a response, and it is not fictitious: "I'm really not in a very good position to give you the thorough judgment you request. I have read all of [his] work which is of very high quality. . . . My acquaintance with him is casual, however, and I cannot say anything else but that he seems a very pleasant person." Nothing unusual here; just the usual perjury and much ambiguity. And the letter does not reveal any degree of pleasure that writing it gave me. Then the punch line: "I think we would be quite enthusiastic if we could bring [him] to Stanford." What department would not want to hire a sterling person like this?

Then there are the letters in response to inquiries asking for a comparison between two candidates, your own students or others. The purpose of these letters of inquiry is to entrap you and have you do the job that the inquiring person should do for himself or herself. To get out of the trap, hitting the ball right back into the other's court is in order: "Because I'm off on a prolonged lecture trip, . . . I hasten to reply to your letter of 13 October, though I can do so only rather superficially. In other words, I cannot go in any detail into [the two candidates'] work, though I would be glad to examine one or the other's work carefully should it come to an appointment."

For reasons not difficult to fathom, I have never been cited as a perjurer by some committee on professional ethics. And, of course, I have myself been the victim of undeserved letters, like the following from the senior staff of the one academic organization I have valued above all others, the Inter-University Consortium for Political and Social Research. After conceding, truthfully, that this was "an extremely difficult letter to write," the letter continued on a more discretionary note:

> The gratitude, respect and affection that result from an association that has spanned twenty years, in my case, and more than a quarter century, in the case of the Consortium, cannot be easily expressed.
>
> Perhaps the best way to begin is to simply state our very deep appreciation. Your many contributions as Official Representative, as Chairman of the Council and member for two terms, and as Associate Director have shaped the Consortium in vital ways. In a very real sense you have watched over the Consortium from its very beginnings, and have been a constant spokesman for the larger scholarly values that the organization was founded to serve. Whatever success the Consortium has achieved has been in no small measure a tribute to your continuing and selfless efforts.
>
> Your influence in less formal ways has been equally important. As friend and mentor to many of us on the staff you have consis-

tently provided assistance and encouragement. The respect that you have shown the staff and its work has been particularly valuable for morale and self esteem. Your willingness to share your professional experience, organizational insights and scholarly wisdom has been a source of guidance for us all.

Amen!

5

The Lonely Crowd —
Students as Products and Peers,
or
If Your Colleagues Only Treated Us
the Way You Do

He knocked, came into the windowless office, and sat down opposite me. This was not the office in which I usually saw students; that had windows. It was the office in which I hid from students to do some serious work, and hence it was windowless—if you can follow the logic of this architectural preference. As soon as I looked at him I knew that something was amiss. I said, "Hello," studied him for what was probably less than a second, then came up with my usual, well-rehearsed opening line: "And what can I do for you today, Bob?" with an emphasis on the "today" to make it clear that we had met before—something that, I had suspicion to believe —some of my colleagues sometimes forget when a student comes in to see them.

Bob, one of our graduate students, looked down at the floor and said, "I'm going to withdraw from school." It wasn't the first time I had heard that, and I could have sent him on his merry way, with a perfunctory "sorry to hear that," and gotten on with whatever I was doing. But I liked Bob, and while on first meeting him I hadn't expected him to be an academic mover and shaker, I thought he was intelligent and, above all, sensitive enough to be a good teacher.

Bob had come to us from a respected private university in the upper South where he had enjoyed a good undergraduate education in political science. He was now in his second year, and I had not the slightest idea that he wasn't happy. I did not try to talk him out of his decision to leave but was interested in exploring his reasons. He wasn't unhappy with our department's program; he wasn't unhappy with Stanford as a place to be; he wasn't unhappy with his fellowship; and he wasn't unhappy with his girl friend. I can't recall all we talked about, but when I finally pressed him to tell me what really troubled him, he burst out: "Professor Eulau, I would stay if your colleagues only treated us the way you do." I found his comment intriguing enough to follow up: "And how do I treat students?" Bob: "Not as students but as future colleagues."

When the Undergraduates Come Marching In

My responses to student interests and needs had been honed at Antioch College, where student feedback to faculty misdemeanor was instant and noisy. Except for this "noise factor," the transition from teaching undergraduates at Antioch to working with graduate students at Stanford was relatively easy. At Antioch individuation had been gospel. And as Antioch was anything but a rah-rah college, the academic atmosphere was more mature than at many other undergraduate colleges. In my early years at Antioch, right after World War II, the place was full of veterans, some of them older than their teacher. Because of the college's work-study program, most students spend five and even more years in school. In my last year there I had a small team of students helping me for several months interview state legislators in Columbus. So "working with" a student was how I conceived of teaching, at both the undergraduate and graduate levels.

I'm equating the Antioch undergraduates with the Stanford graduate students, rather than with Stanford undergraduates. The Antiochians of the 1950s were a very different lot from their age-equivalent cohorts at the university. At least in my early years at Stanford, undergraduates in the social sciences and the humanities did not expect and were not expected to work with a professor. Although I taught very small, seminar-style undergraduate courses, I remember only two or three of the Stanford undergraduates who participated in some of my own research. Because I have written about the Antioch experience elsewhere (Eulau 1996, chaps. 5 and 14), I have to be careful not to plagiarize myself. And modesty should forbid me from reviving the following testimonial, but as it has appeared in public print and says something about the substance and style of teaching at Antioch, I will throw modesty to the winds. Cynthia Fuchs Epstein, now a distinguished sociologist at the City University of New York Graduate Center, researcher and author on "woman's place" in things professional, recently recalled her years as an undergraduate at Antioch:[1]

> The choice of Antioch College turned out to be a good one, not only because I found a lot of intellectually kindred souls there but also because I became attached to a group of students in political science who were studying with Professor Heinz Eulau. Eulau frightened a lot of people because he was so demanding and uncompromising as a teacher, but I was used to being frightened, and it did not occur to me to buck authority, at least not the authority of a person I respected. I was exulted by this brilliant man who made each class an experiment and who assigned us weekly essays on our readings, including a wide range of thinkers such as George Herbert Mead, Robert K. Merton, Paul Kecskemeti, Harold Lasswell, Freud, Marx, and Darwin. Eulau had attracted a group of students who took pleasure in the constant intellectual interaction and interchange his classes offered and who with him explored theory to find new explanations for what caused the varieties and clusterings of human behavior. In fact, of that group of about ten or twelve, a good portion became professors in the social sciences with outstanding reputations. Others went on to become dynamic lawyers in public-interest law. Eulau was one of those facilitators of excellence Merton has written about.

> The Antiochians were simply wonderful because they made me see myself as they saw me. I still have in some album a card I received from the eight students in a course when it was all over. It shows a drawing of my head in various poses but inevitably with pipe or cigarette in mouth, and the heads of the group. Quoting from Luke, one side of the card said: "All . . . wondered at the gra-

---

1. See Cynthia Fuchs Epstein, *Woman's Place: Options and Limits in Professional Careers* (Berkeley: University of California Press, 1970); *Women in Law* (New York: Basic Books, 1981); *Deceptive Distinctions: Sex, Gender, and the Social Order* (New Haven: Yale University Press, and New York: Russell Sage Foundation, 1988). The quotation comes from "Personal Reflections with a Sociological Eye," in *Authors of Their Own Lives,* ed. Bennett M. Berger (Berkeley: University of California Press, 1990), 354.

cious words which proceeded out of his mouth." The opposite side, showing more heads, quoted from Psalms: "We shall not die, but live and declare the works of the Lord." The backside was devoted to Shakespeare: "O, do de, do de, do de." Another card, again from an entire class, had these greetings accompanying a present: "A portfolio—to transport the syntheses of countless thoughts of the week. In appreciation for guidance through the avenues of innumerable dependent and independent variables."

You shouldn't be surprised to learn that one of the card's signers was Cynthia, and another of the signers much later recalled the good times had by all. Here are some excerpts from a letter received on my retirement from Bill Gamson, who for many years taught sociology at the University of Michigan:

> My most vivid memories are of the double credit course in "Politics and Society" in which we wrote a weekly paper on the readings of that week. For most of the students (including me), it was a matter of staying up most of Thursday night to do it. This was a big class and, of course, it never occurred to me at the time what a burdensome task this created for you—weekend after weekend of reading student papers. (You must have been crazy!) And there was never any doubt in any of our minds that you read these papers and were ready to call them crap if that's what they were.
>
> I still remember with delight when you responded so positively to a paper I wrote as a dialogue between theorists and how gently and properly you reminded me to move on when I tried the same device a couple more times. "You're staying at the same level of Socratic disputation" was how you put it.
>
> Not that I would describe gentleness as one of your central personality traits. I recall another occasion when I had just read Robert Lynd's *Knowledge for What* and conveyed my enthusiasm for it to you. "You like propaganda," you remarked, cigarette dangling from the corner of your half-smile. Well, yes, you're right. I liked propaganda then and I still like it.

I never got as close to Stanford undergraduates as I did to my students at Antioch, and I never had anything like this kind of endorsement at Stanford. Occasionally a student might come around to say or write something formally complimentary. And I didn't do much undergraduate teaching, but circa 1968 I let my chairman talk me into teaching a huge beginning American government course, with formal lectures, microphone and loudspeakers, quiz sections, teaching assistants whom nobody had ever taught to teach, and all that sort of ballast. The course was a nightmare. I try to repress this experience in mass education as much as I can, but there was one incident perhaps worthy of remembrance. It remains a testimonial to those times of trouble when we were expected to educate the uneducables.

I had given a lecture on social structure and politics, suggesting two structural dimensions in social relations—one horizontal (called "stratification") and one vertical (called "levels of organization"). On the blackboard, exhibiting all the artistic skills I'm capable of, I produced a neat drawing of a diamond-shaped figure that I thought was a fair facsimile of what I was talking about. I gave several illustrations. At the end of the lecture I asked for questions, as usual, "Is everything clear?" A young woman in the front row piped up. "But, Professor Eulau...." I knew what was coming (I had not taught her never to start a question with "but"). "But Professor Eulau," she asked, "what is *your* commitment?" In my customarily gentle way, I responded, "That, young lady, is none of your damn business."

The Teacher as a Looking-Glass Self

I can't say anything about or speak for my colleagues in the teaching business as to how they see themselves as teachers. I almost wrote educators, as we humble teachers are called in *Who's Who*, not to mention the sophisticated word "pedagogue," much beloved by Victorian thinkers because it is so revealing of the pedantic component of our art. My own social psychology has been largely influenced by James Horton Cooley's conception of the "looking-glass self" and George Herbert Mead's notion of the "significant other" (a concept trivialized in recent times). We tend to see ourselves as others see us. But as others do not see us with the same eyes, this creates a bit of chaos in how we see ourselves.

It's an open secret that most university professors in research universities, so-called, do research to get promoted and/or get rich by way of grants or contracts. In some rare cases a few may even enjoy doing research for whatever psychic satisfaction it brings them. And it is common knowledge that they publish their research findings for the good of humanity, if not for the esteem it brings them among their peers. How students think of them is a very minor consideration when they occupy the grandstand.

Just how difficult it is to enter students' minds was brought home to me when I learned that something I had taken for granted was a novelty to them. I took it for granted that an evening seminar began at a specified time, say 7:30 P.M., as announced in the university's time schedule. As the time schedule did not schedule any other course after 10:30 P.M., I also took it for granted that there was no specified upper limit to student endurance. My notion was that a seminar would go on as long as there was something to be seminared about. Here is one recollection of just how I entertained the seminar crowd. The writer of this memoir is SPSS inventor Norman Nie, who never used one word when and where he could use two. I am therefore liberally cutting what, for the purpose at hand, can be cut.

> In the Spring of 1966, Heinz gave an evening seminar built around the most recent contributions to the then infant field of rational choice.... The seminar began at 7:30 P.M. and the course schedule said that it would end at 10:30. In fact, we rarely left the parlor of the Institute for Political Studies on Salvatierra Avenue [actually, just another street then, now only a walk] before the wee hours of the morning. The participants affectionately dubbed it "The Eulathon." Among our spouses and children it became less affectionately known as the widows and orphans seminar. So heated and lengthy were the debates and discussions that our post-seminar search for liquid refreshment was usually limited to the imminent arrival of the morning milkman.... Given my own teaching experience, I can hardly believe that Heinz kept us enthusiastically at it for 6 to 8 hours at a time.

Perhaps exaggerated *un petit peu*, but correct in the essentials. Few students, especially graduate students, ever feel free enough to say what's really on their minds. Just read the silly things they usually write about their professors in the prefaces of their doctoral dissertations. You can't recognize yourself in them any better than in the obituaries that will be written about you not much later (see Epilogue). They all worship you because of the great ideas you instilled in them. The only way of keeping your sanity when reading these effusions is to reverse them from positives into negatives. For the fun of it, I offer the following table d'hôte.

The Very Model of a Thesis Supervisor

It was well known among the students that despite often lingering doubts about the substance of and the fashionable methods used in their dissertations, Eulau was nevertheless willing to sign almost anything put under his nose, on the condition that he would never have to read the published version. As one of his most loyal woman Ph.D.s so tellingly put it, "Although Professor Eulau was 30 years older than I was when my dissertation was completed in 1974, he was even then a role model difficult to emulate, especially as I was a woman of the feminist era."

Similar encomia are found in other dissertation prefaces: "It is something of an exaggeration to say that my first and greatest debt was to Eulau as my principal dissertation adviser," said Dr. A, now a distinguished research professor. "It is simply false to claim that Eulau's destructive criticism was valuable at every stage of my project from the development of the research design through the writing of the final draft." Another disavowal came from Dr. B, now a dean, who rejected the idea that her "greatest debt and deepest thanks" are due to the professor; "he was certainly not an inexhaustible source of ideas, encouragement, and patience." Dr. C had this to say: "I resented the few hours he spent with me at the beginning of my study during the difficult process of settling on a topic and the careless manner in which he read various versions of my dissertation."

Not all of these survivors were equally honest in assessing what Eulau did not do for and to them. Here is the testimony of one former pupil, Dr. D, who at one time fancied himself to be a radical. His entry in the 1973 *Biographical Directory* of the APSA boasted of these accomplishments: "Benedict Arnold Award on Revolutionary Softball Team." He identified himself as "Provisional Revolutionary Govt., Stanford University, 1971–72." His activities included "Angela Davis Defense Survey, Witness & Coordinator of Survey." Among his fields of specialization he listed these: "Radical Pol. Econ.; Theory & Practice of Marxist Revolution; Bureaucracy; Epistemology and philosophy of science; Third World Countries & Regions, Including Amer. Subgroups." This fellow, of whom I was rather fond in spite or because of his theatrical performances during the revolution, is now a liberal and sober politician in a midwestern state. In his dissertation preface he waxed almost poetic though remaining prosaic (and, for once, I'm quoting what he really wrote):

> In writing this dissertation, the light was in my eyes, the infield rocky, and the umpire poor of sight. I therefore feel no need to apologize for the occasional error, missed insight, faulty line of reasoning, or inductive leaps that caused unearned runs to score. I would, however, like to thank in more than obligatory fashion, those who did not send me to the showers but helped me finish the game, especially my venerable manager Heinz Eulau.

In general, the prefatory excesses were monotonously embarrassing and devoid of empathy or sympathy with a professor who could not defend himself because he had signed the theses before reading the only thing left for him to read—the prefaces. They included all the familiar bromides of academic discourse—enormous debt of gratitude, rare open-mindedness, intellectual honesty, personal involvement, continuing support and guidance, perceptive and pragmatic criticism, crucial insights and comments, commitment to science, invaluable assistance, creative zeal for empirical answers, clear and high standards, professional excellence, unrelenting concern for objectivity, indispensable antidote, constant, patient, and valuable critic, invariably generous with his time, generous in his praise for clarity, rejection of the second-rate, and so on and so forth *ad nauseam.*

One of the more honest prefaces not in need of adjectival reversal came from Dr. E, who had come into the Stanford program long after having shed the teenage quest for a "role model." In fact, he was short of forty, and by the time he had his Ph.D. he was a reasonably mature forty-three. He could afford to be candid. He clearly knew what mentorship is all about:

> I am indebted to Professor Eulau for his intellectual stimulation, for his moral support, for his efforts to get financial support for me while I was a graduate student in the department. He was instrumental in helping me get a National Institute of Mental Health Traineeship. He also taught me that every research endeavor should begin with a puzzle—one which is of significant theoretical interest. I also want to thank him and the group of graduate students whom he organized into a Wednesday, and then a Tuesday lunch group. This was an invaluable forum for thinking out loud, and getting useful feedback from faculty and fellow graduate students. I hope to continue the tradition.

Eulau's recommendation to all young Ph.D. dissertation advisers: insist on reading the preface and make your signing the dissertation contingent on appropriate recognition of your indispensability as a mentor.

The Lonely Crowd: A Little Love Goes a Long Way

Bob, to get back to him, was a member of the small group of five or six grad students, all Ph.D. candidates, that Dr. E mentioned in his preface. They were all "Americanists," in various stages of their graduate career and with widely varying interests. By the time Bob came in to see me, I had met with the group for a number of years at bag lunches. There was some turnover in the group's membership over the years as one or another actually did finish and managed to "get out," as students put it so crudely. I still have a photo of the group that includes Bob and helps to refresh the memory.

The "Bob episode" has come to stay with me and brought to mind earlier experiences involving graduate students. I remember a faculty meeting in some early year at Stanford at which I had to listen to an associate professor who was the graduate adviser and who had nothing but disdain for our graduate students in toto. Indeed, I remember another faculty meeting in those early years that, I think, broke the camel's back. Arnie Rogow had come to Stanford in 1960, and he was no pussyfooter. The chairman—a chair-*man* of the old school—was carrying on about our "products" doing this or that, and Arnie let it be known that he resented being a "Princeton product" as if he were a pound of hamburger coming out of a butcher's meat grinder.

Some years ago, I had a long conversation with the late Marty Diamond, the political theorist, who had studied with Leo Strauss at Chicago. Marty was a master teacher (he once had his picture on the cover of *Time*), and we were members of an APSA committee on undergraduate education that often met in the early 1970s. We had become good friends, I think, despite or, perhaps, because of our widely differing views of what political science is or should be about. Well, one day I asked Marty why it was that Leo Strauss had so many devoted students. It wasn't so much the substance of what he taught as his accessibility and concern for each of his students as an individual person that, Marty thought, accounted for the "Strauss phenomenon." He was always there and his door was always open, while his colleagues were nowhere to be seen. There was of course more to Strauss than that, but this was what Diamond told me. I confess to never having left my office door open, but there are other ways to love your students than sitting in a draft.

While I took some pride and satisfaction in associating some students with my own research, I tried to get interested in the work of others and see it *as they saw it,* rather than in some outsider's perspective. I think it is this "faculty" (call it empathy, even love, if you wish) that makes for being an effective supervisor of a Ph.D. thesis. Well, I never thought of myself as a "supervisor." Alan Abramowitz, now a premier research scholar at Emory University, whose exploits as a student I have celebrated elsewhere (see Eulau 1996, chap. 8, n. 14, and chap. 25, n. 4), was not too far off the falsifiable mark in a letter written on the occasion of my greening as a professor emeritus. It is reproduced here, not in its coherent wholeness but selectively with some corrective interventions:

It's been said that a scholar's work is solving intellectual puzzles. Well, there's one problem—why did so many of the graduate students of my generation end up working with Eulau? How did you manage to turn out so many Ph.D.s?

Well-trained, Alan came up with several hypotheses, one being that "there were no viable alternatives." He rejected this option as false because "there were several attractive alternatives." His next question, implying another hypothesis:

> What could be the intellectual thread connecting students who were working on such diverse topics as voting in congressional elections, the relationship between protest groups and the mass media, the politics of education, and the impact of senior citizens' lobbying?

Alan rejected this hypothesis as well, but it led him to a third, which he evidently thought of as true: "I had to conclude that the only thing we *did* have in common was our adviser."

Addendum
Partial Guide for Graduate Students on How to Become Famous

Step 1. Pick for your dissertation something very simple and give it a big name that, preferably, is of Latin or Greek origin —like "Poliphily" or love of politics.

Step 2. Announce a dissertation with an appropriate title, like "Poliphilic Tendencies in the United States Senate."

Step 3. Make sure your dissertation title is published in the profession's house organ *PS*. It will tell everybody how bright you are.

Step 4. Make sure you have a one-page abstract of your proposal to send to all those who will inquire.

Step 5. A concept like poliphily is clearly not enough: what you need is a three-dimensional typology—true poliphily, ambiguous poliphily, and false poliphily. (A *three-fold* typology is essential—not two, not four.)

Step 6. Give your typology to your adviser, Professor X. He is likely to point out to you that "false poliphiles" are really "true poliphobes" and that your typology will gain in power (both heuristic and explanatory) if you speak of poliphiles, polineuters, and poliphobes. This will eliminate the bothersome value implications associated with terms "true" and "false" and make your typology more scientific.

Step 7. Collect, by all means, data. Code data. Analyze data. Cross-tab data. If no worthwhile results are forthcoming from cross-tabs, do a factor analysis. Discover three factors—I, II, and III. If so inclined, you may also call them A, B, and C. Discover that one factor seems to be loaded on poliphily, another on polineutrality, and the third on poliphobia. Publish your factor analysis. It will give credence to and legitimize your typology (soon to be known as the "Stanford Typology of Poliphiphobism"). Order plenty of reprints for wide distribution in anticipation of requests.

Step 8. Now that you have spent at least a year becoming fairly famous as "that talented Stanford Ph.D. candidate," go back to your analysis. Cross-tab factor types with dependent variables and obtain correlation coefficients. You again get no good results. Consult Professor Y, who is hot on regression and path analysis. He surely will lead you out of the morass. Do what Professor Y tells you. Show him the results and your write-up. He will tell you that you should publish the results, except there being the problem of recognition, your name being only marginally known (provided you have followed Step 3). "Why not list me as co-author? You will get published quicker that way." Do!

Step 9. The ms. has been accepted, but the editor suggests that Professor Y be listed as the senior author. Do not object. Your own fame will be doubled; everybody knows that the junior author has done all the hard work and thinking.

Step 10. Use your own imagination from here on in.

POSTSCRIPT. The original of this Guide had many more steps. My editorial instinct, reinforced by space limitations, told me to cut them.

6

What a (Department) Chair and a Dog Have in Common,
or
the Great Experience of Being Kicked and Kicking Back

The postmodern transfiguration of the department "chairman" into an atrocious-sounding "chairperson" had become academic etiquette by the time I reached this lowest on the lower rungs of the academy's bureaucratic career ladder. For reasons not difficult to fathom, I never made it any farther "up," not even to being an assistant dean. If memory does not deceive me, it was in the late 1960s. And soon afterward some very sensitive persons, I suspect them of having been welfare economists, had the brilliant idea of reducing a chairperson to a "chair."

There had been the alternative of returning to the outmoded term "head." I had always liked calling a department head a head for two reasons. First, the word refers to an organic and not, as it came to be, an inorganic phenomenon. And second, a head is presumably the location of the brain, with far-reaching consequences for expressing one's view of the head—like being able to call him or her a dumbhead, a fathead, a pighead, a sorehead, or what not. You could also say of the head that his or her "head is screwed on right" or that his or her "head is in the clouds," and stuff like that. But calling a department head a chair also has various advantages. A chair is clearly something to sit in or on, needed to sign all kinds of important documents, which usually come in pink, green, yellow, and white, if you are lucky (see chapter 7). This made for successful administration.

The reification of organic headship into inorganic chairship had all kinds of unanticipated consequences. As I found out, a chair can get into trouble—his or her colleagues' doghouse, so to speak. In fact, as the chair's colleagues find it easier on their toes to kick a dog than a chair, they are inclined to mistake the chair for a dog. This imagery of the chair as a dog and what it is all about is rich in other allusions. For instance, the chair is said to have "gone to the dogs." There are, to be sure, some happier attributions, like "every dog has his day." But, in general, the chair often lives "a dog's life," though at times a sympathetic colleague may tell the chair who is kicked around, "this shouldn't happen to a dog."

As a chair, I faithfully performed whatever department chores were assigned to me, but I wasn't much of a university servant, or "local," as Robert Merton would say. I served only once for one year on a universitywide subcommittee. You will immediately recognize that this was an exceptionally important committee: During the year of my incumbency it devoted all its meetings to listening to ethnic groups fighting over the allocation of resources during "freshman week"—the week before formal opening of the fall term when new undergraduates are brought to the campus for orientation and instruction in the mysteries of campus existence. For a number of years, members of various minority groups were brought to the campus a day or two prior to the official starting date of freshman orientation week. Then, in the year before I served on this committee, two handfuls or so of Native Americans were brought in a day earlier because it was thought they had particular adjustment problems not shared by the other minority groups. When the mainline minorities heard about this obvious favoritism, they also demanded an extra day. The committee in its wisdom suggested that it would agree to this if the respective groups came up with a meaningful program for the extra day, and it didn't mean another picnic at the beach or another "acquaintance dance." If I remember, only one group came in with an acceptable proposal, but approving an extra day for them and not for the others would have created more turmoil. So what did this committee do to solve this ticklish issue? It decided to bring the entire freshman class—of whatever skin color—in for an extra day. So freshman "orientation" began on Wednesday instead of Thursday.

I got out of service on other committees by telling the secretary for the committee on committees, when he or she called, that I was regretfully not available on the day or hour when this or that committee, to which they wanted to appoint me, usually met. "I'm available any day or time after four thirty," I said, in the certain knowledge that the administrators on these committees wanted to go home around that hour of the day.

But about the time when I became department chair I also came to serve on three "nonuniversity" committees that interested me for one reason or another. One was a committee of the AAUP set up in the late 1960s to draft a charter for an Academic Senate which, indeed, came into existence and has played a significant role in university affairs ever since. A second committee, involving I think a two-year term, was the Faculty Club executive committee or whatever it was called. It had disastrous experiences during my tenure. It found out that some chef in the kitchen was feeding his extended family at faculty expense and, besides, stole some silver. He was fired. Then we discovered that we had hired a new club manager who had obtained the job with forged credentials; he had to be fired, too.

The third committee on which I served had more sunny sides to it. This was the Stanford Bookstore Advisory Board or whatever its name. It was the most pleasant committee anywhere I ever sat on, for several reasons. First, by accepting membership on this board you became also an "owner" of the bookstore, which is a coop of sorts. To become an owner you had to invest $1.00. This heavy investment would be returned to you upon leaving the board in the form of an honest "In God We Trust" gold dollar mounted on a plaque "in appreciation of your years of service." Second, the appointment to the board was for life or, rather, until formal university retirement made you unfit to read books. Third, the board met only once a year, in October, for a leisurely dinner. The manager would give an annual report with lots of statistical tables but did not tell us what he was really up to. He was never questioned much by anybody about the budget because the bookstore and, it turned out, he and an assistant manager crony made lots of money. In due time both men had to be fired for excesses in spending on perks for themselves and other bookstore *apparatchiki* beyond my ken to describe accurately. It is a hair-raising academic story, though; somebody else ought to tell it

It was nice belonging for many years—perhaps fifteen—to a little oligarchy whose members' postdinner ruminations on the store as they saw it were as predictable as the steak that was invariably served. This was another perk that went with being a bookstore owner. At most other dinner events I ever attended at the Faculty Club the main dish was "Chicken Kiev," probably imported from the Ukraine in frozen crates and correspondingly tough.

The little speeches delivered at these bookstore dinner exercises provide a whiff of what the academic dispensation is really about. The professor of German always wanted second-hand books in German added to the shelves, perhaps, but only perhaps (that is, reluctantly), in some other civilized language, like French or Italian, but certainly not in Chinese or Swahili. He was rather uninterested in whether anyone would buy the books. The professor of physics wanted comfortable "easy chairs" spread around the place so that people could settle in, browse, or nap, whatever their preference. The professor of sociology felt that the store was unduly catering to the tastes of townspeople and weekend visitors, with too many Stanford regalia like sweat shirts, coffee mugs, or cocktail napkins filling space that could hold books—an idea whose time never came. The professor of music thought there should be a café connected with the store, and classical music should be pumped in to offset the disharmonies he heard when visiting the dormitories. He succeeded. The professor of political science—that's me— wanted the store to acquire at least one copy of every book published by every one of the country's university presses, with new books to be displayed on a monthly basis on an easily visible shelf.

Brother, Can You Spare a Dime?

Being a department chair is a highly overrated affair. But, at the annual salary-setting time, it is the chair's unusually pregnant opportunity to take advantage of his elevated position by getting even with his colleagues, whose kicking he must endure. Sitting in his office chair with his dean-handed-down budget figures tumbling before his eyes, he can dream of rewarding friends and punishing enemies. He soon discovers that an opportunity is only an opportunity and not anything real. By the time everyone has or has not received his or her dean-recommended plus-or-minus "normal" increase, there is mightily little left to reward your friends. So the only way to get out of this predicament of losing one opportunity is to take the equal opportunity to punish your enemies and deny them the increase to which they think themselves entitled. That makes you a kind of equal opportunity chair.

Even before becoming a chair, I had learned whereof I speak. The time is spring 1968, the year before being turned into a chair myself, when salaries were set for 1968–69. When I learned that my increase in salary would be minimal, I decided to kick the incumbent chair just a bit and wrote him a long memo, telling him (as if he didn't know) what a great scholar I was. In retrospect, this memo sounds just like the memos I later received from unhappy colleagues when I sat in the chair.

As I look over the ensuing exchange of memoranda, I cannot but wonder whether today's readers have even the slightest idea of what salaries looked like *anno Domini* 1968. In 1967–68, my annual (though officially nine-month) salary was $19,000. This was the second-highest salary in the department at the time, second only to the chair's. That year, my evidently hard-pressed chair saw fit to recommend an increase of $500, by my calculation an increase of exactly 2.63157 percent, just about what my money market bank account pays me today on my hard-earned social security deposits.

I was writing reluctantly, I told my friend the chair (and he is still my friend), because I did not want to imply or express any criticism of his role as chair. This was, of course, precisely what was implied (but it was also implied that I wished to remain his friend). I was certainly aware of the chair's—any chair's—predicaments in the matter of salaries and raises, I emphasized in a kind universalistic mood and mode. Indeed, it was for this reason that in the weeks since receiving my salary notice for the next year I had made no formal complaint. This was a rather disingenuous reason nobody could possibly believe; but it sounded sincere. Finally coming out with it, I said that I was not just disappointed by the minimal raise I was to receive. I felt deeply humiliated.

After this auspicious opening paragraph came two single-spaced pages setting out my accomplishments that ranged from the trivial to the banal, but all amounting to a demonstration of the injustice done me. Yet, being the chair's friend who did not really want to kick him like a dog, I gave him a way out: "Please feel free to bring this letter to the attention of the appropriate University officials."

And that's precisely what he did. "Heinz, I sent your letter on to LM & suggest you make an appn't to see him," said the terse handwritten note I received in reply. Now there was an experienced chair, and I learned a lot from him. Push it up the escalator.

I cannot recall my appointment with LM, the dean in charge, but I still have his memo of 18 July 1968 addressed to our chair. It, too, taught me something, this time about decanal responses to shouting:

> This will confirm that we have adjusted Heinz Eulau's salary for next year to reflect a $1,000 raise from the 1967–68 salary rather than a $500 raise. I must say that I do not regard this raise as in any sense large. Indeed it is probably undersized for Heinz' reputation and contribution. It is not easy in any one year to make raises larger than $1,000 but it is relatively easy to insure that a strong and out-standing member of the department receive $1,000 raises every year for a considerable period of time. It appears to me that Hienz [*sic*] Eulau is such a person and that it would be wise to assure him that different professors have different asymptotes for their salaries and that Heinz is a high one and he can look forward to continued progress in his salary.

Not the best of English grammar, but what the letter really did for me was not the chicken-feed $500 add-on but my having been christened an asymptote. Never having met an asymptote before, I rushed to the dictionary to learn that he or she or it is "a straight line always approaching but never meeting a curve." That made me feel genuinely good about this dean, the university, and the academic world in general.

Using this "case" is somewhat misguided because during my own years of chairship—three three-year terms—the complainants were not asymptotes but whatever the opposite of an asymptote might be. So my most cheerful and cherished moments spent as a chair came when I had Professors X, Y, or Z sitting on the sofa across from my swivel chair, which gave me a degree of free movement without having to get up. This happened every year with the same ones. Professor X was usually given less than the normal increase because we hoped that keeping him low would be an incentive for him to seek a greener pasture at some college where his talents would not be wasted. He didn't really complain and only pointed out what I already knew—that his increase was below the rise in the cost-of-living index. Our strategy didn't work: preferring California sunshine to Dakota snowstorms or Texas hurricanes, he stayed until retirement solved the problem. Professor Y had been what's called a "promising young man" when he joined us. By the time I had to face him, he claimed to have a disease called "writer's block." This disease of his seemed to have developed almost simultaneously with an enduring interest in sitting on as many university committees as his hours permitted. The last time I saw him he assured me that with a Personal Computer instead of a pen in hand, so to speak, he was overcoming his old handicap and was furiously working on a book.

Professor Z was a true academic fighting man. He would come in every year to argue his case on the simple ground of what psychiatrists call paranoia. Everybody was after him—the dean, the provost, the president. When his increase was 5 percent, he wanted to know why it wasn't the departmental average of 5.2 percent. When it was precisely the departmental average of 5.2 percent, he thought that his great accomplishments as a teacher deserved 5.5 percent. He was a tough number to handle. Nothing could ever make him happy.

There are few brownie points to be had in this business of being a chair. Instead, as I learned, there can be a lot of kicking the chair for this or that offense that only chairs can commit, like trying to reduce the number of long-distance telephone calls, or holding the line on search committee expenditures, or stopping the use of department stamps for letters paying one's household bills, or setting a limit on the use of the Xerox machine, or not providing more and better secretarial help, and all this sort of thing that seems so important to otherwise self-denying academics.

My greatest triumph in the battle of the budget was not of my making. My predecessor had been required, like other department chairs, to write an annual report to the dean in which he was to pass judgment on each member of the department in support of his salary recommendations. One wonderful day circa 1968, the contents of these reports appeared in the student-edited *Stanford Daily*, though the editors, in a spirit of true civility rare in those years of wrath, had withheld the names of the particular professors. These, of course, could be easily identified by any insiders. The files holding these departmental reports had been stolen by the storm troopers of the SDS during one of their invasions of administration offices. When I became chair in 1969, I refused to do these reports, and the dean acquiesced in the wisdom of this counterinsurrectionist conduct. It didn't help me much as a budget maker, but at least I could sleep well in the knowledge that my colleagues would never know what I told the dean about them in camera.

Eulau Democracy or Ring-around-a Rosie

I was elected (democratically, by secret ballot) to be chair of the department in 1969 after successfully scaring the only possible opponent out of running by telling him that he simply didn't have the votes to win and that he could save himself a lot of time and face by not trying (and I knew privately that the dean would never appoint him). Actually, this was hardly the best of times to become a department chair. These were the years of the civil rights movement, the Vietnam rebellion and that strange political phenomenon called the New Left.

The high point came the weekend before what was announced to be a "strike"—the refusal of students to attend classes as a protest against the invasion of Cambodia by the U.S. military. How was the department to respond? This was something of a new experience for us because, until then, the department (as a "whole") had never been called upon to respond to anything. To avoid being bothered by students, I called a department meeting at a colleague's house for the Sunday before the Monday of the strike. And, for once, I made a truly magnificent factual observation and policy recommendation. As we had never collectively responded to anything, and certainly not something so unacademic as a strike, so-called, we were in no position to do so now. I therefore proposed that we should do what we had always done—an "every man for himself" policy. (I don't think we had any women on the staff at that time, at least I can't remember any at the meeting.) This was a kind of enlightened anarchy. The proposal was accepted.

The next morning, I appeared before an assembly of undergraduate majors and graduate students. It had been called by some revolutionary group for the purpose of "deciding" how *the* department wanted to respond to the strike call (*the* department now including the students and administrative staff as "decision makers"; the janitorial help could not be identified by our upper-class student *narodniki*, who had summoned the masses). The meeting was held on the lawn in front of our building, and the crowd—perhaps 150 or so—sat in a half-circle in front of some self-appointed leaders and, of course, me. I was introduced by one of our Ph.D. candidates, who fancied himself to be a radical but was really as meek as a lamb when he was alone with me. I got up and announced how I expected to conduct the meeting. "This is not going to be a parliamentary democracy; nor is it going to be a participatory democracy; this is going to be Eulau democracy," I shouted to be heard as a police helicopter appeared overhead to take pictures. "I'll move my eyes from left to right, and anybody who wants to say anything will be recognized, but once my eyes shift, that's it. When we are through hearing people out, I will be going home and you can decide anything you wish. However, I want to make it quite clear to you that the only person I am responsible to is the dean of the School of Humanities and Sciences, and nobody else."

So we had "Eulau democracy" for a couple of hours, then Eulau hopped on his bike and rode home, not to be seen for the next few days. I understood that some colleagues at the Institute of Politics allowed the students to use the Xerox machine to provide "infrastructural support" for the strike and avoid having the building occupied by the revolutionary forces. As far as my other colleagues were concerned, it was in fact everyone for himself for a week or so. Some suspended classes altogether; some met with their classes on some lawn to be eaten up by ants; and some posted notices on their office doors with assignments for the next week. After a week, it had all blown over.

The invasion of administration buildings and, one day, of the computer center had a profound effect on my political sensibilities. I had thought of myself as an ACLU type in matters of civil liberties and rights, and a New Deal liberal in matters of social welfare and economic policy. The first time I saw the students climb through windows into some administrative offices, I very much resented their behavior as an invasion of privacy. The action made me hurry to my own office, from where I removed all possibly sensitive documents, including letters of recommendation I had written for students or colleagues, to the safety of my home. I became something of a "law and order" type.

Those were years of insanity. I remember a huge meeting of the Academic Council (the body of all professors, in peaceful times poorly attended). This was in fall 1970, shortly after the opening of the new school year and before the November congressional elections. The agenda provided for discussion of something called the "Princeton Plan." This crazy plan called for a week's "study moratorium" during which students would fan out into the surrounding communities, talk to "the people" about the amoral and pernicious war being waged in Vietnam, and work for the election of "peace candidates." I remember a professor of English getting up and moving that Stanford adopt the Princeton Plan. If, I thought to myself, all students from Stanford, Berkeley, Santa Clara University, San Francisco State, San Jose State, and all the other colleges in the Bay Area were to hit the streets, the congestion would leave little room for either pedestrian passage or political persuasion, and our neighbors were most likely to resent being held hostage to this mass mobilization. I kept my mouth shut, though, because I didn't expect the enterprise to get anywhere. Fall weather in October still being on the warm side, 90 percent of the students would hit the beaches or do whatever pleased them other than distribute handbills at street corners. I seem to recall that Stanford opted for a one-day, rather than a one-week, moratorium, but I may be wrong. My best guess is that during the "years of wrath" from, say, 1965 to 1972, not more than 10 percent of Stanford students ever attended a peace rally or protest meeting of one sort or another. And this 10 percent was probably a "moving" percentage. I'm reminded of my daughter Lauren's response when I asked her why she had gone to some peace rally—the only one she ever attended. "Everybody else went," she said, satisfying my paternal curiosity. There were other episodes of this order. I have told another one elsewhere. It involved my heroic stand (literally, as in "stand up to") during an invasion of the Faculty Club by the "nonnegotiable demand" forces of the SDS (Eulau 1996, chap. 6).

Fiasco and Redemption

The heavy burdens of my chairships were greatly lightened by a superb department secretary or manager or administrator, Arlee Ellis, much beloved by students and faculty alike. As a result, I could never claim that these intermezzos in an otherwise humdrum academic career seriously interfered with all the other things professors do, like staying home in the mornings to get on with preparing lectures, writing and research, or jet-setting across the country to sundry meetings and conferences. As a further result of Arlee's administrative and budgetary expertise, I could concentrate on what interested me most—building up the best research faculty we could assemble after Harvard, Berkeley, or Yale had taken potential candidates away from us. This activity also finally got me into trouble when I forgot that I was merely an inorganic department chair and not a department "head" with some discretion in the matter of recruiting faculty.

In 1981 I did the really dumbest thing of my academic career I ever did: I agreed not to retire but serve another term as department chair. One day, in January, the dean called me in and asked me to "do a job for him." He was very much aware of a department in turmoil, accentuated by the sudden resignation of a most promising new chair who, for personal reasons, had to move away. To persuade me, he agreed to give us two altogether new billets if we could come up with some very, very strong candidates regardless of field—"targets of opportunity," so-called.

I succeeded in getting one of the two new billets filled, but a second candidate was willfully held up in committee by a nemesic filibuster (for the nemesis phenomenon, see chapter 7). By the time the committee was ready to make a decision, the candidate had accepted an offer from Harvard. Two years later, at the beginning of my last year as superannuated chair, word had reached some of us that another absolutely first-rate scholar was available as a target of opportunity and that he really would like coming to Stanford. As I had suggested but evidently not made clear enough to some reluctant and fearful colleagues, I had always believed that you could not build a first-class faculty by systematic or synoptic personnel planning along traditional subdisciplinary lines. In fact, almost all of my colleagues with the most distinguished achievements had not come to Stanford in the wake of some turf-minded plan to fill this or that conventional slot or having been recruited in the standard way of a "blind" or "open" search.

As far as I was concerned, there was nothing unusual about my efforts to interest the dean in an extraordinary appointment for which he was prepared to give the department billets not otherwise available. Little did I expect the kind of ferocious attack on the sinful activities in which I had been engaging to the detriment of the commonweal. Were it to be properly told, the story of my last departmental retreat after twenty-five years of service would need a poet with a homeric sense of the heroic or a humorist with the true sense of the comic. Although my head was rather thoroughly bloodied on this occasion, it remained unbowed. I came out as well as I did, I think, by letting my fiercest critic have the last word on this occasion, finding it silly to respond. As the great German poet, novelist, playwright, philosopher, and scientist Johann Wolfgang von Goethe, hero of my youth, once put it (in as gentle a translation as I can manage), "Against nonsense even the gods fight a losing battle." By the way, the person whom John Ferejohn, my co-conspirator in this fiasco, and I tried to attract to Stanford was also lost to Harvard where, as I write this, he is chair!

7

The Faculty's Fallacious but Felicitous Faculties,

or

Nemesis and When Not to Love Thy Colleague as Thyself

Once upon a time—the time actually was somewhere between 1938 and 1940—three of us took a course in "educational psychology." We were the teaching assistants appointed to duty at Berkeley for a two-year term in fall 1938. We had been advised to secure, along with the noble Ph.D., teaching credentials that would surely get us a job in one or another of California's junior colleges. The country was still in the throes of the Great Depression. Jobs in four-year colleges or universities were scarce. If you didn't want to starve, prudence dictated working for a junior college teaching credential. We had to take a course in "psych," as our teacher in the School of Education called it. This "psych" experience was enough to chase us right out of the School of Education and its credentialing powers.

According to this psychology of education, the best way to stimulate the minds of the young, especially those not smart enough or too poor to make it into a four-year institution, was to appeal to their "faculties." These faculties were "components" of mental activity, such as knowing, reasoning, memorizing, feeling, even being hungry. They were supposed to be more or less independent of each other. This was good Aristotelian stuff. When I was still a high schooler in Germany, the rationale we were given for having to get through certain subjects, whether we liked them or not, was that they were "good for you," if not good for the soul. History was good for training the memory; Latin grammar was good for clear thinking; mathematics was good for logical reasoning; reading Homer in Greek was good for acquiring verbal skill (as if Goethe's *Faust* were not enough, but we never read that one); studying French was good for good taste; geography was good for spatial understanding (translate: *Lebensraum*); and so on. No wonder I found that course in educational psychology somewhat irritating.

But how clever, from the Middle Ages on, for bodies of men —there were no women—to call themselves "faculties"! If the mind or soul could be so neatly compartmentalized, why not the learned doctors of theology, medicine, jurisprudence, and pedagogy? So it happened that the group of learned men designating themselves "faculties" claimed for themselves special faculties or aptitudes connected with theology, medicine, jurisprudence, and, especially, pedagogy. As academic bodies they were to be the certified and exclusive custodians of some craft, trade, art, or science.

Being a "Regular" Faculty

Just how jealous a faculty can be of its particular faculties and the hypothetical power that goes with them is a matter of record. At least three or four times in each of the three decades of intense interaction with my departmental colleagues, there were occasions for much squabbling about who should be admitted to what was called the "regular" and, therefore, anointed faculty—faculty thought sufficiently competent to be exposed to undergraduates, or vice versa. For a practically oriented person like myself, a regular faculty member was simply someone who was a line in the department's faculty budget and not on some other budget, in or out of the department. So the purists and antipurists haggled time and again over whether Professor X in this or that other department should be appointed as a courtesy professor or an adjunct professor or a consulting professor, or what not, so that his course or courses could be taken for credit toward the major in political science. Nowadays, of course, faculties are not really faculties anymore but subfaculties and sub-subfaculties. For some obsolete reason, however, the "department faculty" has remained a decision-making unit, though its effectiveness is in question. Effective or not, attending departmental faculty meetings remains the true high point of any academic's career. I therefore offer the draft of a one-scene, one-act play not atypical, I think, of real life, which tends to imitate art.

The Great Decision

A One-Act Play with Plot but without Outcome

SETTING: *A smoke-filled room with a dozen or so men and two women (for balance) sitting in a circle around a square table (is it possible to sit in a circle around a square table?); table is littered with paper and wine glasses. One person, feet on table, has eyes closed and snores; another looks dreamily out the window at sun-drenched lawn; a third is noisily opening his mail; a fourth reads the* New Yorker; *a fifth furiously records the nonconversation on large yellow pad (obviously a secretary). And so on.*

Dramatis Personae

Chair, current chairperson of department
Adviser, graduate adviser in department
Boss, former chairperson of department
Secretary, departmental secretary
Professors K, L, M, typically articulate professors
Other People, typically silent professors

Chair: Will the meeting come to order? To order! I have a telephone call to make. Discuss this important item in my absence.

(Chair leaves. There is silence except for one person snoring; then everybody talks to everybody until Chair returns ten minutes later).

Chair: What have you decided? Nothing? You know I'm bound by your decision. If nothing has been decided, I cannot be bound. Let's get on with it.

Adviser: Yes, this is the June review of our second-year graduate students, which, though now held in May, should have taken place in April. So I want all of you to think of this as an April and not a June review. In the spirit of compromise characteristic of this faculty, you will agree with me that May is as good as April or June for this purpose.

Prof. K: I'm not so sure of this as you seem to be, my friend. As you know, there are thirty-one days in May but only thirty days in April, and that may make a considerable difference. On the other hand, I agree that June will not do. With commencement coming on the fifteenth, there are really only fourteen days in June, which really means only two Wednesdays for us to meet, while in May we have four Wednesdays for the June review, and in April we have in fact five. So May is more similar to April than to June, and that's why I will go along with having the June review today.

Adviser: Thank you, K. It makes me feel good to have your support, should I say as always? Let's just take up Jones, who seems to be the only second-yearer who's in serious trouble. I understand he may drop out.

Boss: Good. All the others are okay. So let's go home.

Prof. L: Not so fast, Boss. For all kinds of reasons, we should not let Jones drop out without giving him an opportunity to talk with his adviser. First, he clearly needs advice; second, anyone dumber this year than last should be urged to pay back his fellowship stipend; and third, it is by no means clear whether the chairman should sign the green sheet, the blue sheet, or the yellow one.

Prof. M: Does it make any difference? I think not.

Prof. L: It does. It depends on whether Jones drops himself, is dropped now, or will be dropped after we have reviewed his case. The dean's memorandum on this is not clear—whether a student in danger of being dropped should be dropped before he arrives on campus, after his first year, after the April and/or June review, after having written the first draft of his dissertation, or never. Take Smith. He has been around for nine years and has five kids. Should we not have signed the green sheet for him?

Boss: That's right. I signed his green sheet back in _____. Can't remember the year. Smith came in, said he had a wife and a baby, and my not signing the green sheet would seriously undercut his productivity. I'm glad to hear he has five kids now.

(Another half hour is devoted to haggling over various colorful sheets to be signed or not to be signed.)

Chair: Thank you all so much. But what about the green sheet? Should I sign it for Jones? Can a student insist on my signing it? I need the advice of this faculty. Nobody else is more qualified in this critical matter.

Adviser: There remains the question whether Jones, should he drop out, should not be allowed to first take his language exam. We might waive this exam, in which case the chairman could sign the green sheet.

Prof. M: Don't be silly. If we waive the language thing, why not waive the dissertation? Let's just give him his Ph.D. and good riddance. Ha-ha!

Chair: It's not a bad idea. I then could sign the green sheet.

Secretary: Not quite, sir, there are now two new forms of what you people have called the green sheet: one is red and the other is purple. The red form of the green sheet needs no signature at all, and the purple form can be signed by the graduate adviser.

Chair (disappointed): That would leave me with nothing to sign?

Secretary: Yes, but we could still use the old green sheet for our departmental files, and that would give you an opportunity to sign.

Boss: Splendid! Let's go home.

The Nemesis Phenomenon

The new person never had any doubts about herself or anybody else or anything she said or anything anybody else ever said. She was the most quintessentially self-defined godsend I ever knew. I knew about her mission to do the Lord's work as soon as I read the first memorandum she wrote to her new colleagues shortly after coming aboard. I no longer have the memo, but it has left an indelible impression on my otherwise fallible memory. The memo was distinguished by making not just a "suggestion" but a "constructive suggestion." I like that sort of suggestion because (1) it is, by definition, not destructive; and (2) as a kind of preemptive strike, it precludes your forming your own judgment as to what is being suggested. Obviously, if you find the suggestion unctuous, its fountainhead is likely to become your nemesis.

In reviewing my nemesic experiences, I learned all kinds of things about Nemesis, the original one of Greek and Roman mythology. First of all, nemesis is decidedly of the fertile female sex. For this reason I shall refer to the composite nemesis of this chapter as "she."

There were, in fact, two "divine conceptions" of Nemesis. I shall skip over the first as irrelevant to my concerns here and turn immediately to the second. According to a highly confidential source, a.k.a. EB, this second Nemesis was a "divine entity" but, at the same time, an abstraction: "That the abstraction was worshipped, at least in later times, is beyond doubt...." (*EB* 1974, 7:250). I find it somewhat difficult to swallow the idea that an "entity" can be an abstraction, or vice versa, but, then, the Greeks and Romans had a vivid imagination. There is much food for thought here.

An academic nemesis is a particularly skilled infighter when it comes to issues of turf. Because nobody else can possibly live up to the nemesic turf-builder's own self-declared high standards, her mission is to define, declare, develop, and defend a piece of subdisciplinary terrain. This turf, she evidently thinks, is nobody else's business to intrude upon, though everybody else's business is not immune from condemnation and retribution by the nemesis.

Academic Turf versus *Lebensraum*

The word "turf" is an undignified adaptation of the old-Norwegian word *torf*. "Torf" sounds better to my musically sensitive ears than "turf," but that's something idiosyncratic. It is more important to distinguish between academic turf and *Lebensraum*. Turf refers to the specification of boundaries in intellectual matters and their implementation in personnel decisions. *Lebensraum*, by way of contrast, refers to the faculty's physical environment and well-being, such as good office space, well-lit classrooms, ample parking space and equally easy access to the Internet and a nearby lavatory, and so on.

The struggle for *Lebensraum* is carried on between university schools and departments as well as between individual members of these collectives. I once waged this war over office space, and it is a splendid case study of how my nemesis at the time tried to defeat me in the name of fairness and democracy. How can you fight and win against a nemesis with those virtues on her side?

Shortly after getting out of my second stint as chair in the mid-1970s, the Department of Political Science, then dispersed in several buildings, was to be brought together in a single building, still sometimes referred to as "the old law school." It was a horrible mistake to agree to this move, which involved, for some of us, giving up cozy offices in a relatively remote wooden firetrap of a house on a shaded side street in what had once been a residential area. The "old law school" is a labyrinth of floors, corridors, classrooms, and offices. Its inner space is a wasteland of stacks occupied by dusty, rarely used law books.

Anyway, the high-stakes issue facing the faculty was who would get what offices, the quality of the offices varying a good deal. Some were in remote nooks on the fourth floor of the building, with a splendid view of the hills behind the campus. Others were in the basement, often flooded during the rainy season. A committee was to recommend which option, of several, should be followed in this literally life-and-death struggle for *Lebensraum*. The committee was headed by a professor of public administration, and hence particularly qualified to make an organizationally dysfunctional recommendation. It came up with the unique solution of assigning the offices by lottery, a method thought to ensure fairness. Choice by seniority was rejected as undemocratic, and there were no clear criteria for defining seniority (age, date of Ph.D., length in rank, length in the profession, length of employment by Stanford?).

I quickly assumed the role of nemesis, pointing out the stupidity of the lottery. The building, in its labyrinthine complexity, I argued with some vehemence and conviction of my own correctness in the matter, was ideally suited to bring the members of various subfields into close and convenient proximity for easy interaction and communication. Well, after a couple of hours of sparkling discourse, a vote was taken: my proposal lost, and the lottery idea won.

Then came my triumph. After a number had been assigned to each colleague, regardless of rank, gender, hair color, specialty, or any other mark of distinction, the department secretary performed the sacred task of fishing around for a correspondingly numbered slip of paper in an urn, which really was a flower pot. The procedure was in the best tradition of ancient Athenian politics and modern Bingo. Guess whose number was called first and had the premier choice of an office?

Turf and Nemesic Conduct

Turf in its academic sense is really a strictly nominal concept, though the custodians of subdisciplinary turf, being sensitive in the matter, like to make its territorial integrity a matter of personal honor. So every speck of turf becomes a highly charged bone of contention (if I may be permitted a rather awkward metaphor). Once staked out, disciplinary turf is holy ground to be defended at all costs, and possibly even expanded.

Turf worship, the disciplinary equivalent of territorial patriotism, provides particularly propitious opportunities for the emergence of the nemesis phenomenon. And the occasions for action are numerous and diverse. There is, for instance, the struggle over "billets." The military connotation of this synonym for job or position notwithstanding, the fight over what billets should go to which disciplinary or subdisciplinary field is particularly challenging because it is so classically academic. It is often a fight over something that does not exist, a kind of wish list, elicited by a dean who hasn't any money to make good on his or her promises. It is easy to see how a fight over this sort of thing can lead to prolonged turf battles.

Assuming that a new billet has been secured and defined, the fight shifts to the specification of the professorial level at which the billet is to be filled. This is usually followed by a good fight over the composition of a search committee. There are many scenarios to be written in this connection, but I haven't got the space for them here. Anyway, once a new billet, professorial level, and committee composition have been set, there comes the possibility for an almost infinite variety of nemesic strategies. There is the question of the type of search to be conducted. If the appointment is to be at the assistant professor level, a genuine "national search" is called for. But that sounds simpler than it is. If the search is at the tenure level, the opportunities for nemesic intervention are greater. One can insist on a "national search," even though one has one's own favorite candidate in the wings. If, in fact, there is a single very strong candidate known to a nemesic turf builder, she can suggest that a "national comparison" is sufficient. Even if outvoted, the losing nemesis will have a wonderful chance, by reading a candidate's publications, to make mincemeat of someone she does not like for all kinds of reasons, which need not be revealed. When a candidate is brought in for a visit, she can find fault with his or her seminar presentation, even with his or her personality as not "fitting in," and what not.

If a nemesis has not been successful at one or another station of the search process, she can prolong the struggle by simply being long-winded and obstreperous in committee or faculty meetings, guaranteeing delay and the possible loss of the candidate to some other institution.

It's not much of a puzzle why the academic battle over turf is so closely connected with the nemesis phenomenon. Turf as battleground evidently brings out the best or, depending on your standpoint, which depends on where you sit, the worst in people. It is not at all clear what causes what: Does the turf instinct translate into nemesic behavior? Or is there a personality syndrome disposing a professor to be particularly obnoxious when it comes to jealously guarded turf.

Profile of an Ideal-Type Nemesis

Knowing about the circumstances under which a nemesis arrived —in competitive search, as a target of opportunity, through the back door—is conducive to an understanding of how the nemesis develops her strategy in matters of appointment. If the nemesis arrived through the back door, and if the appointment to be made is one of opportunity, there is a good chance that the nemesis will come up with an unsubstantiated rumor of someone planning if not executing a conspiracy to circumvent everybody else by either putting over a candidate for appointment or opposing him or her. She also prophesies, by way of a method known as self-fulfilling, that this conspiracy will be strongly opposed, letting you guess by whom—a rather ineffective tactic. If the conspiracy is continued, she predicts, it will lead to a bitter, highly divisive struggle. It will seriously damage the department and its relations with the dean.

I will forgo the agony of expectations the nemesis is likely to have concerning the candidate's capabilities as a teacher of graduates and undergraduates. By the time all these questions are answered, the candidate has ridden off into the sunset at Harvard or

New World University. In any case, it all sounds terribly reasonable but is a patent display of nemesic hypocrisy.

At this point, nemesis also proves herself a consummate connoisseur and advocate of even the least significant rule in the rulebook of bureaucratic conduct in the personnel process. With this goes an exhaustive recall of both recent and ancient departmental personnel history. It allows her to point out, with great authority, how the process has been perverted. There will be references to the memo of 1 September, to the exchange of letters of 1 October, to the committee report of 1 November, and to the faculty discussion of 1 December.

If the bureaucratic strategy fails, nemesis will present herself, in the studiously pompous language that is her hallmark, as the incarnation of goddess Democratia. The ability of the department to govern itself, and the little authority its elected representatives have with which to discharge their important responsibilities, have been badly damaged by various maneuvers of her distinguished colleagues, both inside but particularly outside the department. Such maneuvers undermine the legitimacy of the department's bylaws for self-governance and erode the norms of professional collegiality that are essential to the effectiveness of the department's decision-making procedures.

Careful scrutiny of the language used by the nemesis in opposing an appointment is a dead giveaway. I once contemplated writing a lexicon for novices in nemesis spotting or even role taking. The nemesis is likely to be "genuinely distressed" when her opponent has taken it upon himself to do this or that without consulting everybody around the place. She will express "strong reservations," sometimes even the strongest. More than likely, the nemesis will use superdemocratic language, calling for "full, open, and comprehensive assessment" of whatever by "all."

How a nemesis goes about getting ready for collective action is something of a spectacle with mirrors. She will claim for herself a right that she unequivocally denies to others on other occasions. She will find another person's building a coalition (of which she is not a member) "unacceptable." She charges that it involves strong-arm lobbying within and outside a department designed to undermine the nemesis's own benign efforts and block her recommendations. When nemesis does exactly what her opponent is doing, however, she will find her own conduct perfectly acceptable by cutely "calling on" others for support (like the nice ladies who in nineteenth-century novels and movies "call on" their friends to gossip about other friends).

If there is a proposal to be discussed at a faculty meeting that the nemesis finds displeasing, she will let it be known that the item is being forced into the discussion. At the same time she requests in no uncertain terms that something of her own choosing be put on the agenda. If nothing has succeeded with unconvinced opponents, the nemesis is likely to try a little hysteria, especially if she herself favors a quick decision on some appointment dear to her turfy heart. In general, academic faculties do not like to make quick decisions. As her turf's self-appointed spokesperson, the nemesis will tell you, quite modestly at first, that this turf issue is a matter of "grave concern," that not immediately filling a vacated spot on her turf will immediately constitute an enormous gap, and that the damage will be substantial, indeed be "potentially catastrophic damage." She will invariably tell you that she has given much thought (as against everybody else who is thoughtless) to what is at stake.

A favorite strategy to advance the interests of her own turf is to denigrate the quality and success of what is seen by the nemesis as a competing program. Being an indefatigable turf warrior, nemesis will have assembled data and statistics that, for reasons of lassitude, laziness, or laxity, nobody else will check. Armed with these data, she expects to put the enemy on the run, "if not on the ropes," I once heard. Nemesis will show how applications to what she perceives as a wrongly competing turf program have dropped, or that the program's recent Ph.D.s haven't made it to jobs at Yale or Berkeley.

Then there are the graduate students whose otherwise empty minds on departmental politics need opening. Nemesis will flamboyantly report that "expressions of anxiety and concern" have circulated; that dissatisfied students may decide to go elsewhere; that their concern is quite genuine and real. Nemesis then rejects the notion of possibly self-serving motives and protests her own honesty by impugning the motives of some of her colleagues. She hopes that faculty members tempted to entertain the ugly hypothesis that nemesis has incited the graduate students will satisfy themselves by talking with the students most directly concerned—that is, her own satellites.

When the nemesis finds a colleague doing something she does not like, she will speak of his or her "insensitive and clumsy ways." What he or she is doing has "a most unfortunate effect and disturbing implications." Indeed, it seriously jeopardizes whatever the sinner himself or herself prefers. A good nemesis knows better what another person needs than that person himself or herself; therefore, the beneficiary of such bawling out by the nemesis should not dismiss her wisdom as an exaggeration.

To avoid being "personal," the nemesis will cloak herself in the most professional toga available. She will let her victim know that she doesn't dislike him or her "as a person," but she will "object strenuously" to his or her objectionable behavior. She will be "appalled" by her critic's actions, which are "grossly at odds" (not just "simply" so) with her own concept of professional collegiality (on which she has a monopoly). As her own conduct is as infallible as the pope's, she will take immediate exception when the opponent dares to have some doubt about her candor or veracity. Opposing a nemesic recommendation prior to "open discussion" deprives the nemesis of getting a "calm and fair consideration" of her case.

Moral of the Story?

Once I had taken my measure of a nemesis—her godliness, her uprightness, her unselfishness, humility, and so on—my own strategy was to avoid any direct confrontation with this or that nemesis, knowing that there was no way of coming to terms with the descendant of a godly entity who can take on any number of disguises —from aggressor to victim, from democrat to bureaucrat, from expert to know-it-all, from moralist to hypocrite, from hysteric to rationalist, from sycophant to bully. Whatever a nemesis finds mistaken, disastrous, scandalous, unacceptable, or what not in the proceedings of a university department is largely of her own making and, therefore, irremediable. And that's why the whole business is something of a comic tragedy.

8

Life and Representation
on a Company Farm,
or
Professor Quick-Win Hires
Consultant Quick-Fix

It is one of the great miracles of academic existence. You don't get rich living off the fat of the land, even at a richly land-endowed university like Stanford, affectionately known the world over as Senator Stanford's "Farm." Professorial poverty is compensated for by tenure. For those of us committed to social security, tenure is an immutable law of nature and not to be messed with. Low income but high security makes us free to speak our minds. Whether we actually do or do not depends on circumstances. We are easily intimidated. I would not dare to say aloud what I'm about to write in tacit candor.

By the late 1960s my wife and I had parlayed an initial 1948 investment of $1,000, borrowed from her father (of course; what would we academics do without fathers-in-law?), in an Ohio farmhouse (bought for $8,200) into enough cash to buy a *house* on the Stanford campus but not really including the *land* on which the house sits. For people not blessed by Stanford generosity, this is something of a puzzle. First they will just shake their unbelieving heads. How, they will then ask, can you own a house but not the ground it is built on? Nowadays, only the fullest of full professors can afford to pay the necessary bucks for the privilege of having the university as lessor.

So you explain why and how it came about that Stanford, the Corporation, cannot alienate the lands of Stanford, the University. Years ago, the university had begun a housing development for its low-paid faculty, providing generous mortgage terms (in our case 5 percent) and free, if smelly, lake water to cultivate the earth, but she left you otherwise alone to do as you pleased. It made for a perfectly livable arrangement. For the physical maintenance of this paradise, the university extracts a moderate monthly "ground rent."

Well, we have lived here on Frenchmans [*sic*] Road in serene peace and genteel poverty for almost thirty years, at least until recently. A particularly congenial aspect of the social environment, if you can call it "social," is that we were (and still are) surrounded in all directions by other professors who are rugged individualists. They mostly like to be let alone; and they like to pick and choose their friends, on campus or off, as they wish. Then a few years ago, along came some well-meaning citizens whose good intentions have had, at least for us leaseholders, some not altogether beneficial consequences.

Even before this happened, there had been some change as new areas were opened up for residential use. It would be too tedious to narrate in detail just what changed and how it changed. Being one among the huge preponderance of land-leasing, homeowning individualists, I stuck to principle by not paying attention to the deterioration of our surroundings. I noted only occasionally that the more "improvements" were made (filling potholes, building sidewalks, putting up new traffic signs, and so on and so forth), the more what is called the "quality of life" lessened.

These changes were reasonably tolerable until, not long ago, there emerged an organization titled "Stanford Campus Residential Leaseholders, Inc." or SCRL, Inc. As was the case with the municipal reformers of a couple of generations ago, the organization's activities threaten to destabilize the local environment.

The SCRL, Inc. has a board of directors. As boards of this sort are rarely able to direct anything, they have to have an "executive director." This devolution of authority permits the presumably democratically chosen board—I have no idea what the vote turnout is—to advance and defend my interests as a leaseholder jealously vis-à-vis an ever more bureaucratic university. Whether you want to be a member or not, membership in the SCRL, Inc. is "free," that is, there are no dues. I don't know how you can drop your membership; that really makes you something of a captive. The organization's good deeds are made possible by subsidies it receives from the university. These subsidies obviously guarantee its independence as a true bargaining agent for us leaseholders.

As Parkinson's law has it, every executive director needs an "administrative assistant," and the latest SCRL, Inc. *Newsletter* informs us that one has come aboard—"an honors graduate of UC Berkeley." A UC Berkeley alumnus myself, I consider this a splendid choice. Moreover, the new administrative assistant "has several years of solid experience in customer relations and office management." I am not sure what experience in customer relations has to do with what the SCRL, Inc. exists for, but it confirms the suspicion that we have a city government in the making: an administrative assistant to an executive director who serves a board of directors.

Life on the Farm

The mail just delivered (at $.27 per item) an eight-page *SCRL Community Planning Project Final Report Summary*. It seems that a couple of years ago and in control of about $300,000 discretionary money "for improvements to the residential area," the SCRL, Inc. board voted to develop "a plan for phased completion of projects over the next three years." To carry out this benign "effort," for which evidently no competent resident was willing to volunteer, the board hired a "consultant." This obviously objective outsider has now delivered his grand plan for our future as Stanford leaseholders. According to the plan's summary, "the focus of the consultant's approach was to engage the community in a teaching and learning process." His clients seem not to have told the consultant that the "community" is a bunch of ruggedly individualistic teachers who are living here because they want to *teach others*, mostly students, and are something less than eager to *learn* about a community that may or may not exist. "The major tasks" of the plan are said to be these:

- To facilitate a way for residents to discover how much they *already know* about their community.
- To help residents *learn more* about their community, themselves and each other, and
- To provide a common language, shared information base, and fair process for decision making [no period or comma here]

• To elicit residents' concerns and priorities for improving their community.

How can anybody possibly dissent from these noble goals? How can I refuse discovery of how much I "already know" about the place I live in? How can I not want to "learn more" about my community (otherwise nowhere to be seen), myself, and the new couple next door who recently bought the house, and had it totally erased to build a new one How can I possibly continue to live here without finding out whether friend S up the street or friend R across it and I share a common language and an "information base" before we decide on taking our spouses to the movies?

According to the summary, "the primary focus [of the study] was to *build consensus for a shared vision of community.* With consensus on a shared vision, the SCRL board would be able to propose actions with confidence that they will both further the common interest and enjoy broad support." Alas, to test this persuasive hypothesis, predicated as it is on the emergence of a common language, it is important to understand first the "process" the consultant used to arrive at what are called "key findings" and "recommendations."

The Process of Inquiry

I was particularly interested in the process because, as a dyed-in-the-wool social scientist, I have a sense of how this sort of commercial research is done. The first thing is to impress the customer. For this purpose, the summary informs us that "the planning process included a series of activities designed to foster community involvement and participation. These included public workshops, focus groups, a social ecology inventory, a mail questionnaire, newsletters and comments collected from community members." An impressive portfolio of procedures.

The questionnaire was considered "a supplement to the meetings" and was mailed to each leaseholder. Of the "approximately 850 questionnaires" (why "approximately" if "each leaseholder" got one?), 217, or 25.52941 percent were returned. This response rate is claimed to be "well above average for mail-back surveys of this kind." Well, the return rate would be pretty good if your questionnaire were sent to a *random sample* of the population of some city, state, or nation. It's not so hot when sent to a target group that is a *universe* of a highly literate professional elite like university professors and top administrators with a direct interest in what may be at stake. So I'm in fact more impressed by the 75 percent or so of my fellow leaseholders who so valiantly resisted this community activity by not filling out the questionnaire.

Though neither number nor percentage is given, "the most surprising finding was that 'places to walk' was the highest ranked feature in both importance and satisfaction." Evidently expecting the reader also to be surprised by the surprising finding about places to walk, the summary comes to this tantalizing inference: "The community's high value on this activity suggests placing greater emphasis on preserving and enhancing pathways and other areas." From what I note on my own daily walks, this "high value" benefits the persons from all over who now invade the Stanford foothills for their daily constitutionals more than us residents. In fact, the stuff about pathways and such is counter to my interests as a local resident, homeowner, and leaseholder, not to mention professor who needs quiet to read and write books. The more pathways and other areas around the place are "preserved and enhanced," the greater will be the number of people, not connected with Stanford in any way, parking their cars on our street and increasingly in front of our house, polluting the air, making the street corner unsafe by driving above the speed limit, and letting their dogs defecate all over our front plantings.

Were I the good citizen possessed of republican virtue expected by the SCRL, Inc.'s consultant, I would have to go to endless meetings and workshops, possibly a "Places to Walk Focus Group" affair, as was held last year with nine persons doing the walking, if that's what they were focusing on. There I would have the great opportunity to protest this or that preservation and enhancement, and protect my own immediate environment in the hope that it will make life on our street free of unwished-for hikers, walkers, roller skaters, skate boarders, bicyclists, dogs and others whose lives the SCRL, Inc. board is enriching.

Some Quantifications

All the workshops, meetings, inventory something, and focus groups fed the Community Planning Project with one of the world's richest data sets. The largest recorded attendance by the ethereal "community" was at an early "Existing Conditions Discovery Workshop, " held on 9 May 1995, and at a last "Recommendations and Priorities Workshop," on 19 October 1995. Each of these two sessions could boast all of thirty-three participants, but we don't know how many of them were individuals coupled to each other by marriage vows, inspired love, or plain sex. What does the "thirty-three" stand for? Being generous, let it stand for leaseholding households, rather than individuals. That's about 15 percent of those who returned the mail questionnaire and barely 4 percent of all households, truly imposing figures of "community involvement." If you want to be less generous and assume two people per leasehold (and presuming single lessees are offset by children in coupled households), the community participation in these workshops comes to just a bit under 2 percent. And these are the heroic numbers. Of the other six affairs sponsored by SCRL, Inc. and monitored by its consultant, the number of attenders varied from a low six (on 6 May, when the weather was too good to sit around in some stuffy room for a meeting of some sort) to twenty-six in an "Alternatives Exploration Workshop."

Evidently to impress its less quantitatively inclined consumers, the summary reported a total workshop/meeting attendance of 174. Assuming a household being represented by one person and eight opportunities to be seen and heard at these functions, this makes for 850 × 8 or 6,800 potential attendances. This means that the overall attendance rate was only about 2.5 percent (174/6,800). So much for the approach "to engage the community in a teaching and learning process." And one is at a loss to know whether the 174 attenders were a rotating crowd of curious voyeurs or the same hard core of community enthusiasts. If the latter, the attendance picture would look even dimmer.

The "planning process" included two other steps. Residents "were invited to offer written comments at every public meeting, focus group, and through the survey." This thoroughly scientific bag of instruments for gathering information yielded another gold mine of data—"a total of 218 comments (recorded on 213 'comment cards') . . . on a wide variety of subjects." The resulting grab bag of goodies has been "catalogued by topic in a database" that, I suppose, can be "shared" by all who want to live up to virtuous citizenship under the friendly aegis of the SCRL, Inc.

Finally, the process involved the production and distribution to "all households" of sundry SCRL newsletters, though there was gratefully no follow-up that could have informed us about the number of recipients who read them. But, I am glad to note, "one collateral benefit of the planning process was the redesign of the SCRL Newsletter, starting with the first planning issue." Bully!

Key Findings

Turning to the "key findings," I can understand and appreciate their overwhelming import only in the context of the colossal numbers and percentages extracted earlier. In an introductory sales talk on these discoveries, I read that "the most important outcome of the process may be in the improved ability of residents to reach consensus on matters of common interest, and the SCRL's ability to represent its constituency in matters of community concern."

The first "finding" seems to have been that "the [nonexistent, I daresay] community is a 'company town,' with the University in the role of both landlord and employer." This finding is explicated later in a section on "Implementation and Evaluation." It is so totally droll in its political innocence that I want to quote it in full:

> An important insight from the planning process is that the residential area is a part of a company town. Yet unlike most company towns where the resident workers manufacture a product sold by the company, in this instance the "workers" (faculty and staff) embody substantially the entire value of the company [Wow!]. Thus, improvements that promote interaction, or enhance safety, or make the community attractive to new faculty, directly enhance the value of the University's greatest resource.
>
> In this light, community improvements can be valued not as amenities or luxuries, but as fundamental elements supporting a community of scholars.

The concept of a company town is then related to what is evidently also considered a "finding"—"residents *often* express a degree of ambivalence about this state of affairs" (emphasis added). There follows a reference to complaints "often" heard about this or that, but "*most* residents express pride in their connection *to* the University and support of its mission" (emphasis again added). A rather wonderful nonsequitur. I would like to believe that this "pride" is also to be "found" among my colleagues who live off-campus—in Palo Alto or, if rich, in near-by Atherton, and even in faraway San Francisco.

Speaking more to the activists who make up the SCLR, Inc. board than to me or the people I happen to know around the block, another key finding has it that "residents also *often* note that, unlike citizens of a city or town, they have no representational body to which they can address their wishes and concerns" (emphasis added). To remedy this, the summary rather tellingly but illogically reveals, the SCLR "was created by the University administration." So much for *democratic* representation from below in our company town. This is followed by a previously unmentioned item on the SCRL's agenda of "major tasks," namely, that "improving the partnership between the SCRL and the administration was a primary focus of the planning effort." By now there are more major foci than I can focus on.

What is so jolly about all this is the use of the words "often" and "most." As to "often," it's probably misused. It does not tell me whether one or two people often complain, whatever "often" is, or whether some or many complain once. As to "most," one guess is as good as any other.

After all this hype comes what can only be a downer for all good neighbors in search of self-discovery, discovery of others, learning about their community, a common language or a fair decision-making process, and what not. As if one could not infer it from the 75 percent nonrespondents, even among the sturdy 25 percent respondents "residents place a high value on privacy and independence." To leave no doubt about what privacy and independence mean in this connection, it is reported that "a small, but significant, fraction of residents express a preference to simply reduce the ground rent, rather than fund a planning process, new community facilities or functions." These must be the Republicans in the crowd.

There's more ambiguity in this prose than meets the eye. "A small fraction" that is yet "significant?" Statistically significant? Socially significant? Vocally significant? Perhaps merely using the word "significant" makes whatever it is applied to significant. Fortunately, there were "others"—not otherwise specified—who feel that the place (my concept) lacks a "neighborhood watering hole," "a sense of community" and things like that. By "watering hole" is evidently meant an alehouse or pub, not a swimming pool.

Socially more modest seekers of a "sense of community" in the study's convincing questionnaire sample proposed "a neighborhood phone directory or other means of fostering social interaction." You can't say that the Stanford professoriat is not technologically up to snuff.

Some Victories for Humanity

The summary of key findings then turns to "big problems and quick wins." I won't itemize the big problems because they are so big as to boggle the mind. They are said to be "of major concern to a sufficiently broad spectrum of residents that they are voiced in almost any forum in which community issues are discussed." Moreover, solving these "big problems" requires "substantial additional time and effort." So there comes this princely advice, for me the high point in this exercise in hucksterism: "To focus solely on these big problems will mean that results from the Community Planning Project will not be *visible* for months or years to come" (emphasis added). Alas, there are "quick wins" which "can be implemented rapidly." And they have the great virtue of demonstrating "tangible results from the process." Their rapid implementation "*shows* that the SCRL board of directors and the university administration listened to the community." Quick-win implementation "is essential to sustain the momentum for a stronger community generated by the planning effort."

The characteristics that quick wins "generally" have are listed for your philosophical enlightenment as follows:

- They are visible.
- They require no approval other than the SCRL Board and the University Administration [*sic!*].
- They enjoy very broad support, and no known strong opposition.
- They serve a large segment of the community.

There follow, for your enjoyment, some irreproachable examples of "quick wins":

- Installation of benches.
- Installation of entry markers at selected intersections.
- Improvement to the way grounds maintenance services are delivered.
- Installation or renovation of a park or minipark.
- New tree plantings.

You have to be a Stanford leaseholder to be able really to envisage these potentially "visible" accomplishments. The benches will help Stanford undergraduates to do what they do when the moon is full. The entry markers will help the hordes of strangers who come to hike in the hills, park their cars in our neighborhood, and make crossing the street unsafe for us locals, especially on weekends and holidays. More grounds maintenance will transform our partly still natural paradise into a botanical garden. More or better parks will make it possible for us to escape from our run-down backyards and have picnics in public view of anybody who may want to see bare-legged professors broil or fry hamburgers. I do approve of tree plantings. Given our climate, they are surely a "quick win" for the SCLR, Inc. board of directors.

I didn't know, until I read it, that what we had across the street on Frenchmans Road was a "minipark," a concept that has much to recommend itself, at least in leaseholders' physically environmental though not socially contextual consciousness. Until now we have tended to think of it as a fenced-in playground for toddlers perhaps up to age twelve. There are a slide, some cross-beams for the kids to fall off, a covered wooden lean-to to hide in, and that's about it. I visit the facility for about ten minutes every summer when my now eight-, ten-, and eleven-year old grandchildren visit, and I'm desperately in search of finding some entertainment for them. We go over there, they come down the slide and make me nervous by their balancing acts on the beams, and I take lots of pictures as quickly as I can because they will soon want to go home to watch *Sesame Street* or *Police Academy*. I rarely, if ever in a given month, see any kids there, though at night it seems to be a great stop for students to have a quiet rendezvous. I note that something is to be done for or about what is called "Frenchman's Triangle playfield" at an estimated cost of $35,000 (and elsewhere I read that $20,000 has actually been allocated). And the thing is to be completed in 1998 for another $45,000.

What follows under "Implementation and Evaluation," some of it about Stanford as a company town, is unadulterated circumlocution. We leaseholders are now asked to believe that "the planning project has helped to foster an increased sense of *ownership* on the part of the residents for *their* community, and enhanced the partnership between the leaseholders and University administration" (emphasis added). That's sheer bunkum or humbug, have your choice, as is what follows about "partnership" now existing between me as a leaseholder and the university administration.

"Early in the planning process," we learn, as if nobody had ever known, "it became apparent that the study area lacks facilities for community events." The apparition of what is lacking "tends to isolate residents in their homes." God forbid! Isolation! In the thirty-odd years we have lived here nobody around ever invited us to dinner, nobody ever came to dinner. I can now think only of all the new friends we shall make by becoming community conscious; they will surely get us out of our horrible loneliness by meeting with us at a "community center." Because professors are given to conceptualization as a way of life, they are helped along: "The simplest way to *conceive* this community center is to *imagine* a modified single-family residence containing a few small offices for SCLR staff [first priority, natch!], and one large meeting room for SCRL Board [second priority] and other community meetings, with an outdoor patio and garden." What's obviously missing in this model is a swimming pool.

This call on my imagination to conceive of the community

center as a modified single-family residence makes me nervous and suspicious. There is a house on Frenchmans Road. My wife and I happen to live there. This great house seems to have a perfect fit with the imagined community center. There is, by postmodern standards, an admirably large living room that, if you break down just one wall, can be enlarged to hold several hundred participants all at once in any SCRL meeting. It also has lots of small rooms that can serve as offices for the emerging local government and a splendid patio and garden (and even a pool for dips when community discussions get too hot). Could the SCRL, Inc. have their collective eyes on this easily modifiable single-family residence? Fortunately, the community center here to be imagined is "not included in the recommendations within the planning horizon of this process." This bit of pompous prose reassured me that, as the center is only a "long term option" (and hence not visible like a "quick win"), I can sleep more peacefully.

A last section deals with "following through results that you can see." What I can see is a lot of foolishness. First, the Community Planning Project "has generated a great deal of interest and support among community members." Therefore, "to maintain credibility" and "follow-through" (their hyphen, not mine), this "can most readily be accomplished by the implementation of 'Quick Wins.'"

Oh, I almost forgot: one of the Quick Wins evidently implemented already are five "Dog clean-up stations" at an estimated cost of $1,200 each or together, it isn't clear to me. One of these stations has been installed across the street on the little walk that leads to the little playpen, clearly for the convenience of the many mammas or mummies who don't want their toddlers to step into any mess left by a stranger's noblest friend. In a conclusion we are inspired to believe that the project "has built momentum [clearly irresistible] and raised expectations" (how high we can only imagine). And other euphorics.

9

The Rating, Ranking, and Baiting Game,
or
Don't Believe All You Hear
about Yourself Even If True

It began as a Daydream and ended as a Nightmare, both capitalized.

Imagine waking up some sunny morning, discovering that out of several thousand colleagues around the country you are among "the persons recognized as great men by the profession." That's pretty heady stuff. You may be curious to know how this miracle can come about. Al Somit and the late Joe Tanenhaus, at the time not yet great friends of mine but obviously possessed with a sense of humor, told it this way: "When political scientists, relaxing from the burden of teaching, research, molding public opinion, and shaping governmental policy, gather together in convivial discourse, this subject [of who are the "greats" and why] is almost sure to come up." I like that. Missing only was the prescription for the spirits that animate this conviviality. When a former student called to tell me of my greatness, I guess because he wanted to bait me with the news, I had one on the house and convivialated with myself. (All the great quotations here and subsequently come from Albert Somit and Joseph Tanenhaus, *American Political Science: A Profile of a Discipline* [New York: Atherton Press, 1964], 63–76.)

There are some other wonderful things I might quote from the study. Limited space enjoins me to pull in the reins. What it all comes down to is this: while we political scientists do not enjoy the public recognition of "more fortunate professions through such prestigious devices as the Nobel prizes," we can at least assure ourselves and other social scientists that "the great men in political science have made discoveries which, in the framework of their enterprise, are no less meritorious." These fellows *did* have a sense of humor.

From there on, things went downhill. I learned that the greatness of our twenty great men—and in 1964 we were all men, by any count—is "to some degree a matter of opinion"; and that in the absence of "accepted or objective standards" the study does not deal with greatness "in any intrinsic sense" but with a surrogate for it, the opinions of the profession. My own and my fellow greats' greatness turned out to be a simple artifact of Item C-1 of a mail questionnaire that asked, "In your judgment, which political scientists have made the *most* significant contributions to the discipline?"

The best was yet to come. Before I knew it, I was not only a "great man" but—in the chapter's next section, entitled "The Immortals"—a member of "political science's hall of fame." To be fair to the generations, Somit and Tanenhaus divided these hall-of-famers into two groups—those who made "the most significant contributions" before 1945, and those who did so after 1945. The cutoff point for being voted into the political science hall of fame was ten nominations, not a very convincing endorsement if you are told that there were 431 nominators; that is, you could be inducted by getting 2.32018 percent of the vote. The most striking finding of all this analytic effort was that there was an "apparent lack of consensus as to the men who have made significant contributions to political science." Even the great Harold Lasswell, "far and away" the most frequently named with 162 votes over both periods, was still the choice of less than half the respondents. (The next two were Charles Merriam with 131 nominations, all of which were for the first period, and V.O. Key, with 128 endorsements as a "great" in the second period). After some further profound analysis, the two investigators really let me and those like me have it. For all practical purposes, we were impostors who should not have made it into the hall of fame in the first place. At the tenth position, "by normal standards still an honorific position, barely one in twenty (of the respondents) concur." (This translates into about 5 percent. In fact, during the first period the occupant of the tenth position was Fredric A. Ogg, the long-time editor of the *APSR* and a successful textbook writer, with seventeen nominations, or 4.9 percent. In the second period the lucky fellow who made the bottom of the first ten was a great scholar, Harvard's Carl J. Friedrich, with eighteen votes, or 5.1 percent. When numbers get so small, decimal points surely come in handy.) This diffusion of opinion, Somit and Tanenhaus declare, straight-faced, "poses a problem" (to which they promise to return, and they do). With 5 percent "still an honorific position," those of us in the lower ten of the profession's highest twenty are left swinging in the winds of fads and fashions, I suppose. Who are we, anyway?

So it happened that I ended up with just the right number of votes, ten, to make it into the table that ranks the top twenty "great men" for the post-1945 period as measured in the early 1960s. That put me into a tie for seventeenth-to-twentieth place with three others whose company I would not want to spurn—James M. Burns, Karl W. Deutsch, and Dwight Waldo. I don't know anything about their ten loyalists. Mine were all people whom I had met on the occasion of some professional meeting in some hotel swimming pool or downtown pool hall, though Somit and Tanenhaus, at the time still earnest young men at forty-five and forty, respectively, suggested more lofty "elements of eminence," as they put it in the title of the next section.

The rest of this silliness was devoted to an extraordinarily complex typology of the great men's roles and attributes, though our friendly analysts concede that they really don't know what was going on in their respondents' minds (which is just as well). Then, in a concluding section on "Some Unresolved Questions," some sanity returns. Are these judgments well crystalized and stable or casual and transient? Are the perceptions influenced by short-lived intellectual fads? And so on. The answers "can come only from similar inquiries in the years ahead."

There the problem is left hanging, about the evident lack of consensus about greatness. While more consensus is probably found in the physical sciences, lack of comparable data for political science allows us only to speculate, Somit and Tanenhaus concede. Their hypothesis is tantalizing and, perhaps, designed to shock. The low recognition accorded even to the greatest of the great political scientists "springs less from divergent standards of judgment than from a pervasive conviction that there are few men in the profession who have made truly significant contributions." Wow, wow!

Sic Transit Gloria Mundi

It took fourteen years for Somit and Tanenhaus's celebration of the political science hall of fame to become a "seminal" study, at least in the critical discernment of one political scientist, who stood ready to make it seminal. He had evidently not heard at the time that "seminal" is on the approved list of politically incorrect words and should no longer be used, though there are also other grounds for not remembering the earlier study under any label.

The new custodian of fame taking on the quixotic task of updating the earlier trivia was a scholar, then of Drake University, who, I discovered, was a 1963 Stanford A.B. His mistake was, of course, that in his undergraduate years at Stanford he had failed to take a famous course on political behavior, or he wouldn't have spent his time doing something so useless. But I was also attracted to his work by a footnote to Orwell's *Animal Farm* (1946) that seemed to set the right tone for this sort of study of our own particular fauna.

I was deeply disappointed by this revival of the great S&T epic, and not just because my own name had disappeared from among the greats, who were now variously called "notables," "prominents," "persons atop," and "the elect." Being taken out of circulation in fact pleased my populist instinct. Nevertheless, I found it distressing that this new voyeur into the minds of a very dubious sample of 317 self-selected mail respondents altogether forgot about the "great men," "immortals," "eminences," and "hall-of-famers" whom his predecessors had come to praise. My calling the sample "dubious" is not just for statistical reasons. It must take a particular kind of softhead ever to answer the question here posed in its naked simplicity. And by limiting each respondent to three choices, the only thing missing in this fusillade of professional recognition was calling the nominees "celebrities." Moreover, unlike his predecessors, this investigator didn't even tell us just what criteria his respondents might possibly have used to answer the originally open-ended but now restricted question that, in the spirit of true replication, he had adopted as his own.

Instead, there were some other truly enlightening interpolations. Political scientists, unlike "the most prestigious contemporary American intellectuals" who write for journals as diverse as the

New York Review of Books or *Harper's* or *Partisan Review*, do not at all look like eggheads. Instead, the "notables" (discovered in this survey) look more like the nine political scientists who at the time of the study had made the grade into the National Academy of Sciences. In this connection, the investigator had this to say: "I should like to thank Dr. Seymour Martin Lipset for his helpful comments on this paper and, in particular, for suggesting this comparison," that is, the comparison between egghead intellectuals, the study's survey-created notables, and the few political scientists who are members of the NAS. (The quotation here and the following are from W.B. Roettger, "Strata and Stability: Reputations of American Political Scientists," *PS* 11 (1978:6–12.) I cannot resist a good, honest, and direct quote to convey the flavor of all this:

> That is, political scientists have, for some time, discounted the sort of speculative inquiry into the broader social questions which appeals to the general intellectual community. At the same time, they have evolved a set of notables that more closely resembles their representatives in the National Academy of Sciences than it does the notables of the more general intellectual community.

But back to being circulated out of the elite that dominated the early 1970s. One reason for this happy event was that the author had shaved off the lower ten from the upper twenty who had so happily resided in the original hall of fame. And there was unexpected change in the upper echelon. Our investigator was evidently stunned by some respondents nominating four people who were individually known as Campbell, Converse, Miller, and Stokes but a.k.a., collectively, as "Campbell et al." In the tabulations this foursome was identified as "SRC Group." As is well known, in the 1960s this group had made a minor contribution to American electoral research for which they were rewarded by being ranked third in the 1960–70 period with 18 percent of the vote. By 1976 they had lost many admirers but were still on the list, tied for seventh rank along with two sterling individual scholars and a much-reduced 6 percent of the vote. Now, this sort of collective intrusion into the world of individually ranked notables would create problems for any objective and impartial analyst. Therefore, to balance things off as fairness required, this imaginative researcher created his own research team. The newcomer, sharing rank No. 10.5, was a kind of "collective person" identified as "Left Radicals."

The story of how this "aggregate of prominents" came about needs to be told to convey the hilarity accompanying its creation and to give full credit for the contributions it has made to the discipline of political science. Our inadvertent humorist provides this masterful analytic rationale for assembling his strange aggregation:

> Each received one or more nominations by respondents; at no time, however, did any of these individuals receive sufficient mention to merit separate ranking. Indeed, the members of the group as a whole were mentioned by only 5 percent of the respondents during the period "1970–76." Thus, their inclusion, paradoxically, testifies to the general disaffection with the Left which characterizes American Political Science. Despite their prominence in the larger society, the individual members of the Left Radicals have made only a minor impression on the vast majority of members of the APSA.

The gentlemen in question included Ira Katznelson, Herbert Marcuse, Ralph Miliband, C. Wright Mills, James O'Connor, and Bertell Ollman. So it came about that these leftist notables, not being able to impress the vast majority of their colleagues as individuals, came to make it onto the list of the top ten as a collective with a lousy 5 percent combined vote—in the true spirit of the collectivism they individually advocated.

Madness at the Macro Level

Having escaped the fate of being themselves named by their peers as "great men" (which, in my opinion, one was and the other still is), Somit and Tanenhaus had also attended to the rating and ranking game at the macro level—what they called the "status system" of university departments of political science. (This and the following quotations come from Somit and Tanenhaus [1964], 28–35.) The madness of doing this sort of thing is more sociological than the fictive rating and ranking of individuals; at least it does not produce an imaginary hall of fame. If it were not for endless methodological problems that have plagued efforts along this line, there is even a degree of reality in such an enterprise. To this effect S&T quoted and seemingly approved a profound dictum by an old hand at the sociology of higher education: "It is simply a 'fact of life,' declares Bernard Berelson, 'that some universities are better than others.'"

Armed with Berelson's vision of a fact of life, what is there left to say about the relative standing of an academic department in either a putatively objective or a recklessly subjective "evaluation"? The answer is forgone: "not much." It has long been suspected that good universities generally have good departments in most disciplines, and good departments make for good universities. I am truly enraptured to know that, in the esteem of the profession, the Harvard Department of Political Science at one time scored a glorious 2.59 on some index of prestige, while Yale's department, in second place, suffered a humiliating 2.53 score, hence driving the Elis to desperation and a heroic effort to defeat the sons of John Harvard the next time round, as in fact they did.

Now, if you ask why it is that social science research techniques are needed to find out what everybody seems to take for granted in any case, it clearly is not for the purpose of finding out about any old fact of life but about some untested assumptions. As Somit and Tanenhaus so wittily pointed out,

> Offhand evaluations of the comparative strength of various departments are constantly made both in fraternal [with apologies to the sisters] shoptalk—where the subject is second in popularity only to that of desirable staff openings—and in the advising of graduate students. However knowledgeable these casual estimates may be, they are hardly an adequate basis for a formal ranking.

Hardly, surely! I must confess to being as much titillated by the rating and ranking game as are all the raters and rankers, then and now. But I find it somewhat less exciting than the annual, much more carefully monitored and measured ups and downs of the Cowboys or Redskins or my beloved Forty-Niners.

There was also something of the jocular in S&T's discovery of considerable "stability" in rankings over time. This stability, "however gratifying to the departments which have arrived, is simultaneously a major cause of frustration to those attempting to gain recognition." Applying this insight, if retrospectively, to my own department at Stanford when I arrived, in 1957, I can report that it was not even ranked among the top 10 but occupied the suspect No. 13 spot. My Stanford colleagues found this so depressing that they left no stone unturned to rectify the situation and, six years later, we had miraculously climbed into the No. 8 position, though we had to share it with Wisconsin at 2.07 point of the rating scale, leaving us .52 units behind No. 1 Harvard, but gloriously .10 units ahead of UCLA and Cornell.

What should endear the S&T survey of 1963 and all earlier and later studies to all customers in this rating and ranking (and, I should add, baiting) business is their embarrassing methodological candor, especially because there is nothing one would want to call a "theory" connected with any of them. What the plethora of rating studies since S&T have in common is the most tedious description of measurement differences that hardly meet the eye.

Let me be precise about how I "relate" (to use a current item of "polspeak") to all this. I'm only trying to understand the rating and ranking games being played as any other reader would. But what continued to puzzle me through the years was how it came about that I made the list of twenty in the S&T study at a time when I really was a total "unknown." Now, having access to a later and more reliable ACE survey, I can explain that, even though I was tied with three others in spot No. 17, my "case" was unique. Here is the answer to the puzzle.

My alma mater, the University of California at Berkeley, was not always a formidable competitor in the world of interdepartmental combat. Relying on the first-ever academic rankings circa 1925, Somit and Tanenhaus report, "Berkeley was just beginning its meteoric rise." I got there ten years later and, I suppose, the Berkeley department, now somewhere high up in the stratosphere, was undoubtedly responsible for my professional success. At least this is what my friends S&T lead me to believe if I properly understand their analysis.

The time now, however, is not 1935–41, when I dreamed of academic glory in the Berkeley hills, but 1963 and 1964, when two back-to-back surveys unequivocally put Berkeley into the No. 3 spot of what the ACE called the six "distinguished" departments. At this point in time, somewhat later than when I was there, the University of California's and other leading departments, S&T were kind enough to confirm, "continue to play a predominant part in training those who become the profession's luminaries and dignitaries." They note that of the political scientists named ("in a recent survey," not otherwise identified but presumably their own of 1963) as having made "the most significant contributions" after 1945, fifteen had received their doctorates at "distinguished" departments. They then provide the details: "The distribution here was six from Chicago, three from Harvard, three from Columbia, two from Yale, *and one from Berkeley*" (emphasis added). At long last, an otherwise invisible micro phenomenon could be located in the macro world of fierce departmental competition for prestige to which, *ceteris paribus*, he would have to assign his own meteoric rise between 1941 and 1963.

10

Funding, Foundations, and Fellowships,
or
Better Get What You Can While the Going Is Good

Today's mail brought a letter from, unmistakably, the John Simon Guggenheim Memorial Foundation. I know that the letter is from the foundation. The left top corner of the envelope says so; I had received a letter from them last year and the year before, about the same time of the year, I'm not sure how far back. My first inclination is to tear the letter up without reading it; I know what they want. But this letter is heavier than the usual letter—in fact, the foundation paid $.55 U.S. postage to get it delivered. My second thought is to throw it on the pile of unopened and unread letters received since January last from all kinds of charities, philanthropies, and the Democratic Victory Council of California. They have been soliciting my (tax-deductible and taxable) bucks for years. We usually make all our family's donations in December, just before Xmas, to cheer up the beneficiaries of our largesse. This does not discourage all these pen pals from stuffing our mailbox with all the other junk that arrives daily all year long. Curiosity prevails, however, and I open and read the letter.

Before going on, let me report that in 1979–80 I was the appreciative recipient of a Guggenheim fellowship. There was reason for joy. Even before the formal announcement had been made, a highly respected Stanford colleague of mine on the awards committee—in a field I dare not mention lest I reveal his identity—leaked the news at a dinner party; my proposal, he said, had stamped me "the champion of the year's proposal writers" from political science. No problem there: I had a lot of experience with writing my own proposals for funding and reading those of others, sometimes to succeed, sometimes to fail. It's all in a day's work for a professor at a "research university."

It also looks good on your c.v. to have a long list of scholarships, fellowships, awards, or such; and your dean, provost, or even president is likely to take note of your charisma as a fund raiser and pay you some attention. Indeed, a congratulatory letter arrived from Stanford's president himself, telling me that "the recognition given to you and your six Stanford colleagues places the University high on the list of the nineteen leading institutions. Thanks for adding to the laurels of our distinguished faculty ranks. But most of all, best wishes for a happy and productive research fellowship." I don't know about the "but most of all"; it struck me as something of an afterthought, and I don't know where the "list of nineteen" comes from; I guess someone in the president's office did some counting. We evidently came out in nineteenth place; otherwise we would have been in the fifteen, ten, or five "leading institutions."

I'm too lazy to look up the amount of dollars awarded at the time, but it was figured as a "supplement" to my sabbatical pay from the university that was one-half of my annual salary. The award was clearly not what in business language is called a "bonus," above and beyond normal income. It's very important to keep this in mind as this tale unfolds. It has always been my understanding that foundations are expected to receive from the rich and give to the poor. And the rich—a Rockefeller, a Carnegie, a Ford, or a Frick, to name just some classical donors—give because their demonstrable altruism accomplishes two things at once: it assuages their guilty conscience for having made so much money on the backs of others; and it keeps the givers' names alive as great philanthropists.

Learning about Foundations

Some thirty-five years ago, when I was still an innocent, I learned a lot about foundations from a foundation founder whom I knew socially. He had made a lot of money in the liquor business in Chicago, come to live in our suburban California paradise, and, according to *Who's Who* or some facsimile, now considered himself a "professional philanthropist." He presided over a foundation, called "Division Foundation." It doled out small grants for this or that—I could never quite figure out just what. One day I asked him how come the name of his outfit. His reply was inexplicably honest: "Well, some of us had some money and decided to divide it." I thought this was a splendid name and suggested that he might want to divide some of the foundation's funds by funding the pretests of the City Council Research Project I had started at Berkeley and Stanford. Nothing came of it. The trouble with the man was that he wanted not only to give money but also supervise its spending. Even before the research was getting under way, he had all the answers. "No thanks," I thought, and went to the National Science Foundation.

Don't get me wrong. I'm a great admirer of the private foundations. Way back in the early 1950s, reviewing the new Ford Foundation's first statement on its mission, I waxed lyric in writing (publicly) that "until now, no foundation with means comparable to those of the Ford Foundation has ventured so far as to lay all of its golden eggs in the shapeless basket of social science," and stuff like that. I was soon rewarded by a year-long fellowship from the Foundation's Fund for the Advancement of Education, though I am doubtful that there was a causal relationship involved in this fortuitous happenstance. This was both a most charitable and generous fellowship. Its charitable side was its being given for the purpose of improving my learning and teaching. This would not only benefit me but also my students and, through them, mankind. So the fund picked up my entire salary for 1951–52 that was in the neighborhood of $4,800 or so, or $400 per month. (My beginning salary at Antioch College in 1947–48 was $3,700 per annum, or $308.33 per month if figured as a twelve-month salary, or $411.11 as a nine-month salary. Penn State offered me $3,800 at the time. I obviously chose Antioch because it was closer to a railroad track in Xenia, Ohio, than in State College, Pennsylvania.) And, to top this charitable and tax-free award, I also received a generous amount of travel money—enough to take my wife to Europe for two months in the summer of 1952, on the standard budget of $5 a day (for two, of course).

Caveat Guggenheim!

But back to Guggenheim. The letter from the foundation informed me, as probably had previous years' letters, that the foundation has a proud tradition of service to scholars, artists, scientists, and writers that dates way back, and that several thousand awards have been made through the years—"all based solely on the merit and promise of an individual's work." So far, so good, though I have always been somewhat skeptical about the "promise" stuff. Then comes the telltale sentence that let the cat out of the bag: "*There are no strings attached.*" This, in turn, is followed by this strange non sequitur, "There is no political agenda." Now, why would the Guggenheim Foundation be so defensive about two things that, as far as I know, no one has ever accused it of? I certainly do not remember thinking about strings and political agendas when I got my award in 1979.

In another sentence of this portentous communiqué I'm told that "as a Fellow, you understand the significance of the award, and as a donor to the Foundation, you have acknowledged the importance of continuing the tradition." Clever stuff this. While it is true that I made some modest contribution to the Guggenheim Foundation in the past—"modest" because we have other priorities—I have by no means "acknowledged the importance of continuing the tradition." If I did and forgot, I now propose to discontinue the tradition.

What makes me come to this momentous decision? Here it is: the foundation wants to raise X million dollars for twenty additional fellowhips, a worthy undertaking, especially as the foundation "continues to reduce operating costs and to refine investment strategies"—a promise, I suppose. How can one disagree with that? But then comes this little shocker: "In the early days of our fundraising program, many [how many are many?] of the hundred of thoughtful [natch!] and enthusiastic [forever!] Fellows who came forward [being reborn, I suppose] with help offered to 'replace' their original fellowship award for the benefit of new Fellows. We hope that their example will inspire you to do the same, perhaps through a series of five annual gifts."

A shocker, as I said. My 1979–80 award, it turns out, was not an award at all but a loan! "No strings attached!" Holy Moses!

And that's not the end of it. Attached to this charmer of a letter—I wonder which PR firm drafted it—is a chart that informs me of the average amount, in 1994 dollars, of the awards made in the year in which I received the Guggenheim. And to make it all easy, I guess especially for artists and writers who can't count, the chart "includes the arithmetic for a five year pledge." But, generous as the foundation is, it provides for a way out from this arithmetic: "If the number [*sic!*] on the chart is too large for you, move the decimal point over to a more appropriate place." Alas, you don't even have to study the long chart: the Guggenheimers do all the arithmetic for you, to wit:

> The average amount of a Guggenheim Fellowship award in 1979 was $16,055, the equivalent of $30,875 in 1994 dollars.
> You can replace that award with five annual gifts of either $3,211 (5 × $3,211 = $16,055) or $6,175 (5 × $6,175 = $30,875).

In response to these magic numbers I began to move the decimal point in any conceivable direction on both the minimum and maximum calculations, ending up invariably with a big zero or null, wondering all along what old man Simon Guggenheim would have thought of this latter-day mode of making money. And just imagine the unimaginable—having other foundations follow suit in this kind of no-strings-attached "replacement" effort. Should our colleague Herbert Simon return half of his ill-earned (because received in his disguise as an economist) Nobel prize to his Swedish benefactor in order to fund future Nobels in political science?

Big Bucks Are Hard to Get

My mind wanders back into the 1960s and 1970s, settling down in a comfortable chair across from a very nice lady, let me call her Arnice because that's her real name. She's retired now, as I am, but is still there in my memory, as she always is when I need her to straighten out some budget matter. She is unmistakably our dean's fiscal conscience—I can tell because there is an old-fashioned calculator on her desk. Always glad to see me, she invariably reminds me of my colleagues' failure to bring in "big bucks," as she put it one day. I should mention that her ideal money-getter is a very, very famous electrical engineer who does things I don't understand, collects medals and awards the world over, and, above all, brings in big bucks. He happens to be her husband.

Anyway, we have the same conversation. "Why don't your colleagues apply for some funding?" she asks in all seriousness time and again. Or, when in a more aggressive mood, she does not ask but asserts: "Your colleagues ought to get some grants!" She handles all the H&S (Humanities and Sciences) budgets—biology, physics, mathematics, big money-makers. I agree with her, "being funded is wonderful," though we have different reasons for our agreement. She likes to save foundation dollars, I like to spend them. I patiently explain to her how difficult it is to get big project grants in the social sciences. "But you manage," she says, "and Professor North does." We do, I agree, and then I explain that Bob North and I are frontiersmen in research and that not everybody can be at some frontier. "Why not?" she asks. I'm out of gas by then, she shakes her head, and we discuss the budgets as they are and not as they should or could be.

Then everything changed, in the late 1960s or so. I remember the provost calling all NSF-funded project directors together and, using language I sensed to be rather Orwellian, he tried to explain to us that the funded life would never be the same. What he told us, in effect, was that the foundation had placed a "cap" on all grants; that the university in its financial veracity—he really meant "voracity"—sought more and more overhead funding from the foundation (after all, the janitors who cleaned our offices had to eat, too); and that, as the overhead rate, or "indirect costs," so-called, went up, the $$$,$$$ figures in a grant's "direct cost" column would go down. What he didn't tell us was that the paperwork connected with all grants and contracts would also increase in proportion to the increase in the overhead rate. And other stuff I never understood. I don't have to understand, I thought at the time; Arnice will take care of it and me.

One of the files I still have shows that, long after Arnice and I had retired, I resisted "signing off" on my last NSF-funded project with the relevant Stanford authorities. In the years of ever-increasing indirect and ever-decreasing direct costs applying for and holding a research grant had become a bureaucratic nightmare. In the 1950s, and well into the 1960s, one wrote a proposal, sent off three copies to some funding agency, and was awarded a grant or turned down. To do this, one needed the single signature of just one assistant dean, and that was it. By the early 1970s one had to collect, in addition to one's chair's and dean's, all kinds of other signatures from all kinds of faceless paper pushers in some administration building whose sense of business is keen and whose main interest is in seeing to it that the university gets its overhead. These local negotiations are now conducted through a departmental manager, once upon a time called secretary, and it is necessary to have twenty copies or more of every piece of paper.

After my last NSF grant had run out and I had retired, I was asked to write a "final report" on the project. This was long after I had reported what there was to report to the NSF political science program director in Washington. I had soon learned in my weary interactions with the university bureaucracy that, more often than not, all kinds of requests for this or that just go away after a time if you hold out long enough. So, in this case and in a mood of quiet protest, I did nothing. I had underestimated these indefatigable watchdogs of research; after receiving reminder after reminder, I finally gave in and sent them a short piece on the project I had written for the *ICPSR Bulletin* five years earlier, and that made them happy and got them off my back.

In the Clutches of the Graduate Dean

One of the most curious funding episodes came in the early 1970s when, to cap the NSF cap, the graduate dean decided that a department could admit only so-and-so-many new Ph.D. candidates. I don't think department chairs were ever consulted on this nonaffirmative action, but that was not the worst of it. The worst of it was that we could not increase our quota of new Ph.D. candidates, even if we went out to raise our own money. When, in due course, we received funding from NIMH for four annual fellowships, this did not mean we could now bring in fourteen new students instead of the ten allowed us by the graduate tsar. It meant that we lost four university fellowships that would otherwise have been available to us. I had some yelling encounters with the dean's understudy, pointing out to him the obvious—that their policy, if it deserved to be called that, undermined any faculty initiative to raise research or training funds on their own to support graduate students. Of course, the yelling got me nowhere, except to an unbelieving Arnice who, for once, had grounds for shaking her head.

The local arrangements in the matter of graduate student admissions, at least at that time, were most curious. The big dean of humanities and sciences controlled the funds for teaching assistantships (TAs). Although, understandably, he had to hold the line to meet provostial budget limits, he was generally sympathetic to increasing the number of TAs because that would make for better teaching in the large undergraduate classes. The graduate dean's policy, by restricting enrollment, was really counterproductive. We never had enough TAs to fill departmental needs, and some of my colleagues had to go to the law school or business school to find themselves a TA.

Let me get back to those happy days of being funded. "Being funded" is synonymous with "prestige," and it is an important personal attribute in a research university. It gives you an aura of well-being and success (even if the bonanza is less than it seems). You can hire or, better, "support" graduate students, and that, as I just reported, relieves the graduate dean from supporting them. You can charge attendance at some professional meeting to your grant. You can have a drink at the Faculty Club bar with a visiting fireperson by calling him or her a consultant, whether you are consulting or not. You can feel free, except if you make the mistake of hiring your own secretary, who sees to it that you are busy keeping him or her busy. I think that's what being funded is all about, and there is a rather welcome, if ironic, side effect: the well-funded also get the best annual raises because, at least if you put yourself on a budget line and as long as the grant lasts, the university does not have to shell out any salary. And that's the reason why continued funding is so important. Of course, the relationship between being funded and getting merit raises is probably spurious, as both have a common—and unspeakable—cause: some people are just more productive than others.

When I arrived at Stanford in fall 1958, I was assumed to be "funded." I didn't have to tell anybody what this amounted to "dollar-wise" because the grant had been made before I had come to the university and was administered elsewhere. (All I had to do was to cash the checks I received from my patron.) Then, just as I was explaining to Arnice about the difficulties of getting funding in the social sciences, luck struck: even before the NSF formally recognized political science as part of its mission in the behavioral sciences, circa 1964, I had succeeded in extracting what at the time amounted to a huge grant from its Social Sciences Division. Alas, I soon enough learned that this was not necessarily an unmixed blessing.

The grant generously provided to pay the salary of my collaborator, and it provided stipends for a stable of graduate assistants over a number of years (this was before the graduate dean's edict about admissions). In my modesty I paid myself only "summer money" so that I remained a "line" in the department's faculty budget. But with all that summer *richesse,* the authorities at one point thought that I did not need more than a perfunctory increase in pay. My protest was emphatic and loud: I had not only contributed significantly to the maintenance of an "Institute of Political Studies" and the support of Ph.D. candidates, but at the very moment, I had brought in a new three-year research training grant from the NIMH. I once figured out that for the first two decades of life at Stanford I practically paid for my own upkeep when all the moneys I had brought in—professional and secretarial salaries, salary supplements, student stipends, infrastructural direct costs and indirect costs—are added up. So my asymptote (see chapter 6) continued to rise to the bitter end, if barely keeping ahead of the ravishing inflationary spiral that began in the mid-1970s.

The Fortunes of Fortuna

As every schoolboy and schoolgirl learns these days (a more than doubtful proposition), Fortuna, in Roman mythology, is the goddess of fortune. And, culture-bound as they are, they are likely to believe that if they pray to Fortuna, they will come to "make a pile" or, as the dictionary has it, "a large quantity of money or possessions; riches." Alas, Fortuna is really a rather fickle lady: she has the power to bestow good *or* bad on people. Also, the word "fortune" is full of other ambiguities: it can mean luck or chance; and its very opposite, fate or destiny.

It would be nice to believe that there was something inevitable about being able to bring in "substantial"—in the social science sense of the word—research and research-training grants. But if it wasn't so, it was also not all chance. When, in 1961–62, I began planning a major project on decision making in small groups, the groups being ninety-odd city councils, it never entered my mind that the National Science Foundation could be approached for support. At that time the effort soon to be made by Evron Kirkpatrick, the executive director of the APSA, to have political science "recognized" as a discipline within NSF's mission was not known to me.

As I have told the story of the CCRP elsewhere in some detail (Eulau 1996, chaps. 12 and 13), I'll not repeat it here. Relevant is how the NSF funding came about. Fortuna, in her luck-making disguise, had me meet Henry Riecken, who then headed the Social Science Division at NSF, at a conference at Yale in September 1963. I told Riecken about the project, and he encouraged me to apply. Well, the grant came through, and we were in business by fall 1964.

I don't think that Riecken ever thought of himself as a male impersonation of Fortuna. He probably saw his division's making us a grant as a tactic either to make it possible for political science to infiltrate the foundation or, in Machiavellian fashion, to keep it officially out. The latter tactic would help avoid political entanglements with "real" scientists (on the National Science Board that supervises NSF and has always questioned the genuine "sciency" side of social science) and/or with antagonistic congressmen who think we are socialists or worse. Which was what, I cannot say. The fact is: our first grant was somehow processed before political science had been admitted to the sacred circle of the sciences.

Extracting four NIMH research-training fellowships over a period of six years was even more of a long-shot operation. It all happened this way: One day, during the 1966–67 school year, a fellow with the name of Nat Siegel called and introduced himself as chief of the social science training section at the National Institute of Mental Health. Would I be willing to serve on a NIMH team to do a site visit to the political science department at UCLA? They had applied for a training grant. Always concerned about my own mental health but mostly failing (though married to a psychiatric social worker), I said yes. I was curious: I had not known that NIMH was interested in political science, and this chore would give me an opportunity to learn more about it.

The site visit was a disaster—for UCLA, not for me. They had applied for a huge sum of money, it seemed to me ("huge" being a hugely relative term). As I read the proposal and visited around, it was clear that giving them any money would be a wonderful gift package for the faculty members involved in this "training." A departmental entrepreneur had evidently gone around to his more or less research-minded colleagues, perhaps ten or twelve of them, to ask them for a statement of what they were researching; he had then bundled up these statements (covering topics from arms control to sewer treatment) in an "omnibus bill" that provided generous summer salaries for the faculty, amounting to two-thirds of the total budget, with just one-third going to graduate training fellowships that sounded more like research assistantships.

Well, a pleasant time was had by all for two days (site visits are not always pleasant, but the Uclans knew how to do it right on the entertainment front), and the proposal went down the tube fast, even before we left, something quite unusual because site-visit teams are expected to be tight-lipped.

Was it just that Fortuna in the cloak of benign benefactress smiled on me by bringing me Nat Siegel as she had brought me Henry Riecken? I would probably have heard about the program sooner or later from another source, but UCLA's mistakes were a learning experience that I would not have had without the site visit. And going farther backward, I never learned how my name had come to Siegel's attention in the first place. Warren Miller, master fund raiser, once spoke of "research life as a collection of intersecting probability distributions." In part, for sure. But only in part: it helps to be clued into the right professional networks. In the 1960s, though young, we were all "old boys." But this is not to say that Fortuna, goddess of destiny, had nothing to do with our luck.

On Becoming a Philanthropist Yourself

There are, of course, alternatives to foundations and fellowships and all the hassles that come and go with them and the wear and tear on one's nerves. I sometimes marvel that I overcame all the obstacles in the high hurdles for funding and did reasonably well; and sometimes I dream about what might have happened had I inherited a fortune or married a rich lady. Well, that was not my fate or destiny. My current thought in the matter is still very much my original thought before becoming accustomed to foundation largesse: be your own foundation. People ask me sometimes who, now that I enjoy the privileges of retirement, is paying for my travel and hotel expenses when attending a professional meeting. I can answer them in all honesty that it is the rich and famous "Eulau Foundation" that pays for my professional trips. That's just as it was fifty years ago when I first went to meetings at my own expense, and not even with any thought of networking, funding or anything else so vulgar.

11

The Pleasures of Conferencing
and Other Indoor Sports,
or
You Haven't Lived Until Living It Up
in French Lick

Academicians' favorite indoor sport, it should go without saying but has to be said nevertheless, is conferencing. The unique contribution of an academic conference or professional meeting to any mental worker's physical well-being is indisputable. The small round-table conference especially strengthens what German-speaking scholars call *Sitzfleisch*—the ability to remain posted on one's posterior beyond the call of duty. At least so it was when it was the mark of scholarship to be glued from dawn to dusk to some uncomfortable, hard chair in the library's dungeonlike stacks. Nowadays, of course, with computers, printers, copiers, and other gadgets around, scholarly life is a bit different. There is a good deal of standing up and running hither and thither to be done, and one can no longer predict academic advance by the *Sitzfleisch* test. A good conference is the institutionalized representation of the Roman principle, *mens sana in corpore sano.*

There are both costs and benefits involved in conferencing. The costs lie in the danger that one's otic capacity may be overloaded and impaired. As, at a good conference, everybody talks, often at the same time and at cross-purposes, the strain on the auditory system may prove fatal. The benefits, especially to a student of behavior, consist in the opportunity to sharpen one's visual senses as one closely observes and scrutinizes the manners of other conferees—as they fiddle with the pipe they are no longer allowed to smoke as in olden times; as they doodle on a napkin to avoid falling asleep; as they caress their carefully trimmed but ever-itching beards; as they take off their shoes, lift their feet on the table, and exhibit some garish socks full of holes. Skill in observation at a conference is contingent, of course, on one's fortitude in limiting one's own verbal assaults on other conferees to a minimum.

There are other advantages to conferencing as an academic indoor sport. If the conference is held in winter at one of our great universities of the Great Plains, one can enjoy the warmth generated by the joviality of one's colleagues. Properly seated at the conference table, one can stare out the window on snow-covered fields and let one's mind drift toward the next conference, to be held in summer, more likely than not in some air-conditioned, windowless hotel room. In fact, as conferences follow each other with seasonable regularity, they give one that sense of security so essential to the life of the mind.

Not that all the summer meetings meet all of one's winter expectations. I remember sitting in an air-conditioned nightmare of a windowless room in some motel at Swarthmore. It was hellishly hot outside and freezing cold inside. But that wasn't the worst of it. The worst was the wallpaper. It was in black and white lines alternating in waves from floor to ceiling, no other decorations breaking their unending flow. The wallpaper was all around you, producing the dizzying effect of seasickness.

All of this is not to say that conferencing is all mental and physical exercise. It is also spiritual and affective. There is no need to dwell at length on the matter of spirits, though novices at conferencing should be advised to bring their own when the conference is held on some self-denying college campus that has not yet come out of the Prohibition era. Spirits are critical ingredients of a good conference in nourishing good fellowship. I could go on developing a classification of conferences—from the intimate workshop conference with a handful of participants to the mass meetings organized by the learned societies. While some colleagues prefer one type of conference to another, I like them all, being a multi- rather than unidimensional conference-goer. When I was an active and sometimes hyperactive professor, what I found most attractive about conferences is known as the "academic truancy dimension," normatively legitimated by the even-better-known "ethic of truancy." It permits the skilled conference-goer to play hooky from his or her home institution. Understandably, I used to prefer conferences, whatever their size or location, held during the school year, not those that intruded on my vacation. I must confess that I sometimes went on from one conference to the next without returning home to do my teaching, enjoying instead the sights and sounds of the Pacific, Caribbean, or Atlantic. Of course, not all professors accept truancy as a principle. I remember intersecting in three consecutive almost week-long conferences with the late Karl Deutsch, an indefatigable conference-goer. Karl rushed back to Harvard for just one day to teach his undergraduate course before rejoining the conference circuit.

Per Aspera ad Astra

The modal academic's career as a conferee does not usually begin too happily. More likely is attendance at one of the national or regional mass meetings called conventions. There the novice at conferencing will look up and down the corridors for some familiar face—usually the face of a former classmate or less often that of an old professor. The hope is of being introduced to someone not previously on the first-timer's prospective mailing list. This new acquaintance then has a chance to become the obviously lucky recipient of a free copy of the novice's first convention paper, perhaps even of a reprint. Still paying off debts accrued during the long years of study and still being in a state of poverty, the freshcomer will share a room with another assistant professor, who snores, and he or she will take breakfast and lunch around the corner at some celebrated, if greasy, dinette. Because the novice has nothing else to do, he or she may even attend a panel session on this or that to learn how the great ones do it. Except, it seems, the greatest of the great take a dim view of the mass meetings and do not show up, having become accustomed to the more intimate affairs, with all expenses paid and no papers to be "delivered."

I recall an experience of my own, by no means the only one in a long career as a troubadour on the convention circuit. I was invited to comment on no less than four papers by some, in fact, distinguished scholars who, it turned out on reading the papers in advance, did have something to say that deserved some well-thought-out comment. Here is the scenario.

Although there were only two discussants for the four papers, the panel chairperson (who doubled as a paper giver in his own right, so assuring acceptance of his paper for presentation) gave each of us fifteen minutes to cover the waterfront. Let me translate this generosity into reality. The four papers, none of them easy to digest, came to 120 double-spaced pages. As my reading skill is somewhat retarded—I manage only about twenty pages per hour on this sort of thing, though I do better on detective stories—I devoted at least six hours to reading and, hopefully, some reflection. But what happened to me on the panel? With fifteen minutes at my disposal, I had to cover eight pages per minute or, the other way round, I could devote 7.5 seconds to every page. Microanalysts would want to calculate lines per minute or seconds per line or words per time or time per words, but I will forgo this exercise. Anyway, brilliant as my comments were, there was obviously something wrong with the "system." (A system in quotation marks is by definition flawed; the concept has its obviously polemical uses.)

Even worse than the experience with this sort of well-organized panel are my experiences as a paper *giver* at panels of the International Political Science Association. Mostly these IPSA affairs serve the useful function of obtaining highly reduced plane tickets for yourself and your extended family to visit exotic places on various continents. You dutifully "deliver" your paper or mere thoughts to legitimize your expenses to some dean or other benefactor, but then disappear as soon as possible. If you can afford it, you eat well on these occasions, take in opera or theater, visit cathedrals and museums, make side excursions into the hinterland to observe the natives, make perhaps some new friends from Japan or India who become your pen pals for life and want you to invite them to your university so that they can take your picture, and so on.

I fondly recall my first IPSA conference in Geneva, in 1964. I was there alone, didn't know many people, but ran into the late Kalman Silvert, the splendid Latin Americanist, who was also keeping his own company. Together we explored old Geneva and together we broke bread, not really bread but a variety of cheese soufflés for which Geneva is famous. Yes, there was a panel I attended to give a paper—one of no less than fifteen papers "delivered" in the two hours available for this sporting event, including comments from commentators whose number has escaped me. As I recall it, I got up, bowed, read the title and subtitle of our paper, acknowledged my two coauthors, informed the crowd how they could get a copy of the paper, and sat down.

There is no escape from that mandatory big-meeting after-dinner speech at which some well-meaning orator thinks he has something significant to convey to the assembled mass. I remember an evidently unending address by an APSA president. After listening (or not listening) for fifty-nine minutes, Dwaine Marvick and I got up, rather conspicuously and probably in bad taste, only to find all of the nearest ballroom doors locked. Then there was the incredibly dull speech by another APSA president that the official representatives of the Inter-University Consortium for Political Research once had to endure in the ballroom of the Michigan Union (at least I think it was in the Union). Nobody got up; but afterward, I asked friend Jack Dennis of Wisconsin how he had liked the speech. Jack looked up at the ceiling and pointed a finger at the three huge chandeliers and responded, "There are twelve light bulbs out up there."

These are just a few of the pleasures of our professional meetings. Then there are the overcrowded, department-sponsored cash-bar cocktail parties at which the sweat running down one's brow and nose drips into the cocktail glass and people pretend to enjoy good fellowship by standing on their tired feet and pushing each other around. The experienced convention-goer avoids these costly affairs if at all possible. He or she prefers to sit with some old friend in a quiet bar and schmooze about better times before every third-rate Ph.D.-granting department felt impelled to have its own "reception."

Then there are the hinterland affairs. I remember one on "community power," then a hot topic, held at the University of Georgia. The major adversaries were my then freshly minted colleague Ray Wolfinger, only recently discharged from Robert Dahl's pluralistic haven at Yale, and my friend Bob Agger, whom I had met at the 1954 summer seminar on electoral research in Ann Arbor, and who later was the lead author of a big book, *The Rulers and the Ruled* (1964). The two of them were at each other's throats all day long but were equally helpful in pushing an old and overloaded school bus up and around the sharp corner of a steep pass en route to an exotic (and inedible) soul-food dinner on some mountain top.

There was the conference in Tallahassee on public policy, I can't remember when. They took us to some seafood place on the coast, which, horror of horrors, served neither Beefeaters nor wines (not even Gallo's reinforced Thunderbird) nor beer. Off I went with some Florida State graduate student in search of a store to buy some wine. We found one fifteen miles away. By the time we got back to the party, they had all finished dinner and were ready to go back to the Holiday Inn for a well-deserved swim. The six bottles were put to good use by some FSU students.

The Old Boys Become Displaced Persons

I can't recall the dozens of annual APSA conventions I attended in the past fifty years, but some stand out. One was in the early 1970s when the "old boys" became displaced persons. I hadn't paid much attention to the rising women's movement in the academic world, but I vividly recall an incident at an APSA meeting circa 1970. There was a convocation of some kind called either by the insurgent Women's Caucus for Political Science or the conventional APSA Committee on the Status of Women. Not surprisingly, the meeting was stacked with women, and from what I could make out, most of them were graduate students. Their declared or undeclared chief was a young woman whose organizational-political pizzazz was formidable. For better or worse, her scholarly credentials were of lesser distinction. No doctor of philosophy yet, or ever, she was more often on her feet shuffling between a seat in the audience and the microphone on the podium than was good for women's liberation, and she was by no means alone in what looked much like a harum-scarum carnival scene. Call it "participatory democracy." I sat in the audience, next to a most eminent political theorist from a university I cherish. When things on the podium reached the apex of confusion and merriment, I turned to her and asked: "Why aren't you up there with your sisters?" To which impudent question she replied: "They aren't my sisters." No fraternizing for her.

If I sound more flippant on this first encounter with women's liberation in the academy than I should, it is because my concern in this book is our individual and collective fads, foibles, and fumbles, not those weighty intellectual and institutional problems of concern to women that are genuinely and equally shared by right-thinking persons of both genders. But I must confess that I was not particularly attuned to the reviving women's movement of the 1960s, and probably for three reasons.

First, I had trouble with thinking of sex as gender, or vice versa. Having been brought up as something of a Latin-learning grammarian, I knew little of sex, and of gender only as the formal classification by which nouns are to be handled in prose and verse. Later, when I had to study German and French, things became totally confusing. What in German was masculine, like *Der Mond,* was feminine in French, *la lune.* And what was feminine in German, *die Sonne,* was masculine in French, *le soleil.* Somewhere, sometime, something had gone topsy-turvy in the world of gender designations.

Second, I had spent my whole life in the company of women who were reasonably successful and in some cases very successful professionals, including my wife and her associates. The issues of such concern to the young women who rediscovered the gender gap in the 1960s did not *seem* to arise in our circles, even though some of them were there.

Third, I had the good luck of working with many truly excellent and even some brilliant women students, undergraduates at Antioch College and Ph.D. candidates at Stanford. I had absolutely no reason to assume or think that I could not be as much a "role model" for them as for the men.

There was an altercation with the Women's Caucus, in 1970, when I had been made the "official" nominee for president of the APSA. The Women's Caucus was much interested in the election of the APSA officialdom because we were expected to respond favorably to caucus demands for this or that. This was the time when "nonnegotiable demands" were part of the academic culture. Among other things, I was invited to appear before the Women's Caucus to "defend" my prospective "policies" in the matter of women's rights. Although I had no policies to defend, I appeared before a room full of young women, none of whom I had ever seen before. In the course of this debut I was asked whether I would accept caucus recommendations for the appointment of women to APSA committees. According to my friend Jeane Kirkpatrick, one of the two or three faces in the crowd I recognized, I shook my right index finger at the women and told them, at least in Jeane's imitation of my inimitable German accent, "You must do your work!" Then they would have no trouble being appointed to anything; for the time being, I informed my audience, I preferred to appoint women of my own acquaintanceship who were highly deserving without being sponsored by the caucus. By my injunction I meant getting the Ph.D. and doing publishable research.

Many, many years later my friend Ada Finifter, now the editor of the *APSR,* told me that my appointing her to the Committee on the Status of Women in the Profession had launched her professional career within the association. Ada had received her Ph.D. from the University of Wisconsin in 1967 where Austin Ranney and Leon Epstein had been her mentors. She remains a true role model for young political scientists of either gender.

Then there was the episode of my demonstrated sexism. One day I was approached by an agent of the Women's Caucus, who shall remain unnamed, who wanted to talk with me. I had no reason to avoid the talk, having met her before, and nothing in her quite substantial résumé, at that time, led me to suspect that I was in harm's way. I mention this because many years later I was asked, rather ironically, to come to her aid in a discrimination suit she had brought against her university (for the *denouement* of the affair, see chap. 15).

The interview was conducted on some steps leading from somewhere to somewhere in the Los Angeles Biltmore where the APSA was meeting, with people stepping over and around us. Not at all beating around the bush, the caucus emissary asked me to answer the riddle about the surgeon who refused to operate on a son, or something along this line. The "correct" answer was that the person under the knife was *her* and not *his* son. Needless to say, I messed this one up—solving riddles hadn't yet become the standard criterion for identifying the macho males who advocate *Kinder, Kueche, und Kirche.* My flunking the test was reported to the Women's Caucus who, in their wisdom, did not endorse my candidacy for the APSA presidency. Instead, they supported Professor Hans Morgenthau, a distinguished student of *Realpolitik,* whose profeminist proclivities were well hidden. In the subsequent election he lost (3,563 votes), I won (4,711 votes).

After the election the Women's Caucus handed me a list of names of women they wanted me to appoint to the APSA's various committees. I informed them that the list did not include a single nominee known to me, either personally or even remotely as a scholar; and I could not resist giving them a lesson in practical politics that was hardly original—that, in politics, the spoils go to the victor, not the loser. I had enough women in my camp to stock the committees adequately for several years.

Well, it took twenty years before a new generation of caucusites, probably innocent of knowing about all this, made me a "mentor of distinction." In fact, I had directed any number of Ph. D. dissertations by any number of women without any awareness that I was doing something particularly admirable. Given the prehistory of vicarious interaction with the organization, this was an honor I had never suspected of receiving. On 31 August 1991, I was invited to a kaffeeklatsch held at an ungodly 7:00 A.M. at the Washington Hilton, once the battleground of the true believers versus the infidels (see chap. 16). There I received a nice placard, which, appropriately framed and posted on the wall above my work station along with other acknowledgments of this sort, tells the world that it was given to me "in recognition of past and present efforts encouraging and assisting women to enter the profession of Political Science."

I have learned since that this mode of being honored as a mentor of women by the WCPS represents something less than meets the eye. As a more recent inductee has perceptively observed, "Everyone wins in this 'competition.'" It seems that "the only requirement for honoring a nominee is that a letter of explanation and commendation accompany the nomination." During 1992–93, according to Jennifer Hochschild, the WCPS received thirty-five nominations from thirty-four members ("Honoring Mentors of Distinction." *PS* 24 [1993]:770). I infer from this revealing datum that at least one honoree must have received two nominations that year—perhaps it was my old friend Karl Deutsch, described as "deceased," which is not a stylish word to use: "Late of Harvard and Berlin" would have been more appropriate.

Summit Meetings

Then there are the highly regarded and, it seems, often secret rendezvous that I can best denote as "summits." An academic summit is a by-invitation-only meeting at which the invitees are expected to think big and make important decisions for the future of some line of teaching, research, or both. Some of them in fact do have some influence, but some of those I attended did not. This is not to say that they are a waste of the funds spent on them.

Among the summits I remember best was a shindig called "International Conference on the Use of Quantitative Political, Social, and Cultural Data in Cross-National Comparison." Held at Yale, the affair was more than a week long, running from 10 to 20 September 1963. Karl Deutsch, the great impresario, could never do anything in less time; but, then, he was an empiricist with a great deal of imagination. (For a report on the conference and some of the papers presented there, see the volume edited by Richard L. Merritt and Stein Rokkan, *Comparing Nations: The Use of Quantitative Data in Cross-National Research* [New Haven: Yale University Press, 1966].) I had my new colleague Richard Brody in tow, and we lived it up with a lot of beer in some hot, directly under-the-roof suite of one of the old residential houses.

Summit conferences often lead to those cherished personal connections that make the learned life something more than the grind that it can be. While I knew many of the people attending the Yale conference, I met some new ones who, in later years, became good friends, like Mattei Dogan, from Paris, or Erwin Scheuch, from Cologne. I remember best a day's excursion from New Haven to Nantucket with Dogan and two other Frenchmen who, Brody and I thought, ought to learn something about the "real" America. I don't know whether, at that time, our French friends bought this story about Nantucket as an archetype of the real America. The trouble was that my French was worse than rusty and Dogan, at that time, knew almost no English. In his studied earnestness he is one of the most delightful persons I know among our European colleagues, most of them very earnest and intense about political science indeed.

Then there was the NSF-sponsored summit to end all summits (but it did not) held in May 1974 at Lake Lawn Lodge on Lake Delevan in Wisconsin. As it rained incessantly for the three days we were there, we were forced to be indoors and spend the leisure hours in the local pub. I remember a long-into-the-night, well-distilled evening in the company of such recidivists as Norman Nie, John Sprague, Dwaine Marvick, and one or two others of similar irrepressible talent. All of this for the purpose of contemplating "Design and Measurement Standards for Research in Political Science." While some of us had some doubts about the possibility of ever reaching agreement on design and measurement "standards" —a matter on which the conference did not get as far as its convener had hoped, it was a good learning experience.

The funny thing about the summit conferences is that one generally does not remember who said what to whom about this or that groundbreaking item in expanding the frontiers of knowledge. All one remembers are the highly personal, usually hilarious, incidents that in retrospect seem to legitimize one's attendance. There were two week-long summits I attended at the Villa Serbelloni in Bellagio. The first was a conference on the study of elite research in 1970. There were Lester Seligman, then at the University of Oregon, and his wife, Judy. They had shipped, or thought they had shipped, several suitcases of winter clothes to Italy because they were going on to the University of Umea in cold Sweden. When the suitcases did not arrive, Judy and my wife went several times to the Milano Airport's baggage department; to no avail. On the last visit, so my wife tells it, Judy broke out in tears, and a nice Italian *padrone di bagaglio,* full of professional empathy, took pity. "Signora," he said, speaking English in a classical Italian accent, "come back with me and look for yourself." When there was no luggage addressed to the Seligman's, the good man waved an arm across the sea of suitcases and said, "Signora, take any one of them."

Then there was the 1977 Bellagio conference on the germinating study of biopolitics to which I was invited for some reason I could not discover. More memorable than the conference itself was the subsequent motor tour through northern Italy with John Wahlke at the wheel, while I paid thousands of lira for the privilege of driving at 100 miles an hour on some *autostrada*. Now, no matter where we were and what we saw—in Verona, Venice, Ravenna, Bologna, Siena, or Florence—it reminded friend John of something in Cincinnati, Iowa City, Nashville, Buffalo, or Stony Brook where he had lived at one time or another. A true patriot!

A venturesome motor trip from London to Edinburgh, where the International Political Science Association was meeting, featured Warren Miller as chauffeur. It was a venturesome journey not only because driving on the wrong side of the road made it so but also because at our nightly provincial hotel stopovers we had to instruct the resident bartender in the fine art of constructing an American martini, not just pouring Italian vermouth named *Martini* into a water glass.

There was no end to summitry when, by a circuitous route, I came to serve as chair of the Board of Overseers of the National Election Studies. I have never counted the times I have been in Ann Arbor from 1954 on, but they were many, many. Apart from the friends I made or had there, what attracted me to Ann Arbor were, first, the two German restaurants the city offered its natives and visitors; second, State Street's unmatched bookstores, in the early years "Marshall's," a small store, which, as the word "store" is supposed to denote, stored a fine selection of books published in England.

For the first few years of the NES we held conferences in such delightful American facsimiles of Florence, Bologna, or Siena as Rochester, Tallahassee, Santa Fe, Baton Rouge, San Diego, Seattle, and elsewhere. Some of these summits were big, in the number of participants and ideas, and some were small, though the relationship between the numbers involved has not as yet been properly investigated. What I remember best about these affairs are my own efforts required in managing our expense accounts. As chair of the enterprise being also expected to be a host, I invariably ended up with the liquor and wine bills. The trouble was that under the laws of the great state of Michigan or the rules of the University of Michigan, these spiritual necessities could not be recovered on one's expense reports. This created minor problems for our members and guests but enormous problems for me. How was I to recover these truly professional outlays? One way was to deduct them as "professional expenses" on my own reports to the IRS, but I rarely kept all the necessary documentation. Then there was the possibility of swindling on the expense reports submitted to Ann Arbor. I was advised that it would be quite proper to recoup some of these moneys under "porter," "tips," "telephone," or "taxi." When I added up these items, they came to something like $19.99, while a good wine bill at our larger summits came to $199.99. How I solved this very personal problem remains a secret of state.

12

At Last a Little Journal All My Own,
or
Saying No, No, No
Can Get You into Lots of Trouble

One day in late summer 1979, a man with the name of Paul Hoeber appeared in my office. He introduced himself as the owner of Agathon Press, a small New York publishing house. He had been sent by brother-in-law, Bill. Whom could I recommend to edit *Political Behavior*, a new quarterly journal he had begun publishing earlier in the year at his own expense and risk. He had found it impossible to live with his editor, and there had been a divorce. Only one person came to mind. "It's what I had hoped for," Paul said. "One thing, though," I said. "There must be no micromanaging of the editorial wing by the publisher. You print and sell, I edit." We shook hands, and as he departed, he left behind a stack of manuscripts of doubtful quality. I had to get rid of most of them, immediately endearing myself as an editor to all kinds of hopefuls.

I don't know why I so rashly accepted this invitation. I guess it was my studiously cultivated love of language, grammar, and etymology that made editing a favorite pastime. There had even been some years, now long ago, when I had made a living as a professional editor on a liberal "journal of opinion." My years with the *New Republic* (1944–47) make for an interesting story in their own right, but I will not burden the reader or myself with it. Being there brought me into contact with a remarkable person, the magazine's long-time copyeditor, Betty Huling. She taught me all that can be taught about editing.

The literary amateur that I was (and this is meant literally, a "lover of letters"), I had also served at one time or another on one or another associational editorial board, but I had never made it to the top; I mean being in charge of a journal or magazine all my own. Not that I grieved over this tragedy. For reasons I'll hint at, being editor of one of the journals published by the associations is not particularly appealing, though candor requires me to admit that I would have accepted an editorship, had one been offered. Well, none ever was.

As I'm mentioning editorial boards, there are all kinds of them—those to walk on and those to walk over. Some are there strictly for ornamentation. Once you are on, you never get off until the nonexistent call on your time has become so burdensome that you finally resign. Other boards are like boardwalks by the sea. If you are not careful, you will be so swamped by manuscripts that it feels like falling off the walk into the ocean. Still others are there, in part, to help a hapless editor get out of trouble when he has offended some potential contributor by rejecting his or her manuscript and made the mistake of telling why.

These journal boards have become increasingly large in recent years, and appointing their members is really something of a racket. They evidently exist, also in part, to enable the free-riding boarders to list their demanding editorial work on their annual reports to the edification of deans who may or may not take cognizance of their flock's accomplishments at promotion or salary-setting time. In due time the editorial *stakhanovite* will list service, past and present, on half a dozen or more boards on his c.v. The latest issue of the prestigious *American Journal of Political Science* lists all of forty-nine members on its editorial board; it would probably be fifty if there were space for another name on the page. "In my day" (circa 1957–58), to make a day my own, the first board (of which I was a member) of the *AJPS's* predecessor, the *Midwest Journal of Political Science*, had six members under a wise editor, David Fellman of the University of Wisconsin. David was wise because, as he once told me, he relied on my judgment alone when it came to articles on that strange new thing called "political behavior."

How I got to be on the *MJPS* board was something of a comedy. The short version is that I was violently opposed—in speech only, of course—to the Midwest Association publishing a journal with "Midwest" in its title when the issue was discussed at some meeting. The next thing I knew was that, to silence me, I had been coopted into the midwestern establishment by being named to the board of the new journal. I resigned after one year because, in 1958, I moved from rural Ohio to urban California and was still naïve enough to believe that a midwestern journal ought to be edited by midwesterners.

In fact, there seems to be something of a friendly competition for desirable board members among the journals, whatever qualifies a person as desirable. Clearly not be outdone by the great Midwest, the southern and older *Journal of Politics* boasts an editorial board of sixty-four members to the greater glory of the region. More sanity is found at the *Political Research Quarterly* (once *Western Political Quarterly*, $N = 26$), the *APSR* ($N = 22$), and the *Legislative Studies Quarterly* ($N = 20$).

So now I had "my own" journal and could do with it what I wished, editorially speaking. My name appeared as editor on the masthead of the fourth issue of volume 1 (Winter 1979), though I had nothing to do with the articles within. For about ten years, until I turned the editorship over to Richard Brody, my Stanford colleague, life was not the same. As soon as the opportunity presented itself, I got rid of my predecessor's four associate editors and editorial board. I replaced them with an in-house "editorial advisory committee" of nine Stanford colleagues and a bevy of "editorial consultants" who could be called on when I could not call on my Stanford committee for editorial help. It didn't happen very often. And there were some "editorial interns" whose reward for reading manuscripts was to see their name on the journal's masthead page.

The sort of structure we adopted for *Political Behavior* is unlikely to be acceptable in any of our associational journals, where the presumed benefits of belonging to an editorial board must be spread around the country, obviously for "political" reasons. I always felt, from a strictly nonpolitical, practical, and academic point of view, that this was rather silly. An editor can rely on his immediate colleagues for editorial advice, especially if the editorship is located in one of our large departments. I had really learned this when I served on the editorial board of the *Antioch Review*. All its members were Antioch faculty from various fields—philosophy, psychology, literature, history, economics and political science, in-

cluding at times even a bona fide physicist or biologist. In those
pre-Xerox times, manuscripts would be rotated to all members in
the course of a month, and the board would then meet for a long
evening at some member's house, argue about the merits of the
manuscripts, and make its decisions after things had been thrashed
out—a method far superior to the nose-counting of referees from
all over the country and not in contact with each other.

A Hurrah for Bias

My most immediate and, it turned out, most enduring problem as
editor of a journal that aspired to being disinterested and scholarly
was to respond to all kinds of charges of bias when I turned down
an article. In some remote corner of one of my widely dispersed
vertical steel cabinets there is a file still holding, among other
things, some unpublished (read: unpublishable) manuscripts, referee reports, convention papers, and letters to the editor. The letters, on alternate occasions, charged me with being, in alphabetical
order, a behaviorist (obviously "bloody"), an empiricist (invariably
"brute"), an interactionist (hence "gutless"), a Marxist (of whatever the latest "revisionist" brand was), a phenomenonologist (always misspelled, as here), a pluralist ("damned," by definition), a
polemicist (a lover of wars of words), a positivist (of the worst
kind—Popperian), a reductionist (up or down the abstraction ladder), a structuralist (selling out to the French), a structural functionalist (selling out to anybody), and so on and so forth. Nobody
accused me of being a deconstructionist, for which I was grateful.

It is not difficult to guess why I deserved these heart-warming
accolades. Unlike the association- or university-indentured servants
called learned journal editors, I was free to write my mind and
make some enemies. I certainly didn't "speak" it; an editor is a pre-
dominantly horizontal animal; an orator, contrariwise, has to stand
on his feet, which makes him a vertical being. My response to the
hate (but also love) letters was not to respond.

"We" (an editor's modest substitute for "I") had decided to be
somewhat different from the mainline publications by deviating in
our editorial in-house procedure from a currently common practice
of most association-sponsored journals. In this latter-day age of ac-

ademic democracy, these admittedly excellent publications refer *all* manuscripts to external reviewers for earnest appraisal and final judgment on whether to accept or reject, with editors rarely reading anything but an article's title. As this is fact, the editors of the mass-circulation academic journals really do not deserve being called editors. They have become bureaucratic paper shufflers of "communications" (see below). At the time of my joining the fraternity of journal editors, I was not sure whether they were still reading manuscripts themselves, but I knew for sure that they were reading lots of communications about manuscripts like referee reports or letters of protest. I learned that, to protect themselves against possible charges of doing a manuscript an injustice, some editors even distributed referee reports among the referees, including a communication from the editor to the author telling him or her why the editor favors referee McDonald's judgment over the judgments of referees McFadden or McGregor, thus denying the would-be author his or her democratic right of being published. Never must the modern editor simply reject a manuscript without a lengthy communication.

In view of all this folderol, we proposed to read all submissions "in house," with the help of our editorial committee consisting of our trusted Stanford colleagues and some editorial interns. We would reject out-of-hand all those manuscripts that did not deserve careful scrutiny. Actually, you need only read the first and last paragraphs of a ms. to get its measure. By sending out rejection slips as quickly as possible, we expected to be fairer to contributors than if we had them wait for many weeks or months before learning that their manuscript had been rejected; and we avoided make-work for otherwise busy referees. On a positive note, a manuscript not quickly rejected had a good chance of being accepted, possibly subject to revision on the advice of in-house counsel. Apart from saving paper and postage, this procedure reduced both an author's anxiety level and the journal's turnaround time.

For turning down a manuscript, we designed a nice, short form that looked like this:

( ) Sorry, we cannot publish this article because
( ) the topic is of too limited interest

( ) the data base is inadequate
( ) the theory is insufficiently developed
( ) the findings are too weak to warrant publication
( ) the style and presentation are not acceptable

That gave us a lot of parentheses to choose from and work with. We simply tried to communicate with minimal effort. On a personal note (and using the immodest, noneditorial "I"), I think that an editor should have the time-honored privilege of turning down a manuscript "without reason" (giving it the proverbial "pink slip") and should not simply be treated as a glorified clerk and transmission belt. Anyway, after sending one of our brief mementos, I remember receiving a furious letter, out of the inferno of the Midwest but unfortunately shredded long ago. It accused me of unprofessional conduct and several other heinous editorial crimes for doing nothing other than saying no.

Communicatio ad Absurdum

I was keenly aware of the depth of absurdities to which the editor of a learned journal, so-called, can sink. In one recently recovered file I found some Xeroxed pages from a contemporary issue of the *American Political Science Review*. The stuff I read there at the time had evidently made me nervous, though I'm not the type to be nervous. What, I must have asked myself, is big brother or sister *APSR* up to? The *APSR* editorial note was a communication-from-editor on "policy" concerning communications-to-editor from the journal's mass readership. It is so droll that I want to comment on it.

The *APSR* editor's communication informed the several thousand avid readers of the *APSR*'s official journal that "the volume of communications can at times be excessive, so much so that space for articles may be threatened." To soften reader resistance to the policy to be announced, we were told that "most readers would agree that the emphasis of the *Review* should be on articles, not communications." I can quickly agree to this timeless verity in order to get on with it. But only extended quoting will convey the intoxicating flavor of the new policy:

... all communications, like manuscripts, are refereed, and only those that have received referee endorsement are published, which helps to regulate communication flows. Communications, however, typically question or attack previously published articles, and when these letters are accepted for publication, authors feel they have a right to respond and indeed that their responses should appear in the same or the subsequent issue. To attempt to do this would, however, open a Pandora's box. We will therefore adopt the following policy. A communication involving a previously published article will be sent to the authors of the article in question. The authors will be asked whether they wish to respond and given two weeks to do so. The package, communication plus author response, will then be submitted to the regular referee process. Referees will be asked to determine whether both items, only the communication, or neither item, should be published. If authors do not respond within two weeks, the communication will be submitted to the normal referee process. (*APSR* 77 (December 1983):1012)

Since *Political Behavior* was not a mass-circulation journal like the *APSR*, though my publisher would have liked it to be, I was spared from either opening or closing this particular Pandora's box. In any case, it would have been a tough act to follow. As I understand the *APSR's* procedure, a "communication" arrives in the editorial office. It is sent to the author of the offending article, presumably with a letter from the editor warning him or her about the two-week grace period. That makes two communications. The author replies, and that's communication number three. Out go the original communication, the author's response, and another letter from the editor, presumably to two referees; so we now have five communications. Both referees respond (we are not told what their grace period is), and that makes seven communications. But, alas, suppose the referees disagree. There follows another letter from the editor—communication number eight—to a third referee who, it is hoped, will come down on one side or the other of the two previous referees, and that is the ninth communication. Finally, the original communication and the response are published; and that, generously "packaged" so that I am willing to count the two published communications as one, is the tenth communication.

The only problem with this scenario is that it is too simple; it omits a significant contingency. The referees, it will be recalled, are instructed to determine "whether both items, only the communication, or neither item" should be published. But now imagine that some perverse referee recommends that the author's response, but not the critic's communication, be published. There is, of course, a way out: don't publish the article in the first place and only ask the author to respond in advance to his or her likely critics. That would solve the space problem: no articles, only advance responses—a standard procedure in good public relations. And "communication flows" will not have to be regulated; they will disappear.

Controlling for Paranoia

Given the hazards of editing and trying to keep my own paranoia under control, I kept another file in which I stored all the communications possibly needed in a legal action, in case of attacks on my person or property by communication-happy communicators. For instance, there is the irate letter from an irate correspondent who claimed to have sent in a manuscript for publication in *Political Behavior* some nine months earlier. I write back that I hadn't received any such ms. and inquire whether it might not have been sent to the competition. She writes back that, no, the ms. should have come to me, suggesting that, perhaps the Post Office is to blame. I like that and write back that, indeed, the Post Office isn't any longer what it used to be, but that I will be glad to "see" the piece. My new pen pal then sends three mimeographed copies, single-spaced, of an enormously learned paper on "Parallel Cognitive and Affective Processes in the Political Thought of Adolescents." This paper, a footnote informs me, was delivered three years earlier at the annual meeting of the American Psychological Association. Looking through my disorganized personal file on "Political Socialization," I found that, in fact, I had once received a single copy of the paper without any indication whatever that it had been targeted for our little journal.

Actually, I did not hear all that often from irate readers. One day, though, at long last I heard from a really incensed reader who found some statistical measure used in some article unacceptable! Fortunately, I knew little about the substance of the piece, and even less about the statistics involved (in any serious sense, as cultivated by people who are genuine statisticians and do not call themselves methodologists). I therefore did not propose to come down on one side or the other of the controversy or make some Solomonic decision that would give each side its due. I was simply pleased to learn, as if I didn't know, that scholars pay attention to each other and that this controversy was likely to rock the relevant scholarly community. As everybody knows, the stakes of academic disputation are high. So I blindly published this communication and a rejoinder to it, but not several further rejoinders to the rejoinder. Nobody complained.

The victims of my pity, rather than wrath, were the pieces I liked to call *les miserables.* I could spot them right away because there were unmistakable cues that the manuscript had been submitted to at least three other journals before coming "down" to us. Usually these would-be articles had been previously presented as "papers" at the North-to-Northwest Political Science Association or some other local conclave. They usually were secondary analyses of data stemming from survey questions whose ontological status was no longer in doubt; they had been worked over and over again. This allowed the authors to engage in the most mindless multiple-regression studies usually justified as efforts to estimate the contribution of a (apparently randomly picked) battery of independent variables to the explanation of the variance in some dependent variable, for the presumed purpose of testing a model. But as the model was dictated by the data conveniently at hand, rather than by a modicum of mental exertion preceding their collection, it simply amounted to an enormous tautology of limited truth value. Our own preference was for modest studies using fresh data to explore some *terra incognita* by way of some trial-and-error process that usually resembled more a shakedown cruise than the odorless elegance of a regression equation.

Logs and Backlog

Sometimes an editor gets into an editorial bind or, if you prefer it, stew. The name of the bind or stew is "backlog." I was not too sure about the implications of backlog other than that things seemed to be piling up on my desk and often floor (and not just manuscripts but also letters, books, reprints, memoranda, bills, and sundry other items). To get me going, I consulted my beloved Webster, the little handy one, and discovered more about logs and backlog than I cared to find.

As a verb, backlog means what I thought it means—"to accumulate." Flipping around in old *Webster's* to get at the word "accumulate," I discovered that there is nothing explicitly said about backlog. Nevertheless, the definitions of "accumulate" are instructive (and I will spare you the Latin derivation of the word). I found: "1. to heap or pile up: AMASS ["a fortune"] 2. COLLECT, GATHER [a composer *accumulating* one award after another]—*vi:* to increase in quantity or number." This surely was food for thought. If I heaped or piled up enough manuscripts, I would be amassing a fortune —not a bad prospect for one accustomed to impecuniousness. But, then, even if *fortuna* did not smile on me, Webster holds out another promise: by collecting and gathering manuscripts I might succeed in accumulating all kinds of awards that have not as yet come my way. Why old Noah or those who followed him in piling up words in a dictionary picked on composers as accumulators of awards escapes me. College professors might have been candidates, or baseball players and other worthies. The Merriam Company, publisher of *Webster's*, seemed to be a bit arbitrary in its choice, perhaps also being in the business of piling up (and selling) musical scores. I could not pursue this line of inquiry, nutrient though it appeared to be. After all, I was in search of backlog, not of fortune or awards.

Optimistic by nature, I looked at the sunny side of manuscript backlog. And being something of a reluctant functionalist along with my devotion to probability, I persuaded myself that if backlog were dysfunctional, there had also to be something eufunctional about it. As manuscripts were flowing in at an ever-increasing rate (in quantity or number, as the friendly Webster says), my editorial eyes became sharper and more critical; the acceptance-to-rejection rate declined, or the other way round, the rejection-to-acceptance rate increased. That should have made for a better journal in the long run, even if the present looked dismal. In any case, I always had a neat stack of accepted articles in process, enough to fill more issues than a no-backlog situation could possibly warrant. The only way to get out of this jam was to be rather ruthless—which was not my nature and caused me much pain. Some contributors were understanding, having the foresight of foreseeing the foreseeable. Others were not: they wrote or called inquiring about the state of their contribution and my state of mind.

A Confession and an Apology

In general, the editorial life was relatively relaxing because Vera McCluggage and Susan Zlomke, my loyal and highly paid assistant editors, did most of the initial screening of the incoming manuscripts. They would send me little memos that, in exhausting but unambiguous language, said yes or no. Sometimes I had to say yes all by myself, an action few editors dare to engage in these days. We had received a methodological piece by a team called Bishop, Oldendick, and Tuchfarber, and my associates thought that this threesome was one of those old Cincinnati law firms of German descent, and they refused to touch the thing. The article's concern was the harmless art of questionnaire construction and that sort of thing, but there was something of the lawyer's self-righteousness in the authors' charge that practitioners of the odd craft of psephology better watch out before taking another step.

As to "psephology," don't worry if you don't know what it is or you can't say it. This tongue-twister is not of Hollywood making but is of eminently British usage and simply means the study of polls and elections. I first really learned about its use from Austin Ranney, who, in a footnote of his own to a footnote in a book I cannot effortlessly identify, reports that the word was coined by R.B. McCallum (one of the collaborators of the Nuffield Studies of English elections) "from the Greek word for the pebbles which the citizens of Periclean Athens dropped into an urn as their method of voting." Ranney then quotes David Butler, another Nuffielder, to the effect that the *word* "had been intended as no more than an academic jest."

Then there was my own violation of good manners by writing, editing, and publishing my own so critical contribution to knowledge in *Political Behavior.* For better or worse, editorial etiquette generally forbids editors to publish their stuff in their own journal. This was something I finally ignored because, life being short, I could not see myself and my coauthor submitting the piece to another journal. There, I could assume at a high level of confidence, we would receive, after nine months of referee deliberation, the standard "re-submit"; and then, another nine months later, there would come a second encouragement to re-submit, after we had spent at least two months taking care of the first re-submit suggestions. That would total twenty months of suspension *in utero*, more than twice as long as such gestation takes in human reproduction. Of course, there was no guarantee of acceptance. And had the piece been accepted, another nine months would elapse before publication. Being my own editor of a privately produced journal made it possible to transcend the limits of time and etiquette.

If I have said some nasty things about learned journal editors in the abstract, let me reassure my friends among them, past and present, that in the concrete I didn't mean a word of what I said. In fact, I have been "well received," if that is the right word for saying "thanks" to being published at all, by many—Austin Ranney, Nelson Polsby, and Chuck Jones of the *APSR*; or Mac Jewell and John Kessel at the *AJPS*; and several others at other journals I cannot at the moment think of (though I could do some research in the matter; but why?). All of them were superior editors. Above all, I enjoyed being associated with Jerry Loewenberg and his crew, including Jewell and Sam Patterson, at the *Legislative Studies Quarterly*. I understand that these legislative types, accustomed to small print, themselves read or used to read without fail every article coming across their desks.

13

Burps, Blurbs, and the Joy of Having a Book Editor,
or
Mobilizing Your Friends and Fooling Your Readers

"Dear Heinz," the letter began, as most letters of a personal nature do. It could have been "Dearest Heinz," as some old (in both age and longitude of love) lady friends address me; or more simply "Dear Sir," as my bank and telephone company do when they want to sell me something of highly personal interest, like a new credit card without an annual fee or another long-distance carrier. But the letter began as it did, and continued: "Thanks for your humorous note on your new book. The combination of self-deprecating humor + effective self-promotion is critical to success in this business + few pull it off as well as you!"

I like that exclamation mark. As my perceptive wife, Cleo, agreed when I read her the letter, my old friend (as he also addressed me in the middle of the letter, preceded only by "so," as in "so, my old friend") had my number or, as I say when my checkbook balances, "it's right on the nose."

Just a little background to clarify this gaucherie. I had written to a number of friends, both old and new, to help me out in helping my publisher out by writing some blurbish stuff for the dust jacket of a book completed just as I began getting ready for the current funbook. The blurbs, I suppose, would lend legitimacy and authority to the enterprise. "I'm writing," one letter stated, "with an inquiry that is really a request that would require, as all good requests do, a supreme sacrifice. I would like you to perjure yourself on my behalf. It might even be fun." This kind of solicitation was a totally new experience for me. I didn't quite feel that I was engaged in an act of subornation, only that I was close to it. I have written blurbs for others' books but, as far as I can recall, none of my previous authored, coauthored, edited, or co-edited books had ever been graced by blurbs; so I never had an occasion to solicit them.

My publisher, I wrote in another solicitation, has asked me "to supply a number of names of colleagues who would be willing to say some well-chosen and, I assume, relatively few words of a perjurious nature, not about me, but about the book." That last phrase was, of course, written in code. I doubted that my learned colleagues, all busy persons, would want to read 900 or so pages of typescript, and the coded phrase gave them license to talk, counter to manifest request, about me, rather than the book. Among the six blurbs adorning the back of the dust jacket, I learned that I am "one of the founders of modern political science," "a leading scholar of social life," and, to top it all, "a wonderful raconteur and a formidable social scientist." Who would not want to buy a book by this *Wunderkind?*

Just why publishers insist on this sort of nonsense escapes me. For one thing, nobody believes them; and if this is so, they are unlikely to help the publisher market a book. Indeed, as they are not believed, they may even be counterproductive. Anyone who knows me knows that I am not this, that, or the other the blurbist says I am, and that's good enough cause for not buying the book. Then, too, once a book is bought by a library, properly entered on card or computer and finally shelved, the cover has been removed so that the potential borrower does not have the benefit of blurbish wisdom.

Needless to say, given the gravity or, counterfactually, the levity of the matter, I was most cautious in the choice of those whom I would ask to perjure themselves, regardless of whether they had in fact read or not read the long ms. They had to be trusted, and at the same time be representative of various subspecies of *homo academicus* with such critical attributes of scholarly achievement as gender, stature, ethnicity, snob appeal, and so on. As I wrote to one of my editors:

> After much soul-searching I have come up with the names of nine people who may be coaxed to write some blurb for the book. Most

of them "owe me one," as the saying goes. They constitute a nice mixture of privates and publics, old and young (relatively speaking), East, South, West and North, etc., though gender remains unbalanced. But all are smart.

To get back to what publishers want. My own publisher for the book in question expressed herself rather conservatively. Another publisher, a friend of mine at a most distinguished university press, was unequivocally candid in asking me to write a blurb for another friend's book: "I am taking the liberty of sending you a set of proofs in the hope that you can skim it and provide us with a promotional blurb to help us launch the book." So I skimmed and took care of this chore, for a chore it was—not the skimming, which at best took only an hour, but the rewriting of the blurb that went through at least seven drafts requiring three additional, literally back-breaking, hours in front of this PC. Anything for the sake of friendship! It's a professional obligation to be friendly.

Depending on trusted buddies alone for burping and blurbing seems to make publishers nervous. They really much prefer their author's own self-promotional text for the flap copy of a book. As I learned, the blurb I was asked to write for my book "will be used to inform potential readers (nonspecialists as well as students) about [the book's] subject matter, the reasons for its importance, your method of approach to that subject matter, and your conclusions." So far, so good—until I read that all of this is to be accomplished in "approximately 300 words." After these 300 words, there should be nothing significant left for anyone else to say about the book. And just how important these 300 words are appears from the next sentence that "this information will be one of the primary sources for preparing jacket, catalogue, and advertising copy." So I slaved away on these 300 words, a task more difficult than writing the book's 235,000 contracted words. The 300 words presumably tell all that is to be told about the book to get it on the bestseller list, but then I discovered that even 300 words are so many words too many. I was asked to prepare a second "description" of the book that "should aptly summarize the scope and theme of the book in the shortest sentence." This heroic exertion was to be performed for this self-evident reason: "Because advertising space can be severely limited, we [the publisher] sometimes must resort to a very brief summary." Being a good boy and by nature subservient to my own financial interests, I composed the shortest of sentences I could create to let it all hang out: "A distinguished political scientist's report on his personal pathways through the labyrinths of micro-macro dilemmas in the scientific study of politics." That, I expected, would really grab even the most illiterate reader's attention and make him or her buy the book.

I want to get back to the risks I anticipated for my gracious friends who had agreed to perjure themselves for the sake of sound science and the maintenance of the friendship system that makes the academy so lovable to its inmates. There are two types of risk, one inadvertent, one advertent. The first happened to me once, to my great embarrassment. Having published a book with the fine house of John Wiley & Sons, I felt indebted to our editor there, Gordon Ierardi, now in heaven, to write a prepublication blurb for a friend's book, also to be published by Wiley. My few well-thought-out and well-chosen words, as they always are in blurbs, appeared not only on the book's jacket but also in journal advertisements throughout the year of publication. In the meantime, *APSR* book review editor Austin Ranney had asked me to review the book, and the review appeared in due order. Having perjured myself in writing the blurb, I now was faced with the formidable task of making an "honest person" out of my perjurious self. I had no choice but to "build into" the review in exact words the text of the blurb that the publishers were using in the ads. The review had unwittingly become an extended blurb. Call it plagiarism, if you wish. The more immediate risk is being yourself a solicitor of blurbs. I'll show it by way of citing my friends' passionate responses to my request for lending their names *before* they had a chance to read the manuscript and hang on its every word, sentence, paragraph, and chapter.

Professor A's reply: Of course I am willing to perjure myself on your behalf, although that probably will not be necessary. Not only do we and I owe you, but it would be a pleasure for me to endorse your book. Indeed, I very much look forward to reading it.

Professor B's reply: ... I would be more than happy to supply some words (of admiration!) to [the publisher]. I doubt whether perjury would be necessary, but I certainly would not shrink from the challenge.

Professor C's reply: As to your request, my answers: by all means, yes! I'd be happy and honored to provide your publisher with some remarks about your book. Indeed, it would be a real treat. Having read the preface, I find my appetite whetted (or is it "whet"?). So send the tome on.

Professor D's reply: I would be delighted to provide whatever words might be an appropriate adornment for a book that I would, in any case, read with the greatest pleasure and quite possibly assign, in part at least, to graduate students starting to frame their dissertations.

Professor E's reply: [For the first paragraph of this letter, see first paragraph of this chapter.] So, my old friend, I would be happy to try to add a few comments if you like; obviously some areas of overlap more than others [*sic*]. But as a student of history, I will welcome the opportunity to browse through events that predated my participation in the scholarly world!

Professor F's reply: I'm tardy in getting back to you . . . , in part because the prospects for the mail being picked up today do not look at all good. Snow everywhere. Anyway, I shall be pleased to say good things about your book and am sure that I can do so without perjuring myself. First, there's you. Second, I am of Irish extraction.

Private responses like these are good for anyone's soul. I cannot deny having been pleased. It's much too late to instill some modesty in the author (though it can be found, I hope, in his many other, nonauthorial roles). There is really nothing very surprising in this literary drama. My friends came through with great aplomb, but how much of the long manuscript they really consumed I cannot tell; but this is not really the issue here. The point really is to show how the culture of commercialism has invaded the culture of the academy. My friends (or I, as a perpetrator of similar sins) could make much more money on Madison Avenue! Why do we stick around in the academy?

Three Cheers for Chutzpah!

If I were a moralist, I would be upset by this blurb-writing business that, so crassly but conveniently, is enforced by the academic buddy system. I'm not upset because, in the academy at least, everybody but the most naive know what these endorsements mean —very little if anything. But I cannot altogether desist from some moralism. Some years ago I received a communication that put my own recent efforts in the publicity business to shame. Its *chutzpah* was beyond burping and blurbing—outdistancing by far the 300 words my publisher gave me to tell all.

The anecdote involves a refreshing letter, not from some anonymous publisher but from two colleagues who had edited a multiple-authored book on the Congress of the United States (with the inevitable subtitle "Structure and Policy"). The two entrepreneurs assumed, in all innocence, that I and presumably everybody else who received the letter wanted "to have some advance notice of its publication" and "might be interested in this material." Not a bad assumption: I was interested. Continuing their subtle approach, they wrote that "there are a couple of things which we think are interesting about this collection. . . . First and foremost is that it is a high quality collection of pieces which fit together as elements of what we think of as a new approach to congressional research" (there it is, the magic words—"new approach"). Now, this new approach is called "new institutionalism," even though I am reassured that it "has its roots deep in American political thought and also in the roots of empirical congressional research." I felt good knowing that our roots as legislative scholars are rooted, as well as that some well-rooted and esteemed colleagues had a hand in the creation of the new institutionalism. Much of the new stuff, then, was old and reprinted, but the editors informed that they "see these as studies very much related to one another and to a paradigm of research." You obviously can't do without a paradigm these days, although I must note that no text, at least on legislative institutions, has as yet been described as "a paradigmatic approach." (Some people tell me that we are now in a postparadigmatic phase of the social sciences, along with postmodernism and postpositivism, which I always suspected of being paradigmatic progroms [*sic*] rather than programs.)

These ingenious editor-publicists also told us that, in their "attempt to blend the best of the standing research with the best of the newest investigations," they commissioned a number of analysts "to make new contributions in their own areas of research" and that they "have done everything that we can to assure that the quality of these original contributions is of the same high standards as those of the reprinted classics." There is admittedly some ambiguity here, hyperbole notwithstanding. For instance, I don't know how to interpret "original," and I don't know whether the new or original contributions are to be considered "classics" in their own right or by virtue of having been "blended" in with the old and presumably also original pieces at one time. If I assume that they are classics by way of some sort of osmosis, how does the process work? The editors did not let me guess: "To this end, we might add, each of these papers underwent a grueling blind–peer review process much as if they had been submitted to a journal." We are then given the names of these blinded peers, evidently on the premise that blind–peer review makes classical status a sure thing. My mind, feeble as it is, flicked back to Aristotle, Hobbes, Locke, Marx, Mill, and Dewey, who, I have reason to suspect, could never have made it without a blind–peer review.

I must confess to being a bit old-fashioned. I had always thought that it is the business of researchers to research, of writers to write, of editors to edit, of publishers to publish, of advertisers to advertise, and of book reviewers (not being blinded) to review books. It seemed to be an honorable division of labor and to allow for discounts. But here I am, with two colleagues, not their publisher, having told me in advance of publication what good works they are engaged in, how splendid a job they have done, how original or classical the contributions to their book are, how well things hang together in what they call a paradigm, and so on and so forth. And all this in view of, or in spite of, the fact that the book will bear the imprint of a respectable university press. I ponder and wonder what there is left for book reviewers and unblinded peers to say. Well, there are numerous possibilities: admire (or criticize) the jacket's design and colors, find fault with the type as too large or too small, complain about the book's price, and so forth.

An Answer: The Joys of a Book Reviewer

Now, you really don't expect much candid opinion in the blurbs written by editors, authors, or friends of editors and authors. And, as noted earlier, I really fail to understand why they are written. It's presumably different with book reviews. By scholarly consent, it is preferable to read a book before writing a review of it. This would seem to be so self-evident that it should not require mention. The evidence belies self-evidence. Some book reviews appear to have been written without the books having been read, or read carefully, to judge from irate author letters to the editors of our journals. Moreover, reading a book is not enough. One should perhaps reflect on its contents, and if reading a book takes time, reflecting on it takes more time. I now discover that my norms for book reviewing are quite out of date.

I recently received a form letter from a book review editor that instructed me to deliver a review not later than a given date. The U.S. Postal Service being what it is, slow, the letter reached me one week after having been posted. I figured that, given the deadline for getting the review into the editor's hands and allowing for another week to get there, I had exactly twenty-three days to read, digest, and reflect on the book, not to mention writing the review—minus six weekend days when I prefer to settle down with a good mystery. So, in reality, I had seventeen days to do the job, all things being equal which, of course, they are not because I have other things to do than to devote all my time to book reviewing, if you follow this sermon.

Even this reality is an illusion. The book in question is some 500 pages long, including text, footnotes, tables, graphs, and that sort of thing. A book of this kind reduces my reading speed to maximally twenty pages per hour, and probably less, given such facts of life as the telephone ringing, my wife asking me to dump the garbage, or my remembering that the fuchsias need immediate watering; and fuchsias are priority items on my daily schedule. Setting all these distractions aside, 500 pages divided by twenty come to twenty-five reading hours or at least three full eight-hour working days. This does not include some more days for reflection and writing—two connected activities more troublesome than reading. I happen to think that a book review should include at least one idea that is the reviewer's own and not borrowed from the author of the book, but there is no guarantee that one will occur in time for inclusion in the review, and that's the reason why most book reviews in our learned journals are so dull. Needless to say, I didn't make the deadline. In fact, I'm not finished with reading the book at this moment.

The Review Editor as Instructor

Alas, an idea (or, God forbid, several of them) is not really welcome in latter-day book reviews. The instructions from the book review editor suggested as "essential components of a publishable review" (among other components) "an approach which is neither overly laudatory nor excessively critical, but one which instead fairly assesses the strengths and weaknesses of the book." I don't know what, exactly, "overly laudatory" or "excessively critical" are supposed to mean. Presumably, you may say that this is a "good" book or a "bad" book but never that this is an "excellent" book or a "very poor" book, assuming that such judgment is based on some reflection about the book's merits. To be on the safe side, then, give the book a *C*, which is somewhere between a *B* and a *D*, an admirable compromise to keep the editor out of trouble with the author and the reading public properly uninformed. And that's just about how so many book reviews read.

This desiccated and sterilized mandate for book reviewing seems to have something to do with the arbitrary number of words that a reviewer is given. In my own recent case, I was given "about 600–800 words," which clearly, in the good editor's opinion, gave me enough elbow room to take care of the 270,000 words that I estimate to be in the book. Indeed, I dare not write more than 800 words because the editor has instilled the fear of censorship into me, informing that "the space limit is reasonably firm and should not be exceeded to any substantial extent without checking with me." As I'm constitutionally averse to do the required checking, I shall settle for the stipulated length in assessing the book's strengths and weaknesses along with such other "essential components of a publishable review," to wit, "a statement of the author's central theme or message" and "relationship of the book to other related literature." A tall order, to say the least.

There was a time when a book editor would tell us to use "your own good judgment on length" or something like it. And there certainly was nothing like this to appear in an editor's letter:

> We rely upon professional networks and resources for recommendations of prospective reviewers. Of course, we are not always aware of personal ties or professional differences. Therefore, we assume that there are no such ties or professional conflicts of interest which would affect your ability to be a fair and unbiased reviewer.

That little gem really shook me. Having done through the years my quota of book reviews, I must now confess that most of the books I reviewed were penned, as we used to say in the pre–word processor age, by authors to whom I had "personal ties" or with whom I had "professional differences." In fact, book reviews were a wonderful place to unloosen one's biases.

The trouble is that "personal ties" and "professional differences" are orthogonal dimensions. There are friends with whom I professionally agree, and others with whom I disagree; and there are nonfriends with whom I may agree or disagree. What is one to do in this two-dimensional space to be a "fair and unbiased reviewer"? Well, I will leave that to your imagination. The point is that when scholarship was still something of a communal enterprise, one might ask a review editor for a book assignment *because* an author was a friend or *because* one had a professional disagreement with another person. In fact, it was a primary incentive for doing a book review, even though there was the danger of a friend turning into a nonfriend upon his reading a "fair and unbiased" review, yet with the compensatory possibility of a nonfriend turning into a friend on the same ground. The new message clearly is, "never review a book that really interests you," because books of interest are invariably by professional friends or nonfriends (I'm avoiding the term "enemies") in a line of inquiry about which you, as a reviewer, presume to know something. The new message is just an inch away from the fallacy of confirming the consequent: if the review is favorable, the book's author must be the reviewer's friend; if it is unfavorable, he or she must be a nonfriend. One day I received a letter from a nonfriend, as follows:

> You have been one of the few political scientists interested in [topic]. I've been most concerned that the [topic] message has not been getting out to one of its most obvious homes—political science.
>
> Hence, I have a favor to ask of you. I am concerned that my new book come to broad attention. Its title is. . . . I would be delighted if you would write to the editor of a key APSA journal, volunteering to review it. There is much relevant material on [several topics]—not to mention some theory and methods. This way, you get a free copy, and the book gets intelligent, prompt discussion.

How could I possibly resist such a flattering request, not to mention the little bribery scandal involved in getting a free copy? (In fact, I had already bought the book but not read it, so that the bribery issue was rather moot, though the scandal remains.) So, off I wrote to the book review editor, who was agreeable, ordered the book from the publisher, and, in due time, sent it along with the usual form letter and instructions. (The extra copy would of course go to a deserving graduate student.) Though I had asked to do the review, the form letter, so sensitive otherwise to the conflict-of-interest matter, thanked me for my "willingness" to do the review, even though I was given only 600–800 words and an ominous deadline. Then my enthusiasm to do the review was quickly and properly doused, due to my not being an assistant professor in search of you know what:

> It is impossible to say exactly when your review will appear. There is a lead time of almost six months, and whether your review is placed in the first possible issue, or the one following will depend upon space availability, balance among fields and books. Begin looking for publication two issues from now, and you should definitely expect to see your work [all 800 words of it?] come out within a year.

14

Awards and Rewards
for Meritocratic Conduct,
or
Being Surprised on Being Honored
without Even Trying

One day in autumn 1985, overcome by the sweet smell of citrus trees in bloom, two former Stanford graduate students, John Ferejohn and Edie Goldenberg, got it into their heads to "do something" for the old professor on the occasion of his being kicked out of the university. For this worthy purpose they would stage the facsimile of a stuffy, formal retirement dinner that was really designed as a "roast." But this exercise in futility was evidently not enough: they also decided to raise the cash for endowing an award to be given in his name by the American Political Science Association for the "best article published the previous year in the *American Political Science Review*." This was very nice of them, though I am not quite sure what this honoring was *for*—perhaps for the five articles accepted by and published in the *Review* over five decades, not a bad record, though some of them were coauthored; but perhaps also for the equal number of articles rejected. Among the pieces accepted, I am modestly not including the 1972 presidential address to the American Political Science Association, one of the more forgotten classics among the other forgotten annual addresses. The reason for the omission? These APSA presidential addresses are generally immune from the disease of peer reviewing and published as submitted.

There they were, the two of them, sitting under the citrus tree at the Center for Advanced Study in the Behavioral Sciences, sniffing its fragrant delights; and one said something like, "By Jove, Eulau has never won one of those much sought-after and lucrative awards that the American Political Science Association annually distributes among the most deserving." This "deserving" has to be a quality in the eyes of, usually, a three-person committee, itself expected not to have any ax to grind, though it helps any potential award recipient to have at least one friend on the committee. The neglect of our mentor, said Edie in unison with John and John in unison with Edie, "must be redeemed. Let us tax Eulau's former students and, preferably, his rich personal faculty friends at Stanford, in Berkeley, and elsewhere, then approach the APSA Council with an offer of an endowment for an award in his name. This will give him the long overdue honor of having his name alongside and, in fact, ahead (in strictly alphabetical order) of James Madison, Charles Merriam, E.E. Schattschneider, Leo Strauss, Woodrow Wilson, and other such luminaries."

Let me be crystal clear about what transpired that autumn. I had absolutely nothing to do with this conspiracy. In fact, I was abroad, teaching at Erasmus University in the Netherlands, and the secret was not let out of the bag until, full of good food and better spirits, some of my best friends mercilessly roasted me in May 1986. Note my mastery of the inflection called comparison: good, better, best; not "good, gooder, goodest." Why, I wonder, is the English language so perverse?

Now, more recently, thinking back on that glorious event, I began to speculate (even empiricists do that occasionally) whether my experience—not ever having received an award and now being rewarded by having an award given a name that many people cannot even "say"—was unique or deviant or what have you. (For the difficulties involved in "saying" *Eulau,* see the documentation in the Prologue, above). When reserving a table in a restaurant, I invariably do so under "Grofman" or "Polsby." Nobody doubts the spelling of their names or existence. I therefore decided to make a ministudy of APSA awards.

What did I find out? Lo and behold! my case was neither unique nor deviant. None of the notables who were honored by having their name attached to an award had ever themselves received an award—not even James Madison, whose undenied and undeniable immortality should make for eternal eligibility. The trouble is, of course, that once upon a time immortals were really mortals and therefore are not available to pick up any medals or what not. I don't want to be boring, but among those who did not make it as an award winner is the crafty Charles E. Merriam, in whose memory some unreconstructed Chicago behavioralists established an award in 1975. Nor can you find among award winners the suave, liberal Benjamin Lippincott, who, as I understand, decided to honor himself by giving the APSA executive director a wad of thousand dollar bills to set up an appropriate and, indeed, most demanding award. (The award is "for a work of exceptional quality by a living political theorist that is still considered significant after a time span of at least 15 years since the original publication.") Nor was there an award for the learned Gabriel Almond who, as coauthor with Sidney Verba of *The Civic Culture* (1963), should have been a shoo-in for the Woodrow Wilson Foundation Award in 1964. No award came to the beloved and funny E.E. Schattschneider, who had many friends and admirers; or to the studious Leo Strauss, whose large contingent of devoted students must surely have considered, at one time or another, having an award actually conferred on their mentor. Not even the most original of them all, the inimitable Harold Lasswell, was ever rewarded for his greatness.

Leo Strauss died in 1973, just before named awards reached the flood stage. I suppose that, had he lived longer, he would have been a candidate for and winner of the Lippincott, which in its early years went to other German or Austrian refugee and Anglican scholars of a pensive ilk. Then there was the eminent French political theorist, philosopher, novelist, essayist, or scientist (have your pick)—the inconquerable Simone de Beauvoir. Only as late as 1981, when it was both safe and fashionable to do so, did a Lippincott award committee valiantly remember *The Second Sex*, published in Paris in 1949, in the French language, of course. Of fifteen Lippincotts handed out between 1975 and 1993, five went to blue-blooded, American-born theorists of whom only three were card-carrying members of the APSA.

Competition for the prestigious Woodrow Wilson was especially tough in the early 1960s. This award presumably is for the "best book" in political science or international relations, as if there were such a thing as one best book. The 1964 award went to Bauer, Pool, and Dexter's *American Business and Public Policy* (1963)—a worthy recognition. Perhaps the award should have been split that year between them and Almond and Verba. My two colleagues can take comfort from the fact that *The Civic Culture* has certainly outlasted and outinfluenced the winner. My own experience in the previous year was more shattering. John Wahlke and company, authors of *The Legislative System*, had some reason to hope that they would get the Wilson award. Instead, it went—as if to rub it in—to a rather tendentious text in the field of international relations. Well, Wahlke and I had a couple of drinks and forgot that our book was not being recognized as God's best in the 1962 publication year.

Empiricism Forever

By now I hope to have established the authenticity and legitimacy of being counted among the fortunate honorees whose names, in print, are always larger and thicker than the names of the award recipients. This is as it should be: after all, your name as the honoree appears in print every year, while the names of the award winners perish as soon as the fun is over. For instance, how well did the winners of dissertation awards do after the event? As my intellectual horizon is limited, I took a look at the Schattschneider awards for the best Ph.D. dissertation in American politics, handed out since 1972. I was happy to note that the very first recipient was my colleague Paul Sniderman, lured to Stanford out of Berkeley (before such insider-trading was made illegal) with the help of old-boy-network colleague and friend Herb McClosky, in the knowledge all along that he would be a sure Schattschneiderian.

To assess the robustness of the Schatt awards made between 1972 and 1993, I used the "Eulau recognition test," a rather crude but reasonably reliable instrument. Of the twenty-one award winners, the test yielded eleven worthies whose names I could identify as authors of postdissertation books or articles. Expressed in percentages, this comes to 52.38095, which reads like a much bigger number than eleven but isn't. Now let me emphasize right away that this finding may be as much a function of my objective counting method as of my subjective ignorance. It may be that I am out of sync with what goes on in the study of American government and politics; those whom the test did not recognize by name may also have had a distinguished record. As I write this, my mind wanders—as it often does in this postwandering era of political science—to a memorable APSA presidential talk by the great V. O. Key. It was unadornedly called "The State of the Discipline." Key did not find "the state" particularly enchanting and its human "subjects" deserving of awards or honors. Not enough manpower, he held, was being devoted to research and inquiry. Superior empiricist that he was, he backed up his complaint by a little check on the publications of those in political science and international relations who had received Ph.D.s in the three years 1935–37:

> At least one-fourth have not been heard from since they received their Ph.D.s; their theses were not published; nor have they helped to fatten the periodicals.
>
> One-sixth appeared in the periodicals at least once or twice over a twenty-year period.
>
> About a third have published a book (in some cases the thesis) and in some instances in addition an article or more during the first couple of decades of their career.
>
> About a fifth have produced at least two books, although this count includes theses, textbooks, collections of readings, and other items that would scarcely be regarded as books by a knowledgeable dean as he considered a proposal for promotion.

I don't know whether things have improved since Key made his study. There are considerably more of us now, and there are considerably more awards, honors, and prizes to be had.

Another data game is sort of institutional. As I remember it, when I came into the business in the 1940s, there was only one memorable award—the Woodrow Wilson for the "best book," etc. Since then, twenty-three awards have been available at one time or another—the latter specification to indicate that three early awards seem to have died an honorable death. Using an extraordinarily complex temporal mode of classification, we have the developmental profile given in table 14.1 (p. 168).

Make of this what you wish, but let me note that the Eulau award is one of two that came in just under the wire of a moratorium on awards. There was, I was told, some resistance in the APSA Council to these last two. According to likely sanitized Council minutes for 27 August 1986, this always benign and wise

TABLE 14.1

Decade when first awarded	Number of awards
1940–49	1
1950–59	3
1960–69	4
1970–79	9
1980–89	6 (and 3 dead)

body of the people's representatives "reviewed" and "approved" the Eulau and Schuck awards, but also endorsed a recommendation of the Administrative Committee to set up an Ad Hoc Committee on Awards "to examine the number, name, character, financing, and administration of awards, to establish guidelines for the establishment of new awards, and to develop appropriate procedures for the Eulau and Schuck awards." Translated into the language of politics, this reads: we had some doubts, but what could we do without offending Eulau and Schuck? (The latter had a lot of clout on account of the association's female, feminine, and feminist contingents—I never know what's the correct adjective.) Even before the ad hoc committee had a chance to grapple with this weighty problem, the message was clear: future petitioners, beware—it won't be easy from now on to get your best friend into the charmed circle of luminaries for whom an award is named.

Ever watchful of our representatives' actions and the people's right to know, I followed up and found that, indeed, an ad hoc committee was set up (it doesn't always happen) under the sterling leadership of Frank Sorauf (or should I say "under the leadership of sterling Frank"?), with some other honorables as members. The committee reported to the council, on 24 April 1987, that "without some change in Association policy there would be a further proliferation of prizes that would devalue the awards, . . . ," etc. The council then voted (by 15 to 3) "to change the committee's recommendation from 'to limit severely the addition of new awards' to 'suspend for 5 years the addition of new awards.'" Having fulfilled the membership's expectations of statespersonship, the council added some other things about endowments, turned to regularizing the administration of some of the present awards, and ended up with the Eulau and Schuck awards: "the Council reaffirms its acceptance of the Eulau and Schuck awards and approves their statements of purpose as appropriate to the goals of the Association." But, it seems, there remained some "reasonable doubt," as the lawyers have it: "it is also the sense of the Council that to the greatest extent possible the remaining negotiations with their donors be governed by the processes and standards—especially on funding —of these resolutions and motions."

As Marlene Dietrich once told Hemingway: "Ernest, don't mistake motion for action."

As far as I know, no new awards have been added since 1986; instead, the action in search of honor has shifted to the "organized sections" of the APSA. These sectarian groups outdo each other in giving awards, prizes, and other icons of merit, but I'll come to that a bit later.

The Politics of Award Giving

Well, while I try to be present at the annual awards ceremony to rejoice with the winners of the Eulau and other awards, I have not always been able to follow the reading of the citations. Having been to two or three cocktail parties earlier, and having hastily consumed a dinner rich in calories, usually in the company of Ada Finifter, I tend to doze off at the most critical moment. And, I confess, I have probably not read the *APSR* articles that, it has to be assumed, were the very, very best. After all, they had withstood double jeopardy—the heralded process of peer evaluation before being published, and now the much more hazardous process of being selected in competition with several dozen other worthies. As I think about it, the citations, if genuine, at least tell us why the article has been selected, while the editor of the *Review* can hide behind his or her anonymous reviewers.

Nevertheless, having once been chair of the award committee that hands out a most prestigious and the only really rewarding prize, I have some reason to distrust the process involved—from the beginning to the end. The beginning is, of course, the appointment of a committee. That is done by the APSA president, who usually consults, not surprisingly, his or her immediate department colleagues to get the best possible advice. So, if the president is from New World University, there will be a great number of committee chairs, committee members, and recipients variously connected with that great institution. Of course, I am using NWU only as a prototype, not the real thing. The same could be said of, say, Harvard or my alma mater, the University of California (Berkeley, no other). By "connected with" I mean three categories of persons: (1) current NWU faculty; (2) current NWU Ph.D. candidates; and (3) NWU-trained Ph.D.s located elsewhere who haven't learned yet that they are elsewhere and no longer in the womb of their once-nurturing university.

Sometimes the members of a committee know each other extremely well. This is bad for everybody's mental health because they will conspire to give the prize to an undeserving other than yourself. Or they do not know each other at all. This is equally bad because they will expire by declaring a standoff and give no prize whatever, not even an honorable mention. Or the committee will succumb to a dominating and persuasive colleague who tells them how to vote. The committee I chaired had, as comembers, an IR type, then and still today not personally known to me, and a wandering English theorist from whose work I had learned and whom I had met some years earlier when commenting on a paper of his at some jovial conference somewhere in the Caribbean. Anyway, before I could say "b," the Englishman had persuaded the IR man to say "a," and I was left swinging on the telephone line. The award went to a future APSA president who is really an economist, though his bona fides were guaranteed by a distinguished record in policy analysis and long association with political scientists. I can't recall what my own first choice was that year. Because the committee never met eyeball to eyeball, there was no opportunity for a little bargaining. So I went along.

There is a postscript to my experience as an award giver, perhaps to prove how wrong I was in being something less than enthusiastic about the winner's book. Seventeen years later another award went to this winner of the earlier award it had been my duty and pleasure to hand out. "There must be something terribly wrong with my tastes," I said to myself, until I noted that the committee that had bestowed the award was chaired by a close and long-time collaborator of the winner, going back at least forty years when they had coauthored what, at the time, was a remarkable book that should have received an award but did not. But let me discourage any false inference that might be drawn from this. I found to my satisfaction that, in fact, the suspect in this potential conflict-of-interest drama was outnumbered 2 to 1 in the prize committee's composition. A little nosing around showed that the two other committee members, counter to the conspiracy hypothesis, were not connected with the chair and had received their Ph.D.s at New World University; and this was surely enough to authenticate their objectivity.

But to get back to the generic issue of awards, I don't think there ever is a "best" book, article, or dissertation in a single year. I am quite confident that the word "good" could do nicely, like "we give you $250 for a good dissertation in comparative politics and, sorry, we can't give you more." As far as I know, nobody has as yet made a systematic study of books, articles, and papers rewarded and unrewarded by awards to discover the longevity of their authors' fame and influence. This would give our raters and rankers another vast empirical arena for the exercise of their talents as methodologists and analysts of academic prestige (see chapter 9).

"This paragraph," my perspicacious editor noted here, just as I take note of her skill and insight, "is especially interesting given your discussion of codewords for letters of recommendation. Why not refer back to chapter 4?" Indeed, why not?

Award winners constitute a rather curious assortment but, then, our discipline is a grand mélange so that one cannot deny the representativeness of the selections, representation being a big thing in these days of rampant professional democracy. I once cultivated the outrageous hypothesis that the same results could be achieved by random choice, without a committee pretending to have read a hundred books or two dozen dissertations, not to mention four dozen or more articles in the *APSR*. As a result, representativeness would be obtained by cold statistical means, conducive to greater fairness. Anyway, I set out to do a little testing of the randomness hypothesis by looking more closely at the topics in the Eulau award-winning *APSR* articles. For this I relied on the committee citations that one had to listen to in their endless monotony during the annual APSA awards ceremony—a practice that has recently been abolished.

My test met the falsification criterion by undeniably refuting the randomness hypothesis, at least in the case of these awards. The *APSR* being the most catholic of our professional journals, I expected to find that, of the nine awards given so far (as I write), surely one would have gone to an article in, say, political theory of the classical, nonquantitative sort, or to some nice anecdotal and comprehensible piece about what the Supreme Court is doing these days, or to some empirical proof of some profound neo-Marxist hypothesis, and so on and so forth. As the award was not intended simply to reflect its namesake's own intolerant vision of the "best," the choices are completely at the selection committee's discretion. I also found confirmation, in this so-called postbehavioral era, of the hunch I have steadfastly hedged that behavioralism and its offsprings, such as the "new institutionalism" or "social science history" or even "biopolitics," are alive and well. These findings could not have been obtained by theory-blind randomizing: of the nine awards given as I write, five made some reference to the honoree, admittedly undeserved but nevertheless attesting to the soundness of judgment displayed by the respective award committees.

As I review these nine awards, I must admit to some satisfaction, though not with what an award in one's honor does for one's ego, a rather passing matter over the long haul and rather inconsequential when you have departed from this earth. My pleasure is with the survival power of the sundry lines of political science inquiry that had begun in Chicago in the 1920s; that were nurtured there through the 1930s, resurrected by a SSRC Committee and a handful of others in the 1940s, gained reluctant recognition in the 1950s and achieved some (limited) institutional influence in the 1960s, and reached full flowering from 1970 on, after having been declared dead. So, above all, it is indisputable that behavioralism as a catholic and eclectic line of social research has survived the insurrection against it that some unhappy and/or misguided people tried to engineer in the late 1960s. This revolt has almost totally fizzled, due, I think, to the basic soundness of the behavioral persuasion in politics.

The Theme Recovered and Some Loose Ends

I have deviated from my major theme—the creation of a meritocracy by democratic means. You will recall my noting the end of the line, at least for the time being, of the "official" awards given by the APSA "as a whole"—something of an aphorism—when its council put a damper on the blooming multiverse of awards. I lost track of what happened after that, but I recently discovered that "supply side economics" had not failed to impress the council. In its usual wisdom it had approved "the reinstatement of the moratorium on named awards and lectures to be given at the Annual Meeting," an action that, I suppose, will provide the necessary scarcity and maintain the high value of the current awards. Not all is lost, however. The council, according to its minutes of 8 April 1995, also "requests that donations to honor [other] individuals be given to the Second Century Fund with components and activities of the [Centennial Center for Political Science] to be named appropriately in honor of [those] individuals." That's food for thought: no doubt, the council will next want to define the word "appropriately" and "components," lest some cash be sent for inappropriate components of the APSA superstructure, which would undermine what is right and proper in a democracy that celebrates its meritocracy.

In reality, the council's moratorium has long been circumvented by the APSA's inventive "organized sections," of which there were thirty-two by 1994 when I stopped counting. No moratorium had as yet been declared on these establishments, though, I am told, more stringent membership requirements were octroyed in 1995. By this time, twenty of these busy bodies—the pun intended—had created forty-three of their own awards and prizes, sixteen "named" and the rest identified by such intriguingly imaginative titles as "distinguished scholar award," "best book award," "emerging scholars award," "lifetime achievement award," "best dissertation award," or "best paper award." (Taking a leaf from what its members are studying, the champion award giver is the ambitious section on Political Organization & Parties with four awards, two named for my still much-kicking friends Sam Eldersveld and Leon Epstein, one for the late Jack Walker, and an "Emerging Scholars Award" that still awaits being christened.

There are now enough awards and prizes to go around so that, some recidivists notwithstanding, almost every political scientist has a good chance to enter the meritocracy. Moreover, I must also mention another eu-function of this awards euphoria. It represents something of a second line of self-honorification (if the dictionary does not have a word for what you want to say with precision, make it up!). As the number of awards and award winners multiplies over the years, so does the number of colleagues who, by serving on the award committees, get their name into print for all to read, especially their department chairs and/or deans. With some twenty of the APSA's holistic and the sections' thirty-seven segmental awards, and with at least three minds needed to recommend honors, there are now some $57 \times 3 = 171$ devoted volunteers annually involved in this commendable task, or 1,710 over the next decade, provided the moratorium holds and the sections also hold the line (see chapter 2 on c.v. expansion).

I almost forgot the most significant element in this analysis of the APSA's award structure—the donors who so cheerfully open their pocketbooks to make it all possible. Of course, their altruism has well-planned egoistic side effects (you just can't get around self-interest in this era of rational choice). No matter how small your effort in writing a check, your name will get into print as a great benefactor to science; and you know all along that your donation is a tax-deductible contribution to a most deserving charity.

I come to the indisputable conclusion that democracy and meritocracy need not be at loggerheads, as some supercilious dialecticians would have it, and that the American Political Science Association is not ruled by an oligarchy, as the Caucus for a New Political Science used to allege in the days when academic award-giving was still a peanut enterprise.

Alas, the association has not as yet taken full advantage of the opportunity to honor everybody who would like to be honored after having shelled out some cash for the cause of political science. This could be easily done by establishing a "society" within the association. Here the APSA could fruitfully take a leaf from the San Francisco Opera's playbook.

The S.F. Opera is sustained by a "Medallion Society." To be named and listed as a "Founder" of this society, even if you were never there at the society's founding, you must shell out at least $2,500, preferably $3,500 per annum. To be called a "Benefactor," you better have $5,000 or $7,500 to give away. And so on up or down the line through all kinds of "circles" (silver, gold, triple gold, etc.). Just think of all the awards and rewards—medals, titles, prizes, etc.—the APSA and its sections could hand out if they were only thinking BIG. It makes one's mouth water and heart jump.

15

The Fine Arts of Gossiping, Hyping, and Spinning,
or
How the Academic Mind Really Works

I. The Sad Story of Cocktail Party Gossip

As to the story I'm about to tell, you must take my word for whatever small element of truth it contains. I want to tell it because its villain, I will call her Josephine X, is described in Mr. Marquis's *Who's Who in America* as an "academic administrator" in a biographical entry of thirty-seven sturdy lines. Her admittedly highly stylized c.v. in *Who's Who* shows no credit for any books but has an informative half-line given to "contbr. articles to profl. jours." I have always found it intriguing why Marquis abbreviates some but not other words as it does. In the case here: why "articles" in full but journals as "jours?" This will surely confuse any right-thinking, French-speaking academic who wants to find out things about people like Josephine in *Who's Who*.

Some years ago I was called on to testify in behalf of a woman colleague, a full professor at some midwestern state university, who apparently was in all kinds of trouble, which I need not detail here. She had brought a suit against her university over what she complained was the clearly discriminatory practice of giving her the minimalist of minimal annual pay raises that a professor of her status could expect. Though I would not call her a friend, I had known her for many years and, by this time, she had established a fine record of publication in her field, probably a better record than that of any of her male colleagues in an, on the whole, rather undistinguished department.

So it came to pass that I was called to testify in a deposition for the discrimination suit. Up I went into the blue sky across the mountains and into the little chamber where I would be quizzed, under oath, by plaintiff's and defendant's lawyers. As things moved on, I thought I did rather well as an "expert witness," so-called, though I thought that the defendant university's lawyer asked me some excruciatingly difficult questions, like "have you read *all* that's been written" about this or that (answer yes or no), obviously designed to undermine my credibility as an expert. One of the more provocative questions that went right to the heart of my expertise: "Have you ever done research on farm problems?" Answer: "No." Let the rural jury draw its own conclusions as to my expertise.

I must interrupt the proceedings for a moment to digress on some homely virtue. I like to distinguish between what I say in public and what I say in private; and I have always assumed that in the genteel world of academia what is said in private is, in fact, a private matter, said off-the-record, so to speak, giving one some license not available when speaking in public. In this private world we do not by any means expect our words to be sacrosanct; in fact, we assume the opposite—that they will travel in a chain of *private* communications, known as the academic grapevine, to some unknown destination. We call this kind of private talk gossip, and exchanging gossip is one of the few valued side payments that accompany the vicarious status of being an academic. This is so because gossip cannot be included on the lines or read about between the lines of even an extended c.v. But gossip is the cement on which academic social networks are built, and as gossip is just what it is by definition—something private and intimate—we assume that it does not become a matter of the public record, and certainly not in a court of law.

As I discovered in the course of the proceedings (they spent six hours quizzing me), I must have been rather naive in this regard, though I hope that this was a deviant case, the exception rather than the rule, and that the norm of academic gossip being a private thing is alive and well. If it were otherwise, our profession would be in deep trouble, in a Hobbesian world of cutting each other's throats and losing a benefit of unestimable academic value.

My deposition in the case is really the sad tale about the Josephine whose biographical entry in *Who's Who* I have already mentioned. I had encountered her some years earlier at that hub of opportunity for gossip—the academic cocktail party. Upon having been introduced to her, she reminded me that she had been a student at a college where I had taught many years ago. "You probably don't remember me," Josephine said, "but I was a student of yours," or something to this flattering effect. This, needless to say, endeared Josephine to me, for she obviously seemed to have a penetrating mind and recognized that my own memory is somewhat on the shaky side. Being polite, as I try to be at cocktail parties, I probably mumbled something to the effect that, indeed, I remembered her, even if saying so was something of a little lie.

Josephine had been visiting for a year at a think tank in the Stanford neighborhood. I thought of her as just an ordinary professorial thinker who, at the think tank, is supposed to think, while at cocktail parties he or she is supposed to guzzle and gossip. Well, we guzzled and gossiped, and I learned that Josephine was a professor at a state university in a part of the country where neither the weather nor the academic culture is particularly conducive to happiness. But as I thought that Josephine was just an ordinary professorial type, and a woman to boot, I let it slip that I had agreed to testify in a discrimination suit brought against her university. And I evidently said something else that, as this story unfolds, came to haunt me in public. I didn't think much about this cocktail party afterward, and certainly not about the conversation with Josephine; indeed, I did not think about it at all. Were I to think of all the gossip I heard at cocktail party encounters, I would have to write fiction instead of doing social science.

So things were moving along, my testifying under oath to the truth, though most of what I said can only be described as opinion; and how one can state an opinion truthfully is something the lawyers have to work out among themselves. But this only for the purpose of what the lawyers call "laying the foundations."

I can't recall just what foundations the defendant's lawyer had laid for what turned out to be her climactic question to come, other than that she asked me whether I knew the work of Professors A, B, and C in the plaintiff's department, which, truthfully, I did not, undoubtedly further evidence of my lack of expertise, though I did let it be known for the record that the burden of proof was on Professors A, B, and C and not on me. Anyway, with this foundation under or behind me, the defendant's lawyer suddenly sprang this question: "Do you know Josephine X?" I must have appeared rather perplexed but recovered quickly, leaned back, and thought of all the Josephines I could think of. Within seconds, all kinds of Josephines crossed my mind—Josephine Bonaparte, empress of the French; Josephine Baker, symbol of exotic dancing; Josephine Hilgard, respected Palo Alto psychoanalyst; and even Josephine ("Josy") Windermere, whom I had dated in college fifty years ago. But no Josephine X. "No," I said, "I don't know any Josephine X," thus obviously being caught in a big lie and exposing myself to a charge of perjury. "You met her in Palo Alto," the lawyer said, with great confidence. "I did?," said I, again leaning back to let the memory do its computations. It did work. "Yes," I said after thinking as hard as I could, "vaguely, I think at some cocktail party." If not Josephine's image, at least the contours of her ghost emerged out of the computer: "I think she was a student in one of my classes long ago." Having remedied my big lie with the lawyer's skillful help in mental evocation, I was exposed to this shocker: "Isn't it *true* that, at this cocktail party, you talked with Josephine X about the plaintiff and said that she's crazy?" Wow! In ordinary circumstances I would of course have vehemently denied any such gross indiscretion. But here I was, under oath to God and some rural county. "I may well have said something of this sort," I conceded, "but I can't recall it for sure. I say all kinds of things when I gossip at cocktail parties."

And so it went. Long ago I fell into the bad habit of putting my academic friends, colleagues, or enemies into two social categories above and beyond friendship, colleagueship, or enmity—the dull ones with their long c.v.s, on one hand, and the "a little crazy" ones, on the other hand, much preferring the latter to the former. But this usage of the word "crazy" calls for sophisticated between-the-lines understanding. It is one thing to say that someone is "a little crazy" and another for a lawyer to distort an innocent remark made in private in order to attack in public the reputation of a plaintiff (or defendant). What had been going on here?

The answer is "dirty politics." There's a lot of politics in academia and sometimes hot politics because in academic politics there is an inverse relationship between the stakes (low) and the politics (high or hot). But dirty politics is generally eschewed. At least I cannot recall anything else so dirty as happened in this case. What Josephine X had not told me at our fleeting cocktail encounter was that (1) she was not just an ordinary professorial thinker visiting hereabouts but also a bureaucrat at the university that the plaintiff was suing and was deeply involved in the case on the university's side; (2) she would communicate whatever my remark may have been to her university's lawyer in the case; and (3) she evidently allowed the lawyer to make use of a strictly private conversation during the interrogatory.

Just imagine what might have happened if I had denied, in gentlemanly fashion, ever having called the plaintiff "crazy" (or, more likely, "a little crazy"). I would have committed perjury, ended up in the nearby county penitentiary, and become a symbol to the ending of academic gossip. Anyway, I escaped these dangerous alternatives, and I did get it into the record that I resented public exploitation of innocent or trivial remarks made in private, that I considered Josephine's conduct immoral, unprofessional, deceitful, and only designed to discredit the plaintiff as well as to embarrass me as a witness for the plaintiff who, crazy or not, happens to be a distinguished scholar—at the time the only distinguished scholar in her department. Given the fact that this was a discrimination suit, it was as dirty a trick as I can recall in my long and happy career as an academic gossip. But no such indiscrete yet revealing stuff ever even creeps into the "normal" c.v.

The secret irony of this story: the female colleague on whose behalf I testified in this discrimination case was the woman who, many years earlier, when I was a candidate for the presidency of the American Political Science Association, had interviewed me on behalf of the Women's Caucus for Political Science. She gave me the puzzling test about "the surgeon and the son" which I gloriously flunked (see chapter 11).

POSTSCRIPT: I never found out how the case came out, and I really do not dare to care.

II. Titles in Search of a Textbook

Madness is seasonal, in the academy as anywhere else. I have noted, for instance, a high correlation between the opening of the baseball season and the springtime arrival in the mail of several dozen announcements of new or freshly revised textbooks on American government that their authors and publishers hope to get adopted by fall when the baseball season winds down. The correlation is of course spurious. Control for season and you will find that, while the baseball madness is in fact seasonal, the academic madness is yearlong.

Now, this textbook business is as competitive as any business. Just to call a text *American Government* will never do. Instead, you will have to choose among "elements of," or "principles of," or "foundations of," or "essentials of," or "introduction to," or "perspectives on," and so on. Moreover, these introductions, perspectives, elements, principles, or foundations are invariably "new." *American Government* may be alternatively "modern" or "contemporary" or "changing" or "basic." Some of these announcements even promise "understanding."

If you don't trust all these nouns or adjectives, you can rely on subtitles. Modest authors use just two nouns, like "Institutions and Policies" or "Stability and Change" or "Theory and Practice" or "Policies and Politics" or "Conflict and Consent"; or they mix noun and adjective, like "New Directions" or "Changing Expectations." Less modest authors serve up three words, like "Origins, Institutions, and Policy" or "Ideas, Institutions, and Issues" or "Economics, Law, and Policies" or "People, Politics, and Policies" or various other versions of the same sort of thing. It clearly takes a good deal of imagination to come up with three words, and you must never use four.

More venturesome authors will give you a title that doesn't tell you what the book is about, like "The Irony of Democracy" or "Democracy at Risk" or "Democracy under Pressure," or "Unfinished Democracy" or the best-selling "Government by the People" as a synonym for the difficult Greek-derived word "democracy." But, then, these titles require subtitles to bring you back down to earth, say, "The Great Game of Politics" or "The Rules of the Game" or "The Ideal and the Reality" or "An Uncommon Introduction to American Politics" or simply "The American Political System," whether introductory, essential, fundamental, or whatnot.

Somewhere along the line, your choice of a text is facilitated by other adjectives. They presumably tell you about what is called an author's "approach." Approaches are manifold, in alphabetical order: "alternative" or "behavioral" or "constitutional" or "dynamic" or "economic" or "institutional" or "pluralistic" or "processual" or "radical" or, most recently, "neoinstitutional" or "rational" and even "poststructural."

Where the text has been adopted, publishers evidently think, will help you in your own choice. There seem to be two strategies. Either you list just two or three prestigious universities whose repute is nationwide, like Harvard, Yale, or the University of California; or you list ninety-nine or more colleges, from Alpha College to Omega College. There is, moreover, a direct and positive relationship between the reputation of the author and the reputation of the adopting institution. If you are famous, a few prestigious adoptions will suffice; if your name is not a household word, list all the adoptions you legitimately can. For whatever reason, some publishers prefer a single author and other publishers prefer several authors. A single hotshot author is likely to have "produced" not only a book but also many Ph.D.s who can be counted on to adopt the master's text.

As to multiple authorship, three names appear to be the norm, but I have noted an ever-so-slight tilt toward four. Then there is the issue of illustrations—photographs or cartoons that even the most half-witted student must appreciate versus statistical tables or graphs that require something more than knowledge of the three Rs. It's all a question of marketability.

So it goes with the texts that "introduce" the college student to American government and politics, he or she never having encountered the Constitution in grammar or high school. But, then, the local football coach, having recruited "talent," always insists on going back to "fundamentals." The competition between Departments of Political Science and Departments of Athletics is keen, unless they conspire, which is often the case.

Finally, I must note that in this era of paradigmatics no new American government text has as yet been described as "a paradigmatic approach." Anyway, for a professor emeritus like myself it is most refreshing to know that I don't have to write, review, or adopt a textbook of any kind in this season of madness when publishers offer us so much old wine in new bottles. How about *American Government and Politics: A Refreshing Approach?*

III. Spinning the Spin at Stanford

Everybody knows what a spin is, I suppose. Once upon a time it was an honorable term used on all kinds of occasions for all kinds of purposes, as when I made up endlessly drawn-out stories and told them to my children to get them to sleep by midnight. This conception of the "spin" has been perverted into its opposite, the "sound bite," which has become the half-minute, million-dollar prime-time equivalent of the old "short story" and strains the political brain's capacity for absorption.

As a result of all the fast-moving technological developments in communication, the spin-spin has moved from the sports pages to the front pages. Nevertheless, I don't think that the concept of the spin-spin has as yet fully penetrated the academy. It always lags somewhat behind Madison Avenue, at least until a Madisonian is hired to do some spinning and spin-spinning. I learned about all this only recently. My experience needs to be shared. It involves the great university that, until I retired, provided bread and butter and occasionally a spin but never a spin-spin.

When I read about the spin-spin, I immediately wrote an earnest memorandum to Stanford's provost, the honorable Condoleeza Rice, a political scientist, with whom I once co-taught an undergraduate seminar on political elites the world over. I have no idea whether the memo was received because I have never received a response. University administrators do not like to be reminded of the errors of their ways.

"Stanford's Grand Plan to Promote the University," I read in one foggy morning's *San Francisco Chronicle* (25 November 1995), the paper I have to dig out of the bushes every other day despite repeated complaints to the outfit that distributes the paper. What I resent about this mode of delivery is not that the paper gets wet because of a superior irrigation system, but that I cannot fish it out of the dirt wearing my slippers and, therefore, have to either put on shoes or do it barefoot. I would have long given up on the *Chronicle*, were it not for the unperturbable Mary Madison, the paper's "correspondent" who covers the scene at Stanford University. Nothing, it seems, ever alarms, agitates, upsets, or troubles this fearless reporter who lives off Stanford press releases and, occasionally, interviews unhappy professors. Lest there be any misunderstanding, "Madison" in Mary Madison is not a pseudonym but the reporter's real name. I don't know whether she was born a Madison and a distant descendant of one of my heroes in American political thought or whether she acquired this noble name by way of matrimony.

Well, that morning's news from Stanford was that the university had a "new game plan"—the words, at this point, are valiant Mary's—in which "school officials are being asked to use six specific words, including 'incomparable' and 'stunning,' when they talk about the university."

This first paragraph roused my interest, though I'm not sure whether, in retirement, I am still a "school official." I overcame my reluctance to read further by reminding myself that I never thought of myself as an "official" of anything but as a university professor. I was told by Mary that "the half-dozen descriptions are included in a new thirty-page 'strategic communication plan.'" Because the reporter puts the plan in quotation marks, I assume that it is Stanfordian and not Madisonian language. I am trying to read this the way my cousin Marion in San Francisco and thousands of other Stanford watchers are likely to read it, without immediate access to any other source, and certainly not the document itself.

The plan, according to intrepid Madison, "suggests the best ways to promote the university to outsiders, alumni, parents, prospective students, and, believe it or not, faculty, foundation officials, and potential donors." I could hardly trust my eyes but then recovered: by the grace of good fortune, I am not an outsider (I live in the campus ghetto), not an alumnus (in fact, I'm an alumnus of the competition across the Bay), not a Stanford parent (my kids were too smart to apply to their father's employer), and not a prospective student (though I'm occasionally contemplating taking an advanced workshop in gerontology); and I'm no longer a member of the faculty and surely not a foundation official. As to being a potential donor, this story ended all thoughts about giving or leaving anything to a university that has a strategic communication plan providing for only six words with which to communicate. The one good thing about the plan, then, is that a professor emeritus like myself is evidently not a strategic subject or object of the plan.

Let me cite in full the next paragraph of this wonderful story in the *Chronicle,* lest there arise any ambiguity from selective quoting: "The plan suggests the best possible spin for winning support for Stanford in an era of shrinking university budgets and increasing competition for public and private grants, gifts and students."

It would have been nice if the story had ended here, with its emphasis on "spin." No such luck. Instead, fearless Mary reports that Stanford's director of communications, "who devised the plan, cringes at that description." It isn't quite clear what the DoC is cringing at or about, whether his own handiwork or Mary's description of it. Anyway, as I rarely cringe but now had the strong urge to do so, I took off from the breakfast table in search of the household *Webster.* There I found two definitions: (1) to draw back, bend, crouch, etc., as when afraid, shrink from something dangerous or painful, cower; and (2) to act in a timid, servile manner; fawn.

Have your own pick from this menu offered by the *Webster,* but it really doesn't matter whether it's one or another definition. For now our faithful reporter again quotes the DoC: the suggestions are "not a spin, but a description of what we think Stanford is." Wow! If there ever was a spin-spin, that surely is it. The suggested words are not spin but a "description" of Stanford! In a spin-spin you deny that your spin is a spin but everybody else sees right through your denial as a spin on the spin. And, remember, up to this point in the *Chronicle* story we have learned only about two of the magic words that will sell (or should I say, sell out?) Stanford to outsiders, and the like, as well as to the faculty, and the like. The best was yet to come.

The DoC's moment of insight into what Stanford is really about, according to Madison, came in this way: "[DoC] selected the six key words after watching a thirty-second television commercial produced by Stanford and shown on sports programs during the football season."

Infelicitously, we are not told who wrote the TV commercial "produced by Stanford." It couldn't have been the late senator himself, though his lady love Jane had left all kinds of instructions behind. So I did a bit of speculation. My first choice was, of course, the Athletics Department, but I rejected that option because I doubted that the department has the verbal wherewithal for this sort of thing. Then I thought of the Career Planning & Placement Center, but they are much too intelligent to produce this kind of folderol. I doubted that the Admissions Office had anything to do with it, though they might have been consulted. Then I thought of President Casper as potential author. That alternative I also rejected because, humanist that the president is, he would be using weightier, more humane words than offered by the plan to describe the university—words of Latin, Greek, or Greek-Latin, perhaps even German, origin. The Stanford Historical Society, composed of sexa- to octogenarians, I am sure, will be totally traumatized by the six words and cannot be suspected of being their author. That leaves the DoC himself, who, perhaps, is a closet wordsmith in addition to being a self-denying spinmeister.

But on with the interview our correspondent conducted with the cringing communicator:

> The words, "challenging, vibrant, pioneeering and incomparable" are flashed on the screen with a backdrop of the campus, he said. After that, it was easy to add the words "Western (as part of pioneeering), boundless and stunning."

I should be wordless by now but, then, there might be some folk who do not watch Stanford's mostly second-rate football team on TV; these deprived souls need to be told, therefore, about all the wonderful words flashing across the screen that they are missing. I reminded myself, though, that our women basketball players are vibrant and incomparable and deserve all the acclaim they get.

I once again hoped that the interview had come to an end. But no: "The word 'excellence' was considered because 'it does describe Stanford,' [the DoC] said, but was discarded because it is overused."

This little pearl led me to speculate on who these overusers might be; they couldn't possibly be the people in the DoC's own Department of Communication Services, as it seems to be called. They must be the faculty, I concluded, except that faculty prefer "distinction" to "excellence." One is invariably a "distinguished professor" but at best only an "excellent teacher." Had the DoC thought about this? No! Instead, the report on the interview continues, and I'm quoting the *Chronicle*'s helping hand who quotes the DoC:

> "My idea was to see if we could all use the same terms, so that Stanford would come to mean the same things to people," he said. The goal is to communicate the idea of the "essential Stanford," what defines the university and differentiates it from its competitors.

God forbid! The man has an idea. Or Thank God! The man has only one idea. Should I be fearful or grateful? Perhaps the rest of the story will restore my mental equilibrium (Stanford's medical plans do not provide for any disequilibrium that might be produced in one's psyche by its DoC). There is more:

> Under the word "boundless," for example, the plan notes that Stanford spans "more fields of endeavor than our Eastern competitors." According to the suggested script, Stanford, is "open, accessible, inclusive: open to any student of exceptional merit, not just the wealthy. Selective and exclusive, but on the basis of merit."

That clearly knocks out Harvard, Yale, and Princeton, and only leaves Berkeley to be outcompeted. I do admit, however, that Stanford's fields of endeavor are not only for football but also baseball, golf, and track; and there are courts of endeavor where tennis and basketball are cultivated. There is even a pool for swimming. These gladiatorial arenas are not only open and accessible to exceptional students but, as the word "selective" implies, their caretakers (called coaches) are forever recruiting the less wealthy, whose future is in professional sports.

Then comes this dispensation from above: "DoC stressed that the communication plan does not prevent Stanford staffers from creating their own ways to boost the university. It is meant as a guide." This blow *for* academic freedom struck me as most reassuring because, after all, the professors need not stick to the six words made available to them by the helpful strategic plan; they need only worry about "boosting" the university. This is in their own interest, obviously, because successful performance of this chore must be reported in their annual reports to dean and provost, if they want a merit raise.

The story's finale, not inappropriately, has a musical theme. Here are the Stanford spin-spin maestro's own words, as quoted in the *Chronicle:*

> "Rather than a detailed symphony score, it is meant to be a jazz tune, allowing you to do your solos and improvisations.... If enough of us can consistently sound the right notes, the result will fulfill the definition of melody: a rhythmic succession of single tones organized as an aesthetic whole."

I'll let any creative genius like the DoC play his solo part but, though an emeritus, I have a few spirited suggestions for consideration by the provost that might rein in our spinmeister, on an ascending scale of severity (to let the punishment fit the crime):

1. Lend him to Ross Perot for his next presidential campaign.

2. Exile him for ten years to Hollywood to write vibrant words about stunning beauties of the screen.

3. Trade him to Harvard in exchange for at least two assistant professors of philosophy.

4. Fire him outright for misuse of hyperbole, as you would fire the football coach who does not deliver the goods.

POSTSCRIPT. Talking around the campus, I found that this spin on the spin in the *Chronicle* had escaped most locals, who prefer to get their Stanford news from the campus newspaper. They therefore missed this marvelous specimen of the double spin and its hilarious message. Instead, some of them were outraged and demanded an end to the nonsense. And, I understand, the administrators obliged. So a great opportunity to modernize Stanford's image was lost.

16

Trauma, Valium, and a Cocktail
Called Martini,
or
Surviving Revolution in the Trenches
of the Hilton

"Valium and martinis don't mix," the good Dr. McNeil told me when I asked him to give me a prescription for the new wonder drug that by the early 1970s had become the intellectual elite's favorite tranquilizer. I don't know why valium is called "valium." The dictionary tells us that it is the "*trademark for* diazepam" [*sic*]. I consulted a couple of my doctor friends, but they were not very helpful. Chemists are even less likely to know, and as none is nearby I won't take the trouble of hunting one down. My secret hunch, never revealed before, is that valium is not really diazepam but a placebo; and that's probably the reason why I argued with the good Dr. McNeil, whose advice I have always taken on all other matters.

"And why would you want it? You don't need it," Ian—that's his baptismal name—asked and averred in a pastoral manner. "I'll never survive what I'm in for without it," I replied and then told him what was ahead of me. For an entire year I would have to sit through thunderous meetings of the Council of the American Political Science Association. I had sat through them before, earlier as a member of the council and in the past year as the president-elect. I really didn't have much to do but enjoy the palaver. But now, in fall 1971, I was to be a real president, and that meant that I would have to preside over the council.

"Tell me more about this council," the Doc said, and I told him about it. In reply, he introduced me to a new word of evidently clinical significance: "This council of yours seems to suffer of a severe case of logorrhea." That, of course, left me speechless, and I quickly changed the topic. I didn't have the vaguest idea of what the disease was about, but I wouldn't give him the satisfaction of admitting that I didn't know. I simply resolved to introduce the term on the first opportune moment into the vocabulary of behavioral political science.

This particular doc was a good fellow: I had gone to him since coming back to California in 1957, and I had religiously seen him once a year when he would have his nurse weigh me and take my pulse. After this ceremony he would give a whack to my knees, clearly to determine whether I was still of sound mind. Then we would suck on our respective pipes and contemplate things, like the ways of the APSA Council.

During the year that followed, 1971–72, I occasionally took the valium along with a martini to avoid whatever trauma might be in store for me, but the predicted dysfunctional effect did not disturb my equilibrium as I ever so vaguely "recognized" flying hands whose owners wanted to speak, but whose thunderous words passed me by as if they had never been uttered.

The Cocktail Called Martini

Before going on with the traumatic but also sometimes hilarious year I had living with the APSA Council, I cannot but emphasize the importance that the cocktail called "martini" had in the council's deliberations. Most of my colleagues were not fortunate enough to be able to mix this cocktail with valium, except I think for one female councilperson who brought a fairly large leather case full of pill bottles and boxes from which she periodically tossed one, two, or three items into her mouth. I could observe her easily because as a persuaded but rarely persuasive feminist she always sat opposite the head table to demonstrate her opposition to everything that was going on. The pills did not have the calming effect on her that valium plus a martini had on me. She talked a lot and made little sense.

All of this convinced me of the critical importance of the martini in the pursuit of political science. I engineered a resolution instructing me to "report back" whatever I could find out about the cocktail called martini. Ever mindful of our scientific traditions, yet equally sensitive to what is going on at our disciplinary "frontiers" or "cutting edges," I recommended that by proper devotion to the martini the council could make a pioneering and lasting contribution to a permanent comeback of the classical academic cocktail party. Indeed, as a result of the council's firm stand in the matter, no longer need we sip today the insipid, cheap, and usually lukewarm white wine that was the standard mind quencher at academic gatherings during the cruelly ascetic years of the revolutionary 1960s. At that time academics also sported beards and blue jeans at their wine parties to symbolize their being of the "people" opposed to the war in Vietnam.

In my brief report to the council I began with the cocktail called martini as the dependent variable. Though, when properly prepared, a martini can be a drink you can depend on for desired effects, I pointed out, martinis can assume highly variable values, ranging from condensed to watery, depending—and hence a dependent variable—on whether served individually by the glass or collectively by the pitcher. Fortunately, I reported, there is no etymological obfuscation with the word "martini." As the friendly Mr. Webster himself so informingly informs us, this is a noun that "prob." [*sic*] comes from the name *Martini*, which may strike the novice on the contemporary cocktail circuit as rather redundant but constitutes a profound etymological finding. (At this point, my ever-alert editor's marginal note informs me that "James Bond only drinks martinis, and always wants them stirred, not shaken—or vice versa, I may be remembering this incorrectly. If you are discussing martinis, surely you have to mention 007.")

On the ontological side, things were more complicated and troublesome. According to Mr. Webster a martini is "a cocktail made of gin and dry vermouth; *also:* one made with vodka instead of gin." The reference is, of course, to Noah Webster (1758–1843). There is some conflict of opinion on Webster's qualifications for defining a martini or, for that matter, any other cocktail because he may have been a teetotaler.

I was forced to mention, first of all, that there is *no* hyphen between "cock" and "tail," something that must puzzle every ontologist. Obviously, a cocktail *without* a hyphen differs from a cock-tail *with* a hyphen. Mr. Webster again came to my rescue. A cock-tail of the hyphenated species is "1: a horse with its tail docked. 2: a horse not of pure breed." It follows that any inference from cock-tail to cocktail is not justifiable on either etymological or ontological grounds.

There was much debate in the council over the second definition of a cock-tail, for the cocktail called martini is obviously not "of pure breed," as pure gin (or vodka) is clearly being adulterated by an ever so infinitesimal drop of vermouth. As might have been expected, there was much disagreement between the empiricists and the philosophers on the council concerning the measurement of something that is "infinitesimal." The empiricists were understandingly ambivalent on measurement values close to zero. Is the ratio of 20:1 sufficiently different from the ratio of 25:1 to make a fuss about? The option varies with the social environment. While some hosts generously inquire, "How do you like your martini —very dry, dry, or not so dry?" others simply serve from a pitcher something that tastes more like water than even the not-so-dry martini. Genuine martini lovers like myself tend to opt, if at all possible, for the purest version of a martini that altogether eschews the vermouth as an additive.

Now, the etymologically confusing aspect of all this is that the nonhyphen cocktail probably does come from "cock + tail," and for once there was unanimity among the councilpeople that the definition of a cocktail involves a much higher level of abstraction and lower level of operationalization than the definition of the martini, to wit: "an iced drink of distilled liquor mixed with flavoring ingredients." But this agreement did not last long, for there was the empirical problem whether the conventional olive in a martini can be considered a "flavoring ingredient." Some heretics denied this and argued for the legitimacy of substituting an onion.

A second Websterian definition of a cocktail, I discovered and reported, is that it is not really what it claims to be but, and quoting again, "something resembling or suggesting such a drink; *esp.*: a mixture of diverse elements (fog and smoke in equal parts—a city cocktail familiar to all—*New Yorker*)." When I first expounded my theory of the cocktail called martini some years ago, my friend Sam Patterson wrote me as follows: "You should know that the first cocktail was made in Elmsford, New York, in 1776. It was served in a pub called Halls Corners by a barmaid named Betsy Flanagan. The back of the bar was decorated with tail feathers. When a drunk called for a glass of 'those cocktails,' Betsy made him a mixed drink and put a feather in it. Thus cocktails." Sam did not reveal his source for this vitally important piece of trivia.

This left the council with the methodological problem of how the APSA membership should be instructed in the lost art of holding a martini or manhattan glass. It was agreed that there are three techniques. If you hold the glass by its base, using the full hand —thumb and all four fingers—is advisable. If you hold the glass by the stem, the thumb, the index finger and the middle finger will do. If you hold the glass by its rim, by far the most sophisticated technique, only thumb and index finger are needed. Which technique is to be used in turn depends on the holder's position. If lying down, as in Roman-type bacchanalia, modal among assistant professors, use of the full-hand/five-finger procedure is advisable. If sitting, first down and then up as associate professors are likely to do, the thumb/two-finger technique is appropriate. If standing, as full professors must at cocktail parties to show their important presence, the thumb/index-finger method is the most proper because it's the most elegant.

As the discussion proceeded, I could not help but reminisce about the good old days when the president-elect, Bob Ward, my friend since graduate school days in Berkeley, and I used to drink our rye or bourbon straight, at times chasing it with a small glass of beer—a practice that preserves the integrity of both the whiskey and the beer. This uncomposed combination of pure whiskey and pure beer is generally known as a "boilermaker." The great virtue of the boilermaker is that it leaves any possible mixing of the elements to gastral chemistry and, hence, does not require the kind of tiresome "shaking" that mixed drinks, so-called, entail. On this account alone, therefore, the boilermaker is procedurally cheaper than, but substantively superior to, either the martini or the manhattan. History confirms this theoretical insight. In the classical era of intemperance, a boilermaker cost $0.15 (ten cents for the whiskey, five cents for the beer chaser), while a mixed drink cost $0.25. That, of course, was before a martini was a combination of fog and smoke in equal parts.

The High Moral Politics of the APSA

My fear of impending trauma as a gavel swinger turned out to have been driven by the fallacy of misplaced concreteness. Neither my longing for valium nor my elaborate study of the cocktail called martini could have possibly prepared me for the comedy of errors that marked my first council meeting as president in early December 1971. At first I did not know what was going on; then I could not believe what I heard; and, this being early in the morning without valium and/or martini having been had, I was almost immediately compelled—counter to my preference for a quakerish decision-making style—to take total control of the proceedings by as firm a parliamentary ruling as *Robert's Rules of Order* permit a duly elected presiding officer.

This is what happened. Even before the minutes of the previous meeting could be unanimously approved, "subject to such minor corrections as the Secretary may find necessary," holy hell broke out. Apparently the APSA Election Committee had failed to certify the election of a notorious establishment candidate, one Thomas Dye, to the office of secretary, although he had garnered a safe majority of the membership's vote against the combined votes for two competing nominees. This, Dye rightly complained, violated some article in the constitution (of the APSA, not the USA), and he argued that the Election Committee should certify his high status as secretary (and wisely so; for who else could make "minor corrections" in the previous meeting's minutes, as was soon moved?). Dye apparently preferred to spend the day hassling over this instead of visiting the National Gallery.

At this point—I don't know how much time had gone by—I made my momentous parliamentary ruling. According to the minutes, "Eulau ruled that the matter of the election of the Secretary of the Association would be taken up at 4 p.m., December 10th." By then, clearly, I figured that the martini-soaked, drowsy council colleagues would be able to give this crisis their fullest attention. I should mention that the local uproar—after all, we were in D.C. —did not discourage Dye from remaining seated without being certified, for all of the day's Minutes were written by no other than Dye himself.

Four o'clock rolled around and things reached an immediate

boiling point. So hot and distrustful was one side in this dispute, the Women's Caucus for Political Science, plaintiff, that they asked for permission to tape the verbal war about to take place. That lion of lions, Jerry Loewenberg of Iowa, moved the thing along, to the effect "that the Council request the tapes be turned over to the Association for checking the minutes or whatever purposes the President may wish."

The president wished for nothing more than getting out of the meeting and doing what he likes best about APSA meetings—meet with his friends in the bar. So everybody voted for the taping, except the noncertified secretary, the executive director, and the president, who abstained.

The facts of the case were these: when the names of candidates for secretary were submitted *prior to* the September 1971, business meeting, the Women's Caucus had nominated a lady named Judith, and the Caucus for a New Political Science had nominated a lady also named Judith. While in those revolutionary days it was difficult to distinguish between the two caucuses, it was even more difficult to distinguish between the two Judies. Then, apparently, a deal was struck between the two caucuses and the first Judith was announced to be the candidate of the CNPS as well. But, when the mail ballots were sent out, both names appeared as candidates, thus splitting the antiestablishment vote.

There we were, assembled at four o'clock in the afternoon of December 10, in the year of reckoning, 1971, receiving a "Petition on Behalf of Judith X and the Women's Caucus for Resolution Ordering Reballoting for Office of APSA Secretary and for other Relief." This wonderfully pompous title, I immediately sensed, threatened to lead to all kinds of disputation about just what "other relief" the petitioners might have in mind. I therefore asked my colleagues to devote five minutes of quiet reading to the document as a whole before asking any questions or making any statements. I won't detail all points of the petition here, but only its truly high points.

First, the petition asked for an "official announcement" by the council that one of the two Judies had not been anybody's candidate, and that the council "regrets any distress the erroneous listing on the ballot may have caused her." When I subsequently encountered this Judith at some meeting or other, I did not note that the erroneous listing had caused any lasting distress. She was as peppy (I almost wrote "peppery") as always.

Second and third, the petition asked that the election for the office of secretary be voided and a new election be held. But, believe it or not, before the new election could take place, the voided votes of the two Judies were to be combined and tallied as a single vote outcome "so that the combined total may be more reflective of the combined voting strength of the Women's Caucus and the Caucus for a New Political Science." As I said, believe it or not, "two and two makes five" or, in a more philosophical vein, "the whole is larger than the sum of its parts." There followed some threat that "while petitioners are loathe to seek redress... in other fora, they may well be forced to do so unless the Executive Council and the APSA as a whole are more responsive to the need for such remedial relief [wow!] than has been the case so far in this matter." Commendable as the use of the plural *fora* was, how the APSA *as a whole* could remedy this orthographically deplorable situation was not explained.

Next came a response from the Election Committee, through the mouth of Professor Fred Greenstein, then at Wesleyan University. This response completely capitulated to the feminist attack, failed to persuade the council, and made for some great oratory, led by President Eulau himself, who dared to ask if the second Judith "was currently a member of the APSA and learned that she was not." My good friend Nelson Polsby, then editor of the *APSR* but compassionate as always, asked whether a new election was the only means of redress for felt grievances. He received the reply that a new election was "the only rational means of remedy," suggesting how far rational-choice thinking had penetrated our discipline even as early as 1971. Gordon Tullock, really an economist disguised as a political scientist, noted that a new election with an outcome predictable from the first vote was a waste of members' dues. Christian Bay, foremost old political science spokesman for a new political science, argued that it was not really a matter of setting aside any election because no valid election for secretary had been held in the first place. President-elect Ward, a great pacifier and diplomat, noted that the petitioners did not charge fraud or deceit by anyone; but he also wondered what purpose other than a punitive one the petition could serve. The attorney for the petitioners denied that any punishment was on anybody's mind and that the petitioners only intended to ensure the legitimacy of APSA elections.

After all this wisdom had been proclaimed and the opening call for the cocktail hour had long passed, the president asked non-certified Secretary Dye to present his views. Taking note that those who would want to hold a new election had invoked fairness, justice, and decency, Dye pointed out that these virtues had been on his side all along because, in the absence of fraud, setting aside the judgment of the membership already rendered would in fact violate the three virtues. At issue was the first principle of representative government, nothing less. The election returns showed him, Dye, to have garnered 4,138 votes against the combined Judith-Judith vote of 2,931. A new election, Dye complained in the Minutes written by himself for the council and hence unmistakably correct, would "force me to run again for an office which I won fairly with the support of an overwhelming majority of the membership." After some rhetoric unmasking the "dissident elements" in the Association, Dye closed on the high note that the council was morally and constitutionally—in that order—obliged to accept the majority judgment of the membership.

Everybody's barks were worse than their bites. Evidently a "miniconference" was held between (unnamed) representatives of the council, led by that senatorial look-alike savant of U.S. senators and their ways, Donald Matthews, and the petitioners' agents. The outcome of the negotiation was one of the strangest motions ever made by professionals presumably expert in legislative procedure. It noted various technical foul-ups on the part of the petitioners but blamed insufficiently clear Rules of Procedure for them. It then "in theory" (that is, on paper) upheld the recommendation of its Election Committee to hold a new election and the "moral right" of the parties to call for it; but then, "in practice," it appreciated an agreement apparently reached between the parties *in camera* "not to call for such an election and their acceptance of the election results for Secretary." The motion also directed the president and the executive director "to prepare appropriate apologies to the three candidates for Secretary at the last election." I have absolutely no recollection of ever preparing, not to say delivering, any such apologies, and I am pretty sure the executive director also did no such silly thing. The motion was approved, with Caucusite Bay opposed and now-legitimate Secretary Dye abstaining.

A Tantrum and the S-Word

So overwrought am I recollecting the trauma of my first experience as leader of several thousand stalwart political scientists that I almost forgot an episode at the next council meeting some months later. Recounting it admirably requires fewer words because the facts of the case center in a single word not often used in academic circles.

It will be recalled that the late 1960s and early 1970s were a time of turmoil, in the universities and adjoining streets, as well as in the learned societies of which the APSA is one of the most important in the life of at least half of the country's political scientists—half because it has been estimated that another half manage to get along without it. These people have not learned what I once learned from my friend Chuck Jones when driving through the hilly byways of Iowa, I can't recall when, though both of us were attending a conference in Iowa City. This was before I had become an APSA functionary, and I was complaining to Chuck about the organization. To which he replied, rather emphatically, as if thinking of his lovely wife Vera: "She's the only one we've got."

The disease, known as "responsiveness to non-negotiable demands" of the underprivileged, dispossessed, excluded, and so on, really came to harass the APSA relatively late, during the presidencies of David Easton (1968–69) and Karl Deutsch (1969–70). As the association responded, mostly financially, to women, blacks, chicanos, the foreign born, and whoever else wanted a piece of the cake, the raids on the organization's equities, carefully accumulated over the years by a foresighted executive director, threatened to turn a solid cake into a mushy pie. To put a halt to this exhaustion of the reserves, President Lane recommended the establishment of a trust fund as a "prudent protection of the Association's endowment and a guarantee of continued future Association income from the interest thereon." There was the usual bickering about it in the council, but it had become my job to appoint a committee to implement the proposal. I appointed as non-ex-officio members two former presidents, Pendleton Herring and Harold Lasswell, and as chairman the hard-working Austin Ranney, recently editor of the *Review* and later, as was to be expected, a president. Other members were the president-elect, that is, Eulau, and the treasurer, Don Matthews.

As things threatened to get out of hand, the committee acted with deliberate speed and, in short order, produced an amendment to the APSA constitution establishing a "Trust and Development Fund." What Chairman Ranney's report failed to mention was that the committee, minus the treasurer, held its first meeting in early December 1971, around a swimming pool at a luxurious resort on St. Thomas in the Virgin Islands. In defense of this otherwise nonacceptable choice of *situs* it needs mention that, though obviously beyond the reach of the membership's custodial attention, the meeting did not cost the APSA a cent because it was held in connection with a conference sponsored by the Social Science Research Council, which footed all bills.

In general, nuisance committees of this sort are easily forgettable, but this one is not. It was a great experience to sit there, under an umbrella protecting us against the winter solstice sun, with Pen Herring and Harold Lasswell, sipping away as only these two masters could, and listen to them reminisce about their years as assistant professors and writing articles for the "old" *Encyclopaedia of the Social Sciences*.

So, in May 1972, at the second of the fateful year's council meetings, the efficient Austin reported on all the work he had mostly done by himself alone on the trust fund proposal. This, in turn and due course, led to a memorable exchange between councilman Christian Bay, the leading spokesman of the CNPS, and the president. I had known Christian for many years and, before he began acting up like a proletarian at professional meetings, considered him to be a notable theoretician of the "behavioral revolution." Just a couple of years earlier, before this fateful APSA meeting, both of us had sat on the council of the ICPSR.

Then came our encounter at the 1972 APSA Council meeting over the trust fund proposal. According to the Minutes, "Bay argued that the Trust Fund 'would further strengthen the ruling oligarchy,' and he moved to delete recommended items . . . which required Board approval for expenditure of Association Trust Fund capital." There followed the usual quibbling about this or that in the wording of the text, but in the end the Trust Fund was approved, with only Bay voting no, and two abstentions (from otherwise caucus-friendly members). Up to this point things had remained fairly gentlemanly. They changed later on. At one critical juncture, according to the Minutes, Bay "accused Eulau of trying to 'reaffirm the hegemony of a past paradigm.'"

Well, I had enough of this sort of silliness and, again according to the Minutes, "directed Bay to 'cut out the shit.'" Alas, this quote is incorrect and does not represent either my actual words or my feelings in the matter, for what I really said was, "For Christ's sake, Christian, take the shit out of your teeth." I don't know whether the exchange between Bay and me was occasioned by his or my having a tantrum, but it was probably bound to happen after years of frustration for both of us. Christian died in 1990 at age sixty-nine.

All's Well that Ends Well

When I returned a year later from abroad and attended the 1973 annual meeting of the APSA in New Orleans, all the tantrums and traumas of the previous four or five years had been forgotten. Instead, as I later learned from a report on the meeting by the Honorable Nancy Boland Edgerton (a.k.a. Nancy Ranney), "two of the best-attended events during the week were an address by Nelson Rockefeller and an enormously successful Jazz Concert which drew to a close with Heinz Eulau leading the Olympia Marching Band from the hall" (*PS* 7 [Winter 1974]:9). Friend Nancy has an unimpeachable imagination!

Epilogue

De Mortuis Nil nisi Bonum,
or
Better Write Your Own Obituary
Before It Is Too Late

As the closest thing to being born is dying, this epilogue is devoted to a morbid but potentially exhilarating topic. For instance, if, after having been identified as one of your academic discipline's "greats," you still have any doubt about your status, just read your obituary in the *New York Times.* The reason for wanting to make the *Times* is that this highbrow paper has its own peculiar sense of humor. "George B. Craig Jr., Entomologist Feared by Mosquitoes, Dies at 65," the paper reported on 23 December 1995. I didn't know Professor Craig, but I'm sure that mosquitoes the world over rejoiced on reading his obituary. Of course, to have your obituary in the *Times* in timely fashion, you must arrange for dying on a day when nobody else dies. If too many people die at the same time, you as a "mere professor" are likely to be crowded out by clearly more deserving obituarians—artists, writers, venture capitalists, athletes, politicians, what have you, unless you are a Nobel prize winner, a notorious madam, or something like that.

I don't know whether there really is something like an "obituarian" as the subject of an obituary, though the dictionary provides for an obituarist, presumably the person who does you in. I made up "obituarian" because it seems to follow, rather logically and rhythmically, titles like octogenarian or, if you live that long, nonagenarian or centenarian. "Obituarian Professor So-and-So" sounds so much better than "the late Professor So-and-So."

If you don't get your name into the *Times* and you are, as I am, a political scientist (though I also fancy myself to be something of a humanist), then consult *PS,* the house organ of the American Political Science Association. There you will surely find yourself memorialized in a section called "In Memoriam." It will disabuse you of any naiveté about your celebrity status. In this kind of final tribute, you are not only great but the greatest. There has never been anyone just like you. You will also discover that you are likely to be the victim of double jeopardy. Having been named "distinguished service professor" or having been given some "lifetime achievement award" while alive, you must now live up to all this hype in your grave. The trouble is, of course, that as the celebrated object of a necrologue, you can neither enjoy all the false things said about you nor, if so inclined, protest them, for you are no longer a *Homo erectus* and in a position, literally, to do so.

Therefore, and a weighty "therefore" it is, if you have even the slightest doubt about your own greatness, you better sit down as soon as possible and write your own obituary. For that's the only way you can make sure of its accuracy, as well as enjoy it. For one thing, as you so clearly were a true champion in teaching and research, and a wonderful human being in spite of it, who knows you better than you do? For another, you just can't trust the oleaginous nonsense others will write about you.

I have no idea how far back you must reach to discover the "In Memoriam" section in the annals of the association. At the time when I took my Ph. D. prelims (a kind of professional baptism), on 1 April 1939, to be precise, the *APSR* reported a death as just another item under "News and Notes: Personal and Miscellaneous," no special fuss being made about departing colleagues. In this memorable issue of April 1939 (vol. XXXIII, no. 2)—an era when political scientists could still decipher Roman numerals—the compiler of the news was no other than the managing editor himself —the redoubtable Frederic (no "k") A. Ogg—he of the publishing team of "Ogg and Ray." By this time, Ogg and Ray's magisterial *Introduction to American Government* was in its sixth edition (price, $3.75) and the more vulgar *Essentials of American Government* was in a "revised" state (priced, appropriately, at $3.00).

One of my favorite latter-day compulsions—"latter-day" not because they are saintly but because they developed rather late in life—is to read the *New York Times* "Obituaries" before turning to anything else. Otherwise, if I were to read the paper sequentially, I would never get to page A14 or B15 before day's end and the arrival of the next morning's paper with its new portfolio of obits. Hence I would miss what is really news. The compulsion became noticeable about the time I turned seventy-five and my kids for the first time put on a real birthday party, as if it were the last. That was in 1990.

Shortly afterward, sitting at the breakfast table and opening the *New York Times,* I found myself no longer turning to the sports page first, as had been habit for decades, but to the tragic personal news of the day. That is the fact. But what is the reason for my more and more enjoying this rather odd compulsion? And why do I enjoy it and, worse, admit it, even though it is not proper etiquette to do so in my social circles, increasingly limited to septuagenarians and octogenarians endlessly talking about backaches, nursing homes, medical insurance, and so on—anything but the final departure? Is it simply perverse curiosity that drives readers to obituaries? Or is it the sheer requirement of not missing an important departure that calls for extending one's condolences to a grieving family?

Always being inclined to be more candid in my mother language than in Portuguese or Chinese, I come up with the *Schadenfreude* hypothesis. It is a word difficult to translate and comprehend. The dictionary's "malicious pleasure" or "gloating" does not really catch the scent of the German expression. Besides, it is too close to "malicious gossip," which is intended to hurt another person. *Schadenfreude,* though directed at some disliked person, is a highly privatized syndrome, perhaps but not necessarily shared with a third person. It never reaches and becomes known to its target. Indeed, the trouble does not lie in *Freude,* which refers to pleasure or enjoyment or delight; it lies in *Schaden,* which can be translated into "malice" but also into "pity."

Now, I reject the notion that compulsively reading obituaries is due to my enjoying anyone taking off from this earth. So, when I have this obit-induced sense of *Schadenfreude,* it cannot possibly refer to malice but must refer to pity. In fact, most of the obituary page's subjects have been so sick that death must be a great relief, to them and to the people whom the clergy afterward so sanctimoniously call their "loved ones." By the way, I never liked referring to persons, people, or humans of either gender as "subjects." That's probably the reason why I did not become a psychologist. In my once-upon-a-time business of survey research, we referred to "respondents" or "nonrespondents," which clearly tells us something significant about them. The irony is that I never heard a comparative psychologist call his or her rats or monkeys "subjects," even after killing them.

In part, then, and I want to emphasize "in part," what the obituary does for me, through the medium of *Schadenfreude,* is to pity the deceased for not really having been able to enjoy all the wonderful things now said about him or her in the obituary. "Serves him right" or "serves her right," I say to myself, that he or she must endure these encomia *in absentia.* Had he or she written their own obituary, there would be no *Schadenfreude*—a concept so ambiguous for an attitude so ambivalent.

There is another side of the *Schadenfreude* hypothesis when it comes to obituaries. What right-minded person would want to deny that there is at least some element of honest enjoyment for survivors in reading these things, for the simple reason that says, "how lucky I am to be still alive and kicking, while my dear old friend is gone?"

In Memoriam of the Lions

Schadenfreude or not, I hate to see people obsequiously mutilated in obituaries, especially in those collectively written by a committee, as they often are in Stanford's faculty-staff weekly, *Stanford Report.* I usually do not read these because, by definition, any faculty member at Stanford (and any other of the top 100 research universities), alive or dead, is a "distinguished" something or other. I am more inclined to pay attention to the obits that appear in *PS* because, if I knew the deceased, they can remind me of something shared in the past but otherwise forgotten. Sometimes one may even learn some interesting fact, as when the obit says that Professor X was born on 31 December 1899, which makes him or her a nineteenth-century relic. But in general the *PS* remembrances are no more truthful than those found elsewhere. I sometimes wonder just why it is that some of them are written in the first place and sent in to be published. Nobody believes them and surely not the distinguished and now extinguished professor himself or herself.

"Deceased" is another one of those highly technical words from the Latin that should never have crept into Middle English. It comes from the past participle of *decedere*, to depart, and is a composite of *de + cedere*. The latter translates into the English "cease," like in "cease and desist" which means, when applied to the topic at hand, that you should end, stop or discontinue doing something (like breathing, I suppose). From what I can figure out, "desist," coming from the Latin *desistere*, means pretty much the same thing. So, I wonder, why not replace the ordinary-sounding "the deceased" with the more triumphant "desister" (just like "resister")?

Just for the fun of it I studied the obituaries of some 100 sturdy colleagues whom I had known and still remember more or less reasonably well, all lionized in *PS* since its inception in 1968. The first issue of *PS* had four items "In Memoriam," two of men I had some contact with at one time or another. One was George Galloway of the Legislative Reference Service, Library of Congress, who was sixty-nine when he completed "a long and distinguished career as a political scientist." I once had some correspondence with Galloway, shortly after we had published *The Legislative System*. At the time I had nothing better to do than have the brain-numbing idea of having Congress itself fund a "self-study" by way of an interview survey with all its members, in both House and Senate. As an action-research project, the questionnaire would be designed by—who else?—a special committee of congresspersons and staffers, and so on and so forth. My naiveté had no bounds. I received a nice letter back from Galloway telling me it was a great idea but, "at this time," unlikely to get anywhere.

Another early item was for Willmoore Kendall, who was only fifty-eight when he completed what Charles Hyneman, in the obit's very first sentence, courageously called his "stormy career." Because I had found Willmoore to be a most fascinating character, I want to add my two bits to what, in all likelihood, is one of the more candid obit profiles ever written, leaving it to others to tell other (true!) stories about him.

Kendall was visiting at Stanford during academic 1958–59, my own first year there. He had an office down the hall, and we would have lunch from time to time at which we thoroughly and sometimes raucously disagreed with one another about the universe and all things in it. But there was respect, and I was not surprised by the episode I am about to recall.

One early afternoon I was peacefully sitting in my office, when in stormed Willmoore with something in his hand that looked like the reprint of an article, gesticulating furiously and shouting at me: "This guy does not know who God is, how in hell can he not know who God is? You can find God on every penny, nickel, dime, and quarter." Of course, he was right as I found out after checking up: God is on every true coin of the realm—"In God We Trust." So much for the separation of state and church.

The next and last time I saw him was in the early 1960s at some professional meeting wherever—perhaps the southern. Evidently being in a forgiving mood, Kendall gleefully told me that he was now heading a conflict-free department at the University of Dallas. Being overwhelmed by the news, I asked, "How come?" Said Willmoore: "Well, I'm the only member of the department."

Unfortunately, or maybe fortunately, episodes like these do not usually get into an obituary, though Hyneman, in his *PS* piece, acknowledged that things between Kendall and Yale University had become so conflictual that "his service was discontinued by mutual agreement of teacher and institution"—another way of saying that he was "bought out" when there was no other solution. In the end Hyneman turned panegyric, suggesting that "few of his generation in American political science can match his claim for attention over the decades immediately ahead." In certain circles, at least.

Ingredients of an Ideal-Type Obituary

There aren't many types as colorful as Willmoore Kendall in our business. Most of us live lives less virulent than his. That's the reason, perhaps, why our obituaries must make heroes even out of those of us—most of us—who can only claim to be pygmies standing on the shoulders of giants. I have resisted the impulse of writing a Weberian, "ideal type" obituary; but I could not resist the impulse of at least assembling some sinewy ingredients for doing one. If properly constructed, this ideal type would represent an exaggeration of its empirical referents and, hence, would be presumably useful as a heuristic device. To facilitate the process, I have compiled a partial list of possible ingredients on which future obituary writers can draw when lost for words or feelings. The highly selective and somewhat atypical examples in a potpourri of types have been culled from my study of the 100-odd *PS* obits of people I had come across or crossed up at one time or another. To save space, I have edited some of the statements without, I hope, in any way distorting their direct words or indirect meanings.

- [He] was a great man in all the ways that greatness is measured among scholars. He dazzled his students . . . , and he provoked them with his continually sharp questioning.
- His death at the age of 52 brought to a close a life of extraordinary achievement. . . . His intellectual contributions were conjoined with a literary craftsmanship that carried his ideas to a wide and admiring audience. . . . Coming generations of scholars will remember [him] and many will carry on in the tradition he so eminently represented.
- A seminal writer on American politics, compelling teacher, irrepressible raconteur, guiding force in professional associations, and political activist . . . he was "relevant" long before that overworked term came into use.
- No teacher of political science in our time attracted a greater or more devoted personal following. But this was something of a puzzle because no one could have wished less for a following on merely personal grounds.
- [His] life was a seminar. He was one of those rare and fortunate human beings who found a métier truly suited to his character. To speak of his "work" would be a misnomer. Teaching and scholarship, talking and reading, thinking and guiding—these activities were not what [he] "did." They were what he was as a man.
- An internationally recognized political scientist who contributed to a reshaping of the discipline and built one of the country's outstanding undergraduate departments, her life had something of a storybook quality.
- He had been one of the most learned and creative political scientists in America and Europe, who during his long career deeply influenced many generations of students at Harvard.

The range of his scholarly work was extraordinary.

- He is the only political scientist that I have known who is likely to still be read and studied for the value of his contribution to the knowledge of man and society a hundred years from now.

- [He] had a breadth of interest that was remarkable.... He was responsible for pathbreaking studies.... His work was characterized by its theoretical importance, conceptual boldness, meticulous execution, and graceful writing style. His was a truly creative intellect.

- She reached out to people and they, in turn, saw in her someone who would champion their causes and respond to their needs. Human beings were at the center of her political analyses rather than detached institutions or political structures.... She was a woman of fearless integrity and intrepid mind.

- It was, however, who he was rather than what he did that made [him] so special. He was in many respects a walking Hegelian synthesis, reconciling seeming opposites in his character and behavior in a way that made him both memorable and delightful.

- Surely [he] was one of the most influential scholars of his generation.... Nominally a political scientist, his intellect never was constrained by traditional academic boundaries. He came as close to being a Renaissance scholar as anyone I have ever encountered in [the] academy.

Writing Your Own Obituary

My advice to write your own obituary is easier given than carried out. Not everybody has the skill and *chutzpah* to write his own credible notice in anticipation of the end. But there are nobler ways of memorializing yourself than stealing words and sentiments from others' eulogies. I am convinced that for the purpose at hand drawing on your own resources is more honorable, especially if you have reliable documentation to draw on. For instance, as a reasonably active adviser on Ph. D. dissertations, you can use their prefatory "acknowledgments." They will celebrate your super-duper contribution to the writer's first and, in many cases, sole *opus magnum* (see chapter 4). Then there is more up-to-date material in the letters you may have received on the occasion of your retirement. Although usually solicited by a well-meaning impresario, these materials are more credible because the rosy glow of recollections is clearly more reliable than the manic effusions of an obsolete dissertation preface.

For the purpose of classifying various raw materials of this sort, I first developed a complex binary code. It permitted easy placement of all statements that were formal, banal, hypocritical, corny, schmaltzy, and so on (0 or minus); and of all statements that were falsifiable (1 or plus). As the ratio of the falsifiables to the rest was about one to ten, I could safely ignore the stuff in the zero category. In dealing with the few remaining positive or plus items, I soon found that even the simplest coding system was unmanageable for the purpose of transitive ordering. For instance, there were fraudulent allegations about my teaching and research. I therefore decided on a generational set of categories for depositions from former students and on a nondescript catchall category of other denunciations.

I came to teach at Stanford in fall 1958, and though I had a hand in some Ph.D. dissertations as a second or third "reader," it took some years to bring along my "own" crowd. Among the first Stanford cohort were two characters about whom I could reveal much, but because I do not want to forfeit their friendship, I'll just quote some of their illusions about me as raw material worthy of consideration in any obituary. I begin with the letter written on the stationery of a foundation where the writer had exiled himself for a number of years:

In the labyrinthian way that careers unfold, I write on letterhead that seems far removed from PS 400 [Scope and Method], in that vintage year of 1961. But, as you taught, appearances deceive. Across a quarter-century the lessons of PS 400 and subsequent tutelage cast their shadow, and not least among these lessons is a healthy skepticism about surface appearances. And there are more lessons: nurture the habit of self-criticism, as best one can; respect the complexities of the evidence-inference conundrum; write and re-write, then edit before re-writing; read, but never imitate, the masters; have more than one project underway; fulfill professional responsibilities, professionally; build the scholarly foundation slowly and carefully; you learn more, and have more fun, playing in the big leagues; collegiality, not discipleship is the way to build a science; knowledge can make a difference in the affairs of state.

The other first cohort survivor is an especially fun-loving friend with whom in subsequent years I shared many "happy hours" when we sat on the boards of various national research organizations. His epistle is less abstract but equally deceptive:

> My first learning in modern social science was at your hands when you taught me, "In the beginning was the four-fold table." We advanced through many other matters to the ultimate scientific experience—the counter-sorter—in which you gave me private instruction.

Having made a false statement of fact, this rogue resorted to a false statement of value. He told of a party given by a fellow seminarian in PS 400, a U.S. Navy captain who was also the commander of the campus naval ROTC. The party was held at the nearby Navy Officers Club, including wives "for those of us so blessed," as this fellow charitably recalled, continuing:

> At the close of the evening, and after considerable good spirits of all kinds, my wife remarked to all, while in direct conversation with you, "Why, Professor Eulau doesn't seem at all bad." This was apparently contrary to her prior expectations based on casual graduate student rumor. As it has turned out she was prescient.

I gave up on the first Stanford cohort as hopeless and, in 1964, took off to Vienna, Austria, where I spent the academic year at some brand-new, Ford Foundation-funded institute for "higher studies." Coming back in 1965, I encountered a second and altogether new cohort of graduate students. They immediately gave me the impression of having gotten along very nicely without me. Reminisced one of them, on the stationery of the Office of the Vice President for Academic Affairs of some midwestern university:

For approximately forty students, fall quarter 1965 culminated a year of waiting for your return from a sabbatical [well, he was doubly wrong on that one]. Adequately primed with a combination of fact and myth, which had been generously supplied by second- and third-year students, we were not disappointed nor surprised when both fact and myth turned out to be true. I will never forget your dividing my first class with you into three sections representing levels of preparedness and demanding that the students place themselves into the appropriate section. Wednesday night studying Mancur Olson and Buchanan and Tullock was not a time for the timid. It was the most rewarding class I ever took.

This seminar evidently replaced PS 400 in the feverish imagination of the second cohort. There is also the flamboyant letter from the indomitable creator of SPSS.

After noting that the seminar dealt with the "then infant field of rational choice, deductive models and analytical political theory," he claimed that "in presenting such a seminar Heinz, as usual, anticipated by a decade the importance of these developments to the discipline." Not completely true, but for obituary purposes quite serviceable. Not everybody was so easily fooled. Another member of this "golden" mid-1960s cohort, saw right through me:

It is the fate of an eminent scholar and teacher like yourself to set in motion ideas and careers that go off in all sorts of directions—some of them unexpected. Like it or not, for example, you are largely responsible for setting me off as a fellow traveler with the public choice people. What did it was reading Downs's *Economic Theory of Democracy* in your seminar on Empirical Political Theory. You may have intended Downs as an innoculation [*sic*], but I caught the disease. I'm very grateful for being exposed to it.

The cohort of the middle 1960s was, as a group, probably the most distinctive and, as I just said, "golden" I ever worked with. They left just before things got hot on campus, with Vietnam making students both more docile and more interested in what Eulau, making his own well-known popular concessions to "relevance," had to offer. So they kept coming, for reasons so incomprehensible that I shall not venture to deal with them. And I'll leave it at that. Certainly, after all the encomia, hymns, eulogies, panegyrics, and testimonials, no obituary writer, least of all I, can complain about a lack of distorted materials for the task ahead. I tried my hand at it.

Heinz Eulau, Political Behavioralist, Dies at 100

The premature death, at 100, of Professor Heinz Eulau, a political science *savant* of German and Jewish origin but trained in the 1930s at the University of California, Berkeley, was a real shocker to his many friends and enemies, especially his former Stanford graduate students, whom he had persuaded to stop smoking, after himself giving up his beloved pipes; though, indefatigable sinner that he was, he stuck to at least one "Tanqueray-on-the-rocks-with-a-twist" (and sometimes making it a double) per day. Eulau, according to Professor-emeritus John Sprague of Washington University, himself the experienced practitioner of a spirited life style, "was an indefatigable proponent of what is the simplest and most parsimonious in both the theory and practice of politics. His devotion to the veridicality of the holistic theories of state sovereignty and of the individualistic theories of rational choice will remain legendary."

Index